PRA
HEART
MEDICINE

"This book tells a unique and inspiring story—a healing story for our troubled time—a story of courage, vision, truth, and deep love. Drug addiction is notoriously difficult to cure or even treat. Relapse rates are discouragingly high, as are mortality rates. Since all the addictive drugs are also illegal and possession can result in incarceration—the cards are stacked against addiction therapy. Into this toxic psychosocial mix comes the legendary central African plant root Tabernanthe iboga or its semi-synthetic derivative ibogaine, a powerful entheogen used in healing and initiation ceremonies in the Bwiti tradition. Uniquely among other psychedelic plants or substances, ibogaine has the capacity to actually block addictive cravings for long enough to permit an addict to re-establish a healthy connection with the core of their being— given appropriate guidance and support."

> **Ralph Metzner,** former dean of CIIS and professor emeritus, Harvard research associate of Timothy Leary & Ram Dass in the Psilocybin Project, author of *The Well of Remembrance, The Unfolding Self, Green Psychology,* editor of two collections on the science and the phenomenology of Ayahuasca and Teonanácatl

"Elizabeth Bast's *Heart Medicine* is important, and not just because it is a lyrical and touching memoir. Scientific studies of the curative powers of traditional plant medicines are all too often detached from the 'heart,' which is where all true healing occurs. Elizabeth's testimony, therefore, is to be read with close attention."

> **Robert Tindall,** author of *The Jaguar that Roams the Mind* & *The Shamanic Odyssey*

"I stayed up and read 200 pages in one sitting! Bast's writing is so compelling, so present. What a gift she is giving the world with her experience and her exquisite writing. It's the best kind of modern love story: passionate lovers, spiritual awakening, urban addictions, and the rising power of shamanism and plant medicine to help individuals, couples and families step into a new, more enlivened and powerful paradigm of relating. It's not only a fascinating read, it has the power to be a vehicle of healing for so many. There are so many folks right now on prescription medication or addicted to drugs (or hey, even playing Sudoku) who are seeking relief from suffering. This is the perfect story to get through to them. And also for those who are already more aware, what an amazing reminder of what is possible and how to realign with what we know to be true. I'm so heartened to know that her story offers true solution to modern ailments and is now available to the world at large. It's going to grab people and give them a healing just as they read it."

> **Bella Shing,** award-winning writer, director, founder of Sweeter Media

"Heart Medicine is more than a book, it's a fully immersive, technicolor, healing journey. Through down to earth and yet deeply poetic words, Bast invites us into a world of spiritual transformation and awakening. Don't be surprised if some of the magic rubs off on you as you read!"

> **Jessica Graham**, actress, meditation teacher, author of *Good Sex: Getting Off Without Checking Out*

"Once inside of the pages of this book-portal, you will be offered a glimpse into the mysteries of plant medicine. Drenched in Eros, fueled on Agape, *Heart Medicine* is a tale of mystical adventure and healing, in which danger, despair, intimacy and revelation thread through each other to weave a new reality for the tantric priestess Elizabeth Bast and her paramour, the globally renowned spray paint artist Chor Boogie. *Heart Medicine* is a portal that leads the reader on a wormhole journey into healing and self-discovery. It is an adventure story. It invites you to ride the rivers of intimacy and authenticity deeper and deeper into the realm of human relationship."

> **Richard Power,** philosopher, poet, yoga teacher, author of eleven books, including *Cauldron Yoga, Gaian Poetics, & The Way of the Ancient Future*

"A page turner. Elizabeth Bast's poetic words jump from the page. It is both a love story and a lesson to cure addiction. I read her book right before my own initiation with iboga and it helped me to prepare and understand better the potential of this powerful medicine."

> **Javier Prato,** filmmaker, director of *Sacred Plants*

"Bast's story beautifully illustrates the intimate relationship between two people and an ancient healing plant. Her raw authenticity exemplifies the power of the medicine path to face just that, the true essence of our being. Her voice lets us know that we are not alone on this exotic, gritty, and breath-taking path toward healing."

> **Ashley Booth,** founder of *The Aware Project: Rethinking Psychedelics*

"*Heart Medicine* is a soul cleanse. Elizabeth Bast's raw and unfiltered journey connects you to your own untapped medicine. She is a true healer. This is an experience meant to be savored."

> **Alexandra Martinez,** writer, *Miami New Times, The New Tropic*

"Bast's literary gem is an intimate reveal of a couple's soul-level liberation from the largely misunderstood and medically mishandled prison of addiction. This most personal offering strikes a universal resonance with pearl-after-pearl birthed from the trenches of relentless love and a dive into the heart of African shamanism. *Heart Medicine* is a fresh work and invaluable contribution for those curious about one of the most promising means for dissolving addiction at its root. Bast highlights the 'holy wood' from our oldest ancestors, holding the key to not merely reversing addiction, but to helping welcome our wandering souls back home. I recommend a full dose of Heart Medicine! Basse!"

Dr. Joseph Peter Barsuglia, research psychologist, psychotherapist, clinical research director at Crossroads Treatment Center

"E. Bast's book is nothing short of remarkable. She writes with such authenticity on a subject of such vulnerability; love and addiction. Shedding light on a natural Earth medicine that is almost unheard of in the Western world, Bast brings to surface more than a cure for hard drug addictions, but a remedy for our deepest collective wounds and avoidances to true love and intimacy. A true love story indeed, Bast has done a great service to all by writing and sharing this profound experience."

Lillie Claire Love, intimacy coach

"*Heart Medicine* is raw, unbridled story about Bast's relationship with her partner facing addiction and their unconventional journey to sobriety. In a society where we tend to throw away relationships rather than see them as a reflection of ourselves, Bast faces the darkness and bravely tells the truth breathing light to the shadows in her life. This page turner inspires us all shift our perspectives on addiction, dredging into the depths as way to cultivate strength and to reconnect to the shamanic traditions as a path to our inner wisdom. You can feel in every word, Bast has put her heart and soul into this book. It is almost impossible to not to fall in love with her."

Patricia Eastman, retreat facilitator, coach, author of *Pretty Drugs*

"*Heart Medicine* is a game-changer. It's compelling message and exquisite story brings hope and inspiration to all of us who have either suffered drug addiction or watched our loved ones fall into despair and destruction because of it. Elizabeth weaves in their love story, their challenges, and eventually their profound healing and awakening resulting from connection with this medicine and the shamans who prescribe it. It is a heartfelt, exciting story, especially for all those who suffer from the limitations of Western Medicine. It is my hope that this book reaches the widest audience possible. It is a book like no other; its message illuminates a path to profound healing for one of the most challenging health issues of our time."

Mary Frank, writer, producer, radio host

"I couldn't put it down until 3:30am! I am not surprised by how much this story resonates. Reading the book, I feel like Elizabeth and Chor are close friends that I've known for years. The story is so detailed and personal, I felt like I was right there with them through this whole experience. Incredible writing."

Lana Baumgartner, founder of The Pure Way with Lana Shay, co-founder of *Psychedelic Times*, performance artist

"Elizabeth Bast is an artist and a poet who weaves a gorgeous tapestry of true love and true healing like many have never known. She is a potent wisdom carrier and reminds us of the lost art of visionary storytelling to pass down tales of beauty and power from which generations to come will learn from. The story of her and Chor's journey to the heart of Africa and deep healing using the ancient sacrament of iboga is a riveting and inspirational transmission that you will not soon forget."

Maria Teresa Chavez, holistic health & wellness expert, spiritual advisor, founder of *Sacred Earth Warriors Transformational Healing Events and Retreats*

HEART
MEDICINE

HEART
MEDICINE
A TRUE LOVE STORY

*One Couple's Quest for the
Sacred Iboga Medicine and
the Cure for Addiction*

E. BAST

REGENT PRESS
BERKELEY, CA

MEDICINAL MEDIA
SAN FRANCISCO, CA

[Hardback]
ISBN 13: 978-0-9971213-1-5

[Paperback]
ISBN 13: 978-0-9971213-0-8

[E-book]
ISBN 13: 978-0-9971213-2-2

Library of Congress Control Number: *forthcoming*

COVER ART:
The Love Dance
Spray paint on canvas by Chor Boogie

COVER DESIGN AND AUTHOR'S PHOTO
Anandha Ray

Manufactured in the U.S.A.
Medical Media Press
www.medicinalmediapress.com

For the secret keepers

TABLE OF CONTENTS

PREFACE ... xi

IBOGA: AN INTRODUCTION ... xiii

ACKNOWLEDGEMENTS ... xviii

CHAPTERS

1: *Welcome Back* ... 1

2: *Back in The Day* ... 9

3: *When The Fire Was Fresh* ... 13

4: *The Home Haven* ... 20

5: *The Ravenous Dream* ... 24

6: *More and More* ... 29

7: *The Morning After* ... 34

8: *Blood, Sweat, and Tears* ... 33

9: *How In The World?* ... 42

10: *Long Lost Sun* ... 45

11: *Playing With Fire* ... 50

12: *Getting Warmer* ... 56

13: *Searching* ... 61

14: *Reports From the Universe* ... 65

15: *The Scandalous and the Sacred* . . . 71

16: *A Step Closer* . . . 75

17: *The Last Supper* . . . 81

18: *Money Honey* . . . 84

19: *One Spec of Dust at a Time* . . . 87

20: *Not Another Second* . . . 89

21: *Back In The Danger Zone* . . . 105

22: *The Happiest Place on Earth* . . . 109

23: *The Long Road* . . . 119

24: *Back In The Saddle* . . . 126

25: *Storm Shelter* . . . 135

26: *Feeding Demons* . . . 138

27: *Final Countdown* . . . 141

28: *Taking Flight* . . . 144

29: *Welcome* . . . 150

30: *The Doorway* . . . 163

31: *In The Eye of the Hurricane* . . . 174

32: *A New Dawn, A New Day* . . . 192

33: *Wonder and Warnings* . . . 204

34: *Rooted* . . . 213

35: *The Field Trip* . . . 216

36: *Diamond Heart* . . . 224

37: *Five Minutes to Live* . . . 239

38: *Door Number Two* . . . 248

39: *Rewired* ... 267

40: *The Laws of Life* ... 285

41: *Animal Medicine* ... 290

42: *Talking Trees* ... 304

43: *Baptismal Waters* ... 314

44: *Healing the Future* ... 327

45: *Return to So-Called Reality* ... 331

46: *Seeds of Synthesis* ... 334

47: *Temple Dance* ... 348

48: *Fairy Tale Ending* ... 355

49: *Rubber Meets The Road* ... 361

50: *Messenger From Beyond* ... 363

51: *The Marriage of Mater & Spirit* ... 368

52: *Shine On* ... 376

EPILOGUE ... 3787

THANK YOU ... 380

ABOUT THE AUTHOR ... 382

PREFACE

"**A**RE YOU SURE you want me to write about... *that*?" I asked Chor. "It's really fine if I use a little 'artistic license' to keep certain hairy details...private."

Private meaning censored. Surely we didn't have to air *all* our dirty laundry in order to share our story.

"No!" he said firmly, with a clean-burning fire in his eyes.

"Tell everything. Tell the truth. The whole truth. That's the only way." He spoke from that great wellspring beyond himself.

"OK, then."

He was right. The ruthless truth seems to have given this story a soul. So we give you the truth, as best as I can put it into words.

June 2014

IBOGA:
AN INTRODUCTION

Iboga is a perennial shrub native to the tropical forests of Central West Africa. Like ayahuasca, San Pedro (wachuma), peyote, and psilocybin mushrooms, iboga is a psychedelic plant medicine that has been taken ceremonially by indigenous people since ancient times for spiritual initiation and healing. More recently, iboga has been proven to have powerful addiction breaking effects in medical studies and observational research.

When my mother first read my memoir about our experience with iboga (she's a cool mom, alright), she said, "I feel like I've taken iboga just from reading this book." Not everyone needs to take iboga for healing or awakening. Maybe reading this book is enough iboga for you. Maybe there is another kind of medicine for you, for there are many different kinds of mental, physical, and spiritual medicine on this planet to suit billions of radically different human beings.

Is iboga for you? Listen for the quiet call of the soul.

If you are called, approach this ancient medicine with respect and clear intentions. Iboga is not only highly psychoactive and spiritually intelligent, it is also one of the most medically volatile sacred plant medicines. Sustainability issues and ethical sources are a consideration. It also happens to be illegal in many countries, though the politics behind its prohibition are hotly debated. Educate yourself thoroughly, understand the contraindicated medical and psychological conditions, and choose your provider with great care. As shaman Moughenda says, "taking iboga without a qualified guide is like driving a car while blindfolded."

Explore the page on my website dedicated to iboga for up-to-date information, medical research sources, community organizations, integration services, provider listings, and additional sobriety support:

WWW.EBAST.NET

This introduction is for informational purposes only. It is not intended to diagnose conditions, prescribe treatments, or otherwise replace medical advice. There are always risks in approaching plant medicines. Medicinal Media LLC & E. Bast disclaim any liability, loss, injury, or damage incurred as a consequence, directly or indirectly, of the use and application of information presented here.

ACKNOWLEDGEMENTS

IT TOOK A VILLAGE to birth this book. I am deeply humbled and grateful to all those who supported the creation of this book.

First and foremost, I offer boundless oceans of gratitude to our ancestors, guides, and guardian spirits who accompanied us on our journey. I give thanks to my great love, Chor Boogie aka Joaquin Lamar Hailey, for walking this path with me, inspiring me to write, and courageously allowing our intimate story to be revealed. Infinite gratitude to Moughenda Mikala for so generously sharing his tradition, healing skill, stories, and laughter with us. Medals of honor go out to the valiant and kind staff from Iboga House: Michael Dancing Eagle Cassidy, Ann-Mari, and Julia Malone. Immeasurable thanks to my mother for reading the raw manuscript, sharing critical feedback in such a graceful way, and supporting my radical dharma in this lifetime. Deep thanks to our families for the unconditional love, compassion, strength, humor, and skillful support throughout this rollercoaster and public confession. Super sparkly thanks to Polly Superstar Whittaker for being a fierce and fabulous writing mentor. Tidal waves of appreciation to Bella Shing and Drew Freeman for encouraging me to come out from my cave and share my gifts. Zealous pranams to Anandha Ray for the graphic design, photography, shamanic artistry, deep sisterhood, and profound grace. A million red roses to Shamana Ma Sharene and Patrick Riley of Holylove. tv and A List Calendar. A big "woplia!" to George and Georgia Bertelstein, Jeff and Erika Wright, and all our friends from the Medicine Path Native America Church.

Kisses to the feet of the Quimera tribe and the fusion temple dance community. Winks and sultry songs of praise to the wild minds of Danger Wank, my writers group. Thanks to my copy editor, Stephanie Pascal, and my book designer, Mark Weiman of Regent Press, for the passionate professional symbiosis. Incense, arati, and passionate gratitude to Janice Craig of JaniceCraig.com for serving as a true priestess of love.

Blushes and bows to the tribe of artists, poets, bright lights, flaming bodhisattvas, healers, teachers, community leaders, and medicine people for the inspiration and support: Ewa Dauter, Shamani Romans, Michael TonTon'opoulos, Debra Giusti of Debrarecommends.com, Jonathan Dickinson of the Global Ibogaine Therapy Alliance (GITA), Brad Burge of the Multidisciplinary Association for Psychedelic Studies (MAPS), Amber Lyon of Reset.me, April Short, Julian Reyes of KEYFRAME, Magenta Ceiba, the Evolver Network, Reality Sandwich, Miriam Elyse, Kat PK, Eden Rumelt aka Lady Eternal Love, Ashley Rain Turner, Eddie Joe Cotton, Monica Salazar, Dmitry Kras, Philip Milic of Old Crow, Jeff Cook and Gary Cook of Iboga Wellness, Robyn Rock and Mark Howard of Iboga Soul, Steven and Madison Callahan of Roots Healing, Aradia Sunseri, Richard Power, Alexander Friend, Travis Sigley, Beth and Tony, Lizzie Easton-Montes and Trek6, Justin Hamel, Julia Onnie-Hay, Ashok Chippa, Maya Luna, Laura Cirolia, Mara Altman, Mariela de la Paz, Jena la Flamme, Tenley Wallace, Lucid Dawn, Eenor Wildeboar, Tamar Therese, Ayah Buonaugurio, Phillip T. Nails, Elisabeth Millican, Mark Wilson, Jonathan Jay Levine, Megan Rose Woolever, Amanda Elo'esh Johnsen, Lila Rose, Samantha Sweetwater, Rhani

LeeRemedes, Robin Tala, Annaliese, Nana, Kyla Dawn, Marco, Micah BlackLight Lael, Sofiah Thom, Brendan Jaffer-Thom, David Wolfe, Gina, Eileen, Maggie, Eric Waldron, Paul Flamer, Michaelah "Miraculah" Ivie, Leora Pangburn, Shenandoah Ableman, Leila Bazzani, Oshan Anand, Psalm Isadora, John Doffing, Sarah Eden Davis, Wisteria, Sitka, Marja West, Adrian Auler, Alex and Allyson Grey, Shrine, Carey Thompson, Jennifer Michelle Long, Gil Gross, Brooke Waterhouse, and Steve Waterhouse, just to name a few!

Thanks to the scholars and educators who have helped to expand my understanding of addiction and recovery: Gabor Maté, Andrew Tatarsky, and David J. Linden. Thanks to the scholars and psychonauts who have helped to expand my understanding of psychedelic medicine and culture: Rick Doblin, Ralph Metzner, Rick Strassman, Terrence McKenna, Dennis McKenna, Ben De Loenen, Jeremy Narby, Anja Loizaga-Velder, Eduardo Schenberg, Luis Eduardo Luna, Aubrey Marcus, Daniel Pinchbeck, Claudio Naranjo, and Joe Rogan. Deep respect to Howard Lotsof, Norma Lotsof, Jeffrey Kamlet, Kenneth Alper, Dana Beal, Doug Greene, Dimitri Mugianis, Bruno Rasmussen Chaves, Chris Jenks, Jamie McAlpin, Lee Albert, Christopher Laurance, and the other pioneering advocates of iboga and ibogaine, many of whom endured countless challenges in order to serve and educate others.

Thanks to Annie Sprinkle, the matron saint of sex-positive culture and radical erotic art. Without her, I would never have grown the back bone needed to birth this book.

Thanks to all who supported and promoted our

fundraising campaign to produce this book! We are aware of each and every one of you. We are so blessed and honored!

Thank you, the reader, for receiving this devotional creation *right now.*

CHAPTER 1
WELCOME BACK

"And the day came when the risk to remain tight in a bud was more painful than the risk it took to blossom."
— ANAÏS NIN

"Let any one of you who is without sin be the first to throw a stone."
— JOHN 8:7

HE MISSED HIS FLIGHT into San Francisco that night.

He never misses his flights.

His travels usually flowed with military precision.

I have to tell him. Tonight's the night. I can't hold this secret in anymore, I told myself. My secret had become oh so heavy after a few years.

He was able to catch another flight into Oakland airport, arriving at midnight. I was exhausted. My journey to pick him up was stilted by a traffic accident and then a factory fire. Cars backed up. My body ached. So tired. So stretched thin. But there were no shuttles running at that time. I just had to go get him.

Resentment simmered as I sat in traffic. *He couldn't save me like this if the situation were reversed. I was the one with the car and the insurance. So I had to do all the driving. I was the ox in the family.* Or so my story went.

I simmered often, I realize now.

I pulled up, drawn to his favorite siren-red hoodie like a homing pigeon. Broad shoulders slowly swayed side to side, readying to pounce into our car. The stuffed military backpacks he'd been carrying rested by his feet. His long, loose surfer shorts exposed a few inches of this skin, teasing me. I longed to get my hands on his tired body. Chor's travel-weary face looked up. For the first time since we'd met, he'd grown his beard out a little. It was well groomed with thick chops and sharp lines. He looked a little rough around the edges. He'd been working so hard. His once golden skin appeared to be enshrouded in grey smoke. The strong bones of his face were hidden under subtly swollen flesh. His gaze was softer than usual; it floated over and through me. He got in the car and leaned in to kiss me—a tender, full kiss on the lips. *Wow. What a strange treat these days.*

He rarely reached for a kiss anymore when I picked him up from a trip. When he did acquiesce, he'd rush through it, never fully "landing." His homecoming kisses had become about as romantic as an automatic car wash. "Let's just get out of here," he'd grumble, already leaning toward the cave of home. I would be left shivering like an excited puppy panting for pets.

It hadn't always been like that. Once upon a time he planted kisses on me that penetrated my whole being, rooting me to the core of the earth as my mind flowered into the heavens. "Feel how deep this kiss goes," he'd whisper, enveloping me in ecstatic stillness.

The past couple years, I often found myself longing

for him to sink into the present with me and stop time—even for a moment. I could feel his subtle resistance and relentless momentum into an abstract future that never seemed to arrive. Always something more important to do. Always another text to answer. "Just 30 seconds," I would tease, to melt any fear he had of being consumed indefinitely into my vortex of insatiable feminine desire.

"OK, now get off me," he would half-tease me in his tough-guy tone after a few seconds of affection, and then he'd rush back into his inner rat race.

So it went that kisses were harder to come by, timelessness was tough to schedule, tenderness was lost in the shuffle, and a quiet chasm grew between us. Yet, he still routinely professed, "I love you. Yes I DO. You are AMAZING, my queen, star-berry juice LOVE-ness." I clung to those words like a life raft.

Patience, Elizabeth.

—

I could taste the heavy cloud of booze and cigarettes on him that night.

He'd started drinking and smoking heavily during his work trips the past three years. Before that he'd been sober for a decade. And before that...*well, that was a different lifetime altogether,* I thought, *a different person even.*

I'd met him in his sober phase. Militantly sober. So sober, I couldn't imagine him being any other way.

Lying in bed one night, in our early days, we melted into a kiss. He recoiled from the taste of my lips. "Did you...*drink alcohol?*" he asked, aghast.

I had gone to a girlfriend's birthday party that day. We'd had a picnic on the beach.

"Yes, I indulged in half a glass of champagne," I said, straight up.

His face pinched. "But you never drink. I didn't think you drank. *No one* needs to drink. It's poison, all poison."

"I know you don't drink, love, so I never drink *around you*," I responded calmly. "I rarely drink. I partake in wine or champagne maybe a handful of times per year. It's a sacrament for me. I do not abuse the spirits. These rare libations are good for my heart. Yet, I understand that alcohol is not good for you. I support you in your path. We are not exactly the same. I hope you can accept this. I do."

He quieted down. He didn't really agree with me, but he swallowed his judgment and loved me "as is."

Chor had been so radiant in his sober days—pure and focused like a laser.

He was a righteous man without religion. An urban prophet slinging truths: "There's only one emotion: LOVE!" This was one of his favorite catch phrases.

"I am so grateful that you are in my life!" He'd often say to his nearest and dearest, mirroring his sage grandfather.

"Everything...is everything!" he'd laugh, affirming the great cosmic play of oneness.

He kept his body clean. His skin glowed. He spoke the language of love with his words, eyes, and gestures, no matter the subject. He might have been an inch taller, too.

He'd lost some of that light when he invited alcohol back into his life. A cynical scowl now permanently adorned his brow. Though he'd left a trail of brilliant accomplishments in his wake, he rarely seemed truly peaceful.

I accepted him, for he was still my love, albeit a little dusty. My heart led me back to him daily, and I trusted that inner compass.

⁓

After that long, sweet, exotic kiss at the airport curbside, I took a good look at him. What had come over him?

He looked especially weathered that night. Heavy bedroom eyes. His expression, somber. He was living his dream, apparently. Painting the world.

He'd been on the road for most of the past two months. I knew he was overdoing it, burning the candle at both ends. He'd been working himself to the bone, literally, with no sign of slowing down.

His scent was different that night. Strange, sick, synthetic, cough-syrup sweet.

"I think I'm coming down with something," he muttered.

We made it home, and he immediately faded into sleep. I would have to delay my determined confession.

The next day, he lay placid around the house without his usual drive and energy. Generally he was the unstoppable train of doing.

Must have been the flu.

That evening as he lay smeared on the couch, he pulled me to him. Deep, painful breaths. Heavy silence. Then, "Baby, I can't party like that anymore."

"Yeah, love. I can feel it's taking a toll on you."

"Elizabeth...."

More silence. A long sigh. Staccato breaths.

I could see that he was struggling inside of himself. He wanted to tell me something. I coaxed him.

"Love," I said gently, "you can talk to me. I can feel you want to. I'm here for you."

"I...I didn't just drink when I was down in San Diego this time," he said ominously. My heart sank.

"What else did you do, Love?" I asked softly.

"You know what I did."

No.

"Say it, Chor. I need you to just say it."

He looked away, into some other world.

"Heroin. I did heroin."

I fell back on the couch next to him, stunned. We lay looking at the ceiling. The sky fell.

How could this happen? He had left that dead-end road over 13 years ago, long before he met me. His greatest fear had been relapsing. His greatest hope had been staying clean. He had vowed to never return.

"So...do you intend to heal?" I asked. "Are you going to stay away from that shit?"

"Yes," he said desperately. "I NEED to. I can't go

back to that. I'm sorry. I'm so sorry. I feel so ashamed."

"Did you inject it?" I asked bluntly.

"Yes," he answered, soft and open.

"How many times did you use?" I asked.

"A few."

"Did you use clean needles?" I probed with urgency.

"Yes!" he answered emphatically. "I bought them myself."

Then his words grasped, as if for a life raft. "I won't use again. I promise."

Famous last words.

"Do you still love me?" he implored, with all the power and pride drained from his face. A frightened little boy lived in him. "I *need* you. Don't leave me. I love you. Please, Elizabeth—don't leave me."

"Of course I still love you. I love you unconditionally," I paused, pensive, "but living here and being with me does have some conditions. I need to keep this home safe for my son and for myself. I will always love you, but there have to be some boundaries here."

I was a mama lion. My son, Kyle, was just 15 and lived with us part time. I had to protect his heart as well as his safety. He looked up to Chor. He respected Chor's public stance against drugs. I didn't want him to see his hero like this. *What if Chor couldn't stop using? What if he brought drugs into our home? What if...what if?* A million tragic scenarios ran through my mind. Chor was standing in avalanche territory. This could be really bad, to keep Chor in the home right now.

I'd always thought, *I would never tolerate drug addiction in a relationship.* No way. *Not me. That would end the game, if anything would.* But instead I listened to that still, small voice inside of me.

Pray.

Wait.

Listen.

"You must get treatment," I said desperately. "Of some kind. Immediately."

We collapsed in pain and confusion for a while. Breathing. Thinking. Feeling.

I rose up and straddled him, looking deep into his dulled eyes. I formed my hands into eagle claws. I roared in whispers as I raked the air above his heart in long, slow, sweeping gestures. I combed this invisible demon off of him and shook it away into the abyss behind him. Chor just looked at me with wide eyes and indulged this unusual gesture.

You won't take him, I vowed silently to the demon.

"I'm sorry," he said again, and we fell into a deep sleep.

My confession would have to wait yet again.

Chapter 2
Back In The Day

"Art is created at the level of the soul, a reflection
not just of one's self, but of humanity."
— Anandha Ray

"As Infinite Loving Awareness and Consciousness having
a human experience, we are sovereign Beings empowered
with the ability to create Formless into Form."
— Marja West

In the beginning, his dream of success was fueled by love.

It was his prayer that first made me swoon. As we sat in a tea shop interrogating each other on that first date, he rattled off this well-worn daily personal mantra:

"Goddesses and Gods, bless us all and protect us all with your strength, abundance, peace, genuine spiritual love, gratitude is attitude, honesty, willingness, humility, health, wealth, wisdom, knowledge, trust, truth, faith, acceptance, adjustments, intentions, enthusiasm, balance."

He surprised me. With his tattooed, well-honed body, shaved head, and signature proud saunter, he looked more like a refined MMA fighter than "an artist." His iron exterior gave way to a soft heart and deep currents of reverence.

I quickly learned that his masterful art flowed from

a very deep source. Chor wanted to uplift people with his colors. He called himself a color therapist, though I liked to call him a color shaman. His magical implement was spray paint. He painted portals to realms of archetypal wisdom. He brought unthinkable beauty into existence. Third-eye symbols silently sang to the gasping anonymous heart. Faces of the first cosmic lovers looked out from multidimensional sea storms. Regal queens and urban love goddesses emerged from morphing kaleidoscopes, telepathically transmitting the answers to all our human questions. Moving symphonies of every imaginable hue spoke timeless truths. He turned barren city walls, canvases, cars, and any surface that he could legally transform into an eyeful of ecstasy that hinted at a future utopia. His creations were pure visual medicine, before the unraveling faces, before the screaming mouths, before the poison took hold.

We fell in love with the force of two tidal waves crashing together, despite my insistence that I'd never meet my match in this lifetime.

Then we dreamed together. We envisioned our future.

Chor would pray to the Most High every night, out loud, just before bed, "Bless me to find success in the art world—so I can support a family doing what I love."

He wanted to be a papa. He was far more interested in family life and quiet creativity than glamour and glitz. He defied the myth of the tragic artist. He was both a prolific genius *and* a human ray of light—healthy, happy, humble.

We cross-pollinated art.

He invited me to participate in his show at Project One Gallery in San Francisco. "Romanticism" would be our first collaboration. He'd hang his canvases, and I'd bring a dose of dynamic energy to the otherwise two-dimensional viewing. I'd let my superconscious and subconscious minds mingle together in strange outfits in front of people. Some people call this performance art. I call it visual poetry.

Hmm. What would we do? We wondered. We'd never worked with another artist of such a different medium before.

Lovers making art together: *How romantic. Right?*

We churned ideas. We were both used to executing our own visions without any back talk. Chor bluntly dismissed my first few suggestions. My ego was ruffled, and my artistic wings felt clipped. This was not romantic at all. We were like two construction workers hashing out details for a new kitchen sink. I was about ready to excuse myself from the project, and then inspiration struck me with one more vision. "How about this. Paint ME. And another dancer. Not with spray paint, of course. Water-based paints. Airbrush?"

"Yeah, I can do airbrush." His eyebrows raised, and his lips started to curl into the first hint of a smile. "Go on."

"I see an empty frame," I continued, "hanging from the ceiling. Right next to your other paintings. From behind this empty frame, we'll begin a dance. We can play with the border of that frame. We can drip out of it, escape it, assault the audience with rose petals and feathers, and then jump back into the frame. And back out. And in and out. We can literally bring a painting to life and turn spectators into participants. What do you think?" I always loved breaking that invisible barrier between audience and artist, stage and so-called reality. "Come on, baby."

"Yeah! Yeah! Sounds good! Let's do it!" His enthusiasm was music to my ears. I squealed. We placed our art and our hearts in the other's hands.

I recruited a beautiful dancer friend. Our skin was his canvas. Even with two naked women before him, Chor had eagle eyes only for his paint. He fussed over the style, streaks, drips, and full-body composition. We were drenched in his color, from head to toe. We channeled playful celestial nymphs. Our guests sprouted smiles. We kept them on their toes, awake to the art.

Chor had carefully selected his getup for that night. He wore my vintage men's pinstripe suit jacket, a loud T-shirt, and 3-D movie glasses.

Friends and strangers circulated through the gallery. The photo album from that night is filled with shining portraits. Our guests sparkled with delight, their senses and souls sated with aesthetic rapture. Chor and I both beamed with energetic afterbirth.

And so it was that "Romanticism" was the first of several fertile artistic collaborations—and a shining gem in the broader collaboration of our life together.

It was hot, holy heaven on earth for an epoch, but after a few years of wear and tear, our seamless intimacy faded, and prayers were slowly forgotten. Somewhere along the way, our dreams got a little lost.

CHAPTER 3
WHEN THE FIRE WAS FRESH

"ART. Is the willingness to explore the sometimes wild, terrifying, thrilling, joy filled, grief packed edges, through whatever means possible, in order for the world to experience them fully."
— LILA ROSE

"God grant me the serenity to bask in the cleansing effect of life's beautiful messes."
— EDEN RUMELT

"**S**O WHAT DO YOU DO?" people would ask, as they often do.

"I'm an artist," Chor would answer.

When people probed for his medium, he would answer, "Spray paint."

Then without fail, they would say, "Oh, so you do graffiti."

This would become a familiar show.

"No," he would say, "I don't do graffiti. I am an artist that works with spray paint."

Though he first honed his skills with spray cans on the streets of San Diego as a youth, he had come to disown the trendy term *graffiti*. For him it evoked a long-lost street life of gangs, drugs, risky illegal antics, and a slew of near-death experiences.

I'd seen a photograph of him from that era. "Look at that *guy*," Chor had joked about his dated reflection during our visit to his hometown of Oceanside, California. A young man, late teens, peered out at me from the old matte photo paper. Shirtless and lean, baseball cap tilted far off to the side, a studded belt barely held up his sagging jeans, and his boxers boldly peeked out. His mouth opened in a cocky smile as if to flaunt invincibility. His whole body leaned, elbows bent, palms turned up at his sides, welcoming danger—or perhaps dangerous ladies. I imagine him saying, "Yeah! Where's the party?" Those were the days. His first chapters of poison. *Another life.*

I respected his professional trajectory and his desire to distance himself from his toxic past, but the term *graffiti* had some positive associations for me. I was all for illegal art—at least until politicians designated legal public art space in every neighborhood. "Uncensored public art is integral to being human," I'd debate. "It dates back at least 40,000 years to the oldest cave paintings." This made for some spicy conversations.

He wanted to be respected as a fine artist, and rightfully so. He was not a tagger, marking his territory with an alias or slogan or icon whipped up at lightning speed. Yeah, tagging can be a vital creative expression, but it's just a different animal. Chor could spend 30-plus hours just perfecting a few inches of canvas with the tip of his upside-down spray can. He wanted a proper frame and some well-deserved distinction for his creations in the art world.

Chor was a virtuoso. He was a Michelangelo—of spray paint. He had become one with the spray can.

He met certain strains of prejudice in the fierce jungle of "fine art" professionals. With few exceptions, spray paint was devalued. Art forms that bloomed in the streets were devalued. Self-taught artists were devalued. Yet, *he valued himself* and he envisioned himself in galleries and museums—and that's where he would eventually go, one earnest step at a time.

—

His art did take off like wildfire, soon enough.

Demands for his murals steadily came through.

Gallery gigs came in from time to time, never as sensational as he dreamed at the time, but still valuable steps. Private commissions trickled in. He worked every live painting job, however humble. He donated plenty of pieces to charity.

He received some media shine—magazine interviews and news clips here and there. His murals showed up in commercials and music videos. His work was included in a few art books.

His fan base burgeoned. He taught himself the art of social media networking. He went from one Facebook fan to 80,000 in a few years of consistent outreach.

"You're gonna get groupies!" I teased. "You're

gonna have to wear a burqa." It was all humor. I wasn't the jealous type.

"Ah, women are afraid of me anyway. You are the only one for me," he playfully assured me.

I felt his dedication to his art and our love and our vision of family.

His tenacity was a force of nature.

He had thicker skin than any artist I'd ever known. The brighter he shined, the more he attracted criticism and jealousy along with the appreciation. Pseudo art critics and stifled artists would occasionally offer unsolicited verbal surgery for his creations. He'd let all the empty two-cent comments roll off him like rain. "Hmm, that's interesting. Tell me why you feel that way," he'd invite, dissolving the war energy. Once heard, his critics usually softened right up like butter in the sun. His color and beauty would just keep flowing. Such comments would have crushed me once. He taught me how to be strong. He taught me how to take the nonsense, transmute it, and keep on creating true to my vision.

Nothing would stop him, it seemed, even when tragedy quite literally struck.

"I've been stabbed!" He screamed as he limped toward me one early autumn eve. My heart skipped beats. He'd been working on a mural on Market Street in San Francisco. I'd been on my way to pick him up and missed the incident by minutes. A little gang of young thugs had stabbed him twice when he caught them trying to snatch his paint.

I sat through a full night of purgatory with him at San Francisco General Hospital. The trauma center was backed up. Drunks with broken bones, lost souls with black eyes, reckless youngsters navigating bad trips, and old people on their last leg all lay sprawled out on gurneys in the hallways. For a while it felt like an episode of *The Twilight Zone,* and I imagined that we'd end up there forever. He moaned on painkillers for hours, "Why!? Why did they do this to me? I'm just trying to make art!"

I couldn't do anything to ease his distress. So I just sat next to him like a mountain, quiet through his endless rants and shrieks of pain. I stroked his head every once in a while, silently chanting Sanskrit prayers of protection and healing.

Medical tests revealed that they had missed his internal organs by inches. He was finally treated in the wee hours of the morning. The doctor rinsed his wounds with saline, stuffed them full of medicated gauze, and hoped he wouldn't get infected.

Chor went right back to finish painting that mural with his wound still fresh. He turned the trauma into a media circus. He seemed to turn every lemon into lemonade, every tragedy into triumph, and kept on his path like a juggernaut.

⌁

The world beckoned to him more and more, reflecting back to him the monumental energy that he offered.

He bit at all the dream bait.

He spread his color across the nation: New York, LA, Miami. Then over the earth: Australia, China,

Dubai, Mexico, Brazil, Germany, Egypt, Canada. I stopped counting the countries.

My tolerance for his travels was slowly stretched over time. "Just one more trip this month, baby. Something important came up." I rolled with it. Even through all the lonely nights, I loved that my love was doing what he loved.

I ached to be with him when he traveled. I ached to be by his side for his faraway gallery openings and mural unveiling ceremonies, for these were meaningful moments in my love's life. My own work commitments, duties of motherhood, and tricky pet sitting logistics deterred me from traveling most of the time.

"At least you are not a military wife!" He'd respond sharply when I expressed my aches. His glass-a-little-full kind of philosophy couldn't take away this painful feeling that nature was out of balance. I bit my lip and half starved. Patience, I would tell myself.

Fortunately, I had my own obsessions to keep me busy. Life at home alone was loaded with ordinary thrills, creative fulfillment, and cute cats. I taught my niche yoga workshops. I produced a dance festival. I offered holistic health and yogic lifestyle coaching. Random music and performance gigs sated my heart. Various writing and art projects held dominion over my late nights.

Above all, I was a mama. My budding young man kept me busy with sports games, music lessons, and a million errands. As my son found his own sovereign voice, there were endless hearty arguments about everything from house rules to politics to breakfast food. Motherhood required my full presence, participation, and fortitude. Even through the difficult times, I relished these simple days of maternal service.

Blessed with a creative tribe of friends in the San Francisco Bay, there were endless invitations to artsy, communal happenings. I would only occasionally take these opportunities to venture out. They weren't as much fun without my mate, and I would get tired of people asking me where my man was. But I loved the ever-present colorful buffet of options all the same.

And...I had my secret temple. This was a mystical oasis that existed in a hidden sliver of my life. Chor knew all of the secrets about my secret temple, all but one, the one I had yet to confess, the one still throbbing in my chest. But that's a whole Pandora's box, filled with forbidden jewels, ancient potions, forgotten languages, and lost arts. Let me put down a drop cloth before I open that one up.

CHAPTER 4
THE HOME HAVEN

*"The one thing we can never get enough of is love. And
the one thing we never give enough of is love."*
— HENRY MILLER

WHEN CHOR WASN'T painting the world, he
was home, and there was the sweetness.

Love bloomed through all the cracks in the cement
of our routines. We nested nightly for ritual movie time.
I'd rest my head on the mountain of his chest. He'd cra-
dle me and kiss my head and squeeze my cheeks—all of
them. I was his booty-teddy bear, his safe place, his queen.

"This is my wife," he'd always say when introducing
me. I secretly loved it, even though I always told him he
wasn't allowed to call me his wife until we had a true wedding ceremony. We had both wanted a wedding once,
something artistic and nontraditional, but it sounded
like such a laborious and extravagant production. It was
perpetually shelved in favor of other expenses and creative endeavors. A year or so into our relationship, he
got the bright idea to tattoo a thick sienna wedding band
onto his ring finger, and that meant more to me than
gold. *Good enough for now,* I thought.

There were holy conversations about love and
babies. Chor loved to talk about kids more than any
man I knew. "We need to have some babies, Elizabeth!

Yeah, I need to get you pregnant! Soon!" Chor would say with zeal, his formidable warm hand blessing my belly.

"Yes, love. I would LOVE to have babies with you, and I need it to be right," I'd say in earnest. It sounded so beautiful, to have babies with my love, but I wanted to honor the babies we'd bring into this world with a good life. I'd already been around the block, a really rough block, being a mama. "I need to be a full-time mother if I have more children. I will need more support from you, or from the universe." So he kept on working, and I waited.

There were the occasional hot dates and long, quiet walks around our neighborhood.

There was his endless patience for stepping in to share a home with my feisty firecracker son.

There was the way he stood up to my raging ex, armed only with a firm handshake. "Hello, brother." *I'm here now,* he quietly communicated with his powerful grip and direct eye contact at my son's birthday party. He was the first man in my life with the balls to do so.

There was the way my hyperactive dog, Ezmerelda, wholly approved of him. Chor was the only one who could lovingly tame her into sitting still.

There was the way he jumped right in headfirst to Thanksgiving dinner with my clan of eccentric, bookish creatives that always seemed to be on psychedelics—even though they were not. "Yeah, I'd love to go," Chor had said to my shocked face, pretty early on. The invitation was mutual, and he soon welcomed me into the homes of his mother, father, sister, uncles, aunts, grandfathers, grandmothers.

There was trust and truth. Naked hearts, naked bodies, naked minds.

We had our very own little bat cave of love. When Chor wasn't traveling, we were often sequestered at home, nestled into each other, recalibrating, purring. He wanted to stay in when he was with me. He seemed allergic to too much social time, and I was happy to oblige his desire to lay low in my arms.

There was his scent. His scent held a code, an answer, a destination for my soul. My mate. His scent had a compelling sway over me. It was the most intoxicating potion I'd ever encountered: cedar, chocolate, and forest floor after the rain. It went deeper than just biochemistry for me. It was the greater intelligence of spirit revealed through our senses. It was embodied kismet.

And there was the sweet, sweet love. The sweaty acrobatics. The divine intoxication. Sometimes we'd wrestle with our different sensual preferences. But we were sturdy. We'd keep at it. We'd both humble ourselves again and again on the altar of our bed to co-create plentiful moments of earth-shattering, mind-blowing, transcendent union.

I missed him down to my bones when he was away. I prayed for more time together, yet I forged my way through the dry spells. He was not merely my object for gratification, I reminded myself. *Relationship is a practice of devotion as well as a source of fulfillment.* This love filed down my rough edges, burned away my fairy-tale expectations, and tamed my ego.

Yes, love is a practice, but it can be a fine line between devotion and masochism, patience and starvation, selflessness and self-deprivation. I walked these like a tight rope more and more.

CHAPTER 5
THE
RAVENOUS DREAM

"The man of power is ruined by power, the man of money by money, the submissive man by subservience, the pleasure seeker by pleasure."
— HERMANN HESSE, *STEPPENWOLF*

"You are a vessel for that which you desire."
— MIRIAM ELYSE

AFTER A FEW YEARS, his dream became fueled by an ever-elusive glory. It had become ravenous, insatiable, desperate.

He was still driven by an authentic passion for his art, but he'd become a slave to his own ambition.

As the work poured in, Chor worked like a mad man. His cohorts nicknamed him "The Machine." He would paint for 10 to 12 hours straight for weeks on end to meet deadlines for murals and gallery shows. He'd go all day on nothing but dubious energy drinks. No food until 10 at night. Never enough water. He painted until his hands became gnarled, knees ached, shoulders hurt, and organs pinched in suspicious ways.

On the days that he wasn't painting, he would roll out of bed and go right onto his computer and

smartphone, spending 10 to 12 hours straight on the matrix immersed in networking and self-promotion. No sunlight. No fresh air. The only exception being occasional stints at the gym. I'm sure he would have had hair like Einstein, had he not shaved his head.

He'd sit and scowl at his computer. He became increasingly jaded and judgmental. He spewed venomous righteous anger when he didn't get featured in the right magazines or when artists that he deemed as unworthy found more success in the art world than he did.

"Look at that artist! He's just stealing other people's artwork and slapping up his unoriginal knockoffs all over the place. There's no real ART there." The greatest crime, according to Chor, was a lack of originality. Another weighty offense was an absence of well-refined style. "A five-year-old could do that! Why is his shit selling for a million dollars? Why does he have so many fans? (Insert a colorful array of cuss words here.)" I'd hear such spiels a few times a week.

Frankly, I could understand his sense of injustice. Some of these artists didn't have the same level of commitment to their creations. Not even close. They pumped out simple conceptual gimmicks, milked the elitist beast of nepotism, or marketed themselves as hyped-up human commodities. They clearly hadn't put in the blood, sweat, years, and tears that Chor had.

No matter how poignant his perspective, Chor's venom wasn't just flowing outward. It was also poisoning him from within.

His complaints became like a broken record. I couldn't say anything to help relieve him, so I'd just offer my programmed response. "Babe, it takes all kinds to make the world go 'round. Relax. Focus on you. You're on your own divinely timed schedule."

———

Chor began to travel more than he was home. He wouldn't consult with me about his travel plans. He would just *tell* me.

When his travels extended over two weeks, which they often did, I felt our relationship being uprooted. He'd come home with fewer deep conversations. Random acts of romantic reverence became endangered. And we'd have to get used to sleeping together all over again. But he didn't seem to mind the chilly distance as much as I did.

He was as loyal as ever, despite being away more. He still wanted me all to himself. He expressed his moments of jealousy with lighthearted humor.

"What *kind* of party are you going to?" he'd probe when I went solo to an event. "One of those circus orgies?" He teased me with tenderness.

"No, love. It's not that kind of party. You know I would never go to one, not without you, at least."

He liked to poke fun at my openly and shamelessly polyamorous friends, regulars and hosts of Kinky Salon, a notorious Burning Man–inspired private sex club for inventive, sex-positive people. Though Chor and I chose to be monogamous, I still admired this kinky crew for living their lives out loud. They brought their deepest desires into the light and dressed them up in amazing costumes. As ethical sluts, they were honest about their adventures with multiple lovers. They didn't buy society's standard recipes for relationships and instead blazed their own trails.

"Oh, you're just jellyfish," I'd respond with our playful code word for jealousy.

"Just a little," he'd say.

His career continued to blossom, and our connection became increasingly barren. Even when he was home, he often seemed just out of reach. Any time he wasn't painting, he was glued to his phone, even during dinners or movies. He'd become more and more allergic to being present.

I needed to feel our relationship as a garden: watered, weeded, and nurtured with love notes, hot dates, eye contact, and lazy Sunday mornings. To me, our relationship was a living masterpiece, not just the comfortable landing pad that it had seemed to become for him.

Even through this drought, there still existed deeper currents of love. Lucky moments would bring his offbeat, primal affection. He'd hug me in his Incredible Hulk way, pulling me to him and squeezing me until I had to tap out for air. He'd call and text ILOVEU daily. He wanted me close. So close. Every time I'd get up from the couch—or get up from the bed, he'd ask with urgency, "Where are you going?"

He'd always get the same exotic answers: "I'm getting a glass of water," or, "I'm going to pee." For occasional spice, I'd say, "I'm running away with the circus today." I adored these traces of our invisible connective threads.

My mate. My love. My busy, busy love. He'd draw

me to him again and again. I cherished any opportunity to nuzzle into him and feel the rhythm of our breath align. I wanted so much more, yet every little gesture of love was a sweet drop of water in the desert.

———

Though he'd been all over the world by himself, we'd never taken a trip just for us. I always encouraged him to follow his dreams, but I longed for a little balance.

"Please, baby," I pouted, "just give our relationship 1% of the energy you give to your career." It might sound like a pathetic request; if only you knew the Olympian energy that he funneled into his career. 1% would have been the mother lode of romance.

"Don't say that!" he'd respond, as if readying to battle. It seemed to touch a nerve.

"Why not?" I'd ask, but he'd never come up with an answer. Instead he would stare back into his computer screen and turn off my channel. He'd just carry on as before, with enough reassuring professions of "I love you" to keep things going.

Understandably, it's a wild ride being a self-employed artist climbing up out of obscurity. He had to build a name for himself. He lunged at every fertile opportunity he could get, but our flowers at home were drying up. He worked like a god, but he was still very human. He was so focused, but he was getting brittle and bitter.

"Success" would surely find him, but at what expense? I wondered.

CHAPTER 6
MORE AND MORE

"It is impossible to understand addiction without asking what relief the addict finds, or hopes to find, in the drug or the addictive behaviour."
— GABOR MATÉ, *IN THE REALM OF HUNGRY GHOSTS: CLOSE ENCOUNTERS WITH ADDICTION*

MORE AND MORE art shows started filling his calendar. He was expected to mingle. I saw how all the new events on his dance card would dissipate his energy, tease his ego, and push him off center.

After 10 years of strict sobriety, he started sipping wine at these swanky occasions that accompanied his growing slice of fame. I looked sideways at him at first, if only because he'd been so vehemently against drinking for so long. "It's just wine," he would say in the beginning. "It's not like it's drugs. Relax."

Within weeks of tasting the wine, he started guzzling cocktails until he stumbled. Imagine Superman... drunk. It wrenched my heart, this strong and brilliant hero, slurring his words, groping at me, barely able to stand. Sad. I couldn't make love to him when he was drunk. It almost felt like it would have been cheating, for it wasn't even really him. It was just the spirit du jour puppeteering his form.

The alcohol seemed to lubricate his sensitivity to social time. When he was sober, he generally had a far lower tolerance for fancy loitering and small talk. With the liquor, he could stay out late and mingle with rich vampires, hipster art-scene trolls, and wandering jackasses.

The alcohol took the edge off his workaholic trajectory and his aching, exhausted body. I could see plain as day that his life was out of balance. Sooner or later, his body and mind would backlash against the extreme demands he imposed on himself. He needed rest, good nourishment, more water. He needed nature. He needed some form of centering and periodic detachment—e.g., a spiritual practice. I kept offering him invitations to yoga from time to time, though he never accepted. He rarely joined me for my walks anymore. He kept going at full speed, just numbing his wounds.

When drinking, Chor was a barreling train off the tracks. Chaos embodied. A drunk hurricane. 220 pounds of steel gone haywire. His reason would get ravaged. He seemed to have lost his internal compass completely when intoxicated. *Where would he find himself, so lost in alcohol?* I wondered with a shiver. What could I do? I couldn't control him, but I expressed my concerns and I set firm limits around the house. "You can't be around me or my son if you're that drunk. It's not safe," I roared firmly.

Chor quickly learned to keep the alcohol neatly compartmentalized. He kept this drinking demon in his suitcase for the most part. I could feel it. I could hear it. His voice often wavered in our nightly phone conversations when he was traveling. He'd spout off loose and lyrical romantic words.

Normally romantic banter would have been a welcome treat, but it had become a blaring signal of his inebriation, for he rarely expressed his romantic sentiments when he was sober.

Whenever I sought out some fresh effusions of love during daylight hours he'd bluntly say, "Come on, babe, you know I love you. Do you need to hear it *every* day?"

"Yes, actually," I'd say in this particular routine. "We are new beings every day. Organic. Alive. I need your weather report, over and over."

During his drunken calls, however, he was gushingly, even obnoxiously romantic. "Elissssabeth. I love you, baby. I LOVE you. I ammmm gonna come home and get you preg-a-nant. Yes I am. Get ready. Damn, baby, you are sssssso beauty-full...." Etc. Etc.

I loved extra-sweet talk as much as any girl, but I resented that it only came lubricated with liquor. I wished that he could express like that when he was sober and fully present. His romantic heart was a pent-up prisoner inside of himself. I longed for his integration—an inner marriage of romance and reason, eros and logos.

So he drank and drank on these missions away from me. The alcohol left his body poisoned, brain dehydrated, and spirit weak.

In between his drinking binges, he would occasionally explode over minor household squabbles, seemingly out of the blue. "Do you want me to go? Do you?" He'd scream. It seemed he was in a pressure chamber of his own making.

"No, love. Let's just work on it," I said each time. "Nobody's perfect, like you say." He always seemed relieved by my response. I would later learn that this was his way of giving me an "out" as the demon within him grew stronger and the shame in his heart spread like black mold.

—

That night of his confession I realized that this heroin demon, stealthy and devious, had stayed hidden and sleeping inside him for 13 years, whispering to his unconscious all the while, biding its time, waiting for a weak moment and the right company, waiting for its friend alcohol to wear him down and leave him on its dark doorstep.

Was there a way to truly cleanse him of it?

CHAPTER 7
THE
MORNING AFTER

*"All that you are seeking is also seeking you. If you lie still,
sit still, it will find you. It has been waiting
for you a long time."*
— CLARISSA PINKOLA ESTES

*"The most elegant equation in all the Universe: I LOVE
YOU. Apply liberally and unconditionally for quantum
solutions to arise."*
— KAIA RA

THE MORNING AFTER Chor's confession, I went
for a walk alone. Shell-shocked. Heart heavy. I mentally
armored myself for impending devastation, separation,
even death.

Not again. No.

I'd lost other beloved ones to death by recreational
poison. Jeremy, a brilliant 32-year-old with a bright
future, my brother from another mother, was abruptly
erased from the planet one night by a cocktail of cocaine,
vodka, and OxyContin. And Lynette, my sister's lover
of four years and our loyal family friend, was stopped

cold in her tracks by a bad batch of speed. They were wild ones, but not so wild that anyone ever guessed what was coming. Alive, and then suddenly dead. No second chances. They'd left black holes in my heart and immeasurable, contagious pain in the world. Death seemed to be lurking around the corner, so close and so possible.

I communed with the redwood trees around our house. "Patience, Elizabeth," they said in their silent language of steady stillness. The Japanese maple trees offered their feathery auburn beauty tonic. The owls uttered their soft lyrical condolences. The crows cackled, "Lighten up, lady!" A metropolis of tiny birds chattered, "Wake up! Look at us! We are so pretty!" Oak trees taught me the virtue of strength with their sturdy, voluptuous, old bodies. Turkey vultures wandered, whispering, "There is no death. There is only transformation." The fragrant air pierced my reluctant lungs.

We'd escaped the urban stew of San Francisco and found a sweet little casita in a mellow North Bay town a couple years back. A good place to raise kids, we'd heard. Our poisonous situation seemed all the more obscene in stark contrast to the picturesque rural paradise.

Even through my dark cloud, I prayed with every step.

Then, I remembered something...*or something remembered me.*

I had the bizarre feeling that some force from beyond my little self was clawing its way through the watery depths of my subconscious mind.

Indeed, some years prior, I had heard of an obscure sacred plant medicine from Africa called *iboga,* but I couldn't remember exactly from where. Only the vaguest details had registered in my consciousness. I had experienced a few ayahuasca, wachuma, and peyote ceremonies over the years. I had friends who'd studied various indigenous spiritual traditions from around the world. Somewhere along the way, iboga must have come up in conversation.

Iboga...is known to help cure addiction? Did I get that right?

I hustled home to search the internet. The iboga medicine was indeed known to physically and psychologically disrupt all kinds of substance addiction. An addict could essentially be given a clean slate. A complete detox was said to generally take only one to three days, instead of weeks or months. Astoundingly, this medicine eliminated the horrors of opiate withdrawals. Could this offer hope? Or was this too good to be true? I launched into a broader mission of research.

I was devastated to learn that serious heroin addicts generally have a 90% chance of relapse within the first year in our Western medical system. Even the fanciest rehab centers had this meager success rate. Many addicts simply traded in their drug dealers for doctors, switching from illegal street drugs to legal drugs—equally toxic and addictive elixirs such methadone, synthetic opiates, antianxiety meds, stimulants, or sedatives.

I was hip to the importance of harm reduction. Yes, legal drugs alleviated some of the risks associated with the black market, but they did not offer true healing or lasting freedom. Sometimes people in recovery would be "recovering" for years or even decades with such pharmaceutical "drug replacement therapy." I read countless personal reports of addicts who existed as functional zombies with such treatment. People who made it without replacement drugs often struggled against an eternal craving.

Furthermore, abuse and overdoses of legal prescription drugs were all too common. I discovered that pharmaceutical drug reactions were the 4th leading cause of death in the United States, and more people were dying from prescription painkillers than heroin and cocaine combined. A future with big pharma was dim, and I prayed for another way.

I found many stories of complete healing for addicts with the help of iboga—and also with ibogaine, the pharmaceutical extract of the primary alkaloid in iboga, sometimes produced semisynthetically from the Voacanga africana plant rather than the Bwiti sacrament known as Tabernathe iboga.

I also read personal accounts of iboga serving as a potent tonic for the human condition. It was reported to alleviate emotional and psychological issues such as depression, post-traumatic stress disorder, fear, and anxiety along with many physical diseases as well. The medicine could elevate many different beings and treat a broad spectrum of issues. *What a generous plant.*

I also found a few tragic tales of psychological disturbance and even death with iboga on various internet forums, though the medicine seemed to have been misused in those cases. When digging deeper into the threads, I discovered that it had been administered by inexperienced people or mixed with other drugs.

Iboga and ibogaine were apparently rigorous and powerful medicines. The deeply introspective and immobilizing visionary journey was reported to last up to 24 to 48 hours, exceptionally long for any entheogen. It seemed like a daunting commitment.

In the cases where iboga worked, it seemed no less than a miracle. Could iboga get to the root of Chor's demon?

I took council with my sister. I told her everything. Turned out, she knew a legal iboga provider who had reported, "Ayahuasca is a cake walk compared to iboga." Oh God.

This was clearly big medicine—and potentially risky. I had some more homework to do before proposing such a wild idea to Chor.

CHAPTER 8
BLOOD, SWEAT, AND TEARS

"I had been taught to look for monsters and devils and I found ordinary people."
— JEANETTE WINTERSON, *THE PASSION*

"You cannot remedy anything by condemning it."
— WAYNE DYER

THE NEXT THREE DAYS were grueling as I nursed Chor through withdrawals. There was no relief for this kind of ache. He was leveled by the poison and disgusted with himself. I was riddled with shock and anxiety.

The words flashed through my mind: *How did it come to this?*

But there was no time to indulge such ruminations. I had to tend the wounds. I had to keep it together.

Each morning, I flushed his body with a mason jar of warm sea-salted water, as was my own daily habit. Then came the homeopathic doses of wachuma (San Pedro), a highly cleansing and gentle Native American sacred plant medicine. Next, I'd push him into the sauna. I fed him green juice and other cleansing herbs. I massaged his feet and poked at pressure points to stimulate his organs to purge.

Fresh scabs riddled his whole body, evidence of the habitual scratching that accompanied his heroin use. He looked diseased *and* war torn. I anointed his wounds with aloe and medicinal essential oils.

He acquiesced to all my treatments, but he was only half there, too weak and too ashamed to resist. *Would he just dart off for more as soon as he gathered a little strength?* I marched on in spite of my fears, a soldier of love on the front lines, just surviving the day.

I cleansed right along with him. I took the wachuma with him. I pushed myself into the sauna each morning with him. I didn't touch alcohol. I prayed. I opened to guidance from an intelligence that was greater than little me.

Each day he lay melted over the couch like an empty animal hide. Absent was his usual high-velocity, ambitious workaholic momentum. He barely even touched his precious computer.

He distracted himself with extra doses of his favorite legal fix—horror movies played at top volume. They rattled the walls and shattered my nerves. They would fill the house with screams, stabs, slices, and gunshots. The throbbing, manipulative music made my heart pound and cortisol pump. I could barely think straight when those flicks were on. I couldn't understand their charm. They were like nails down a chalkboard to me, definitely not entertainment.

"Love! Turn it down please," I pleaded. *Couldn't he*

just play them at a considerate volume to begin with?

Every time, the same skit.

"NO!" he'd yell back, before turning them down a hair.

Living together requires compromise, I'd remind myself with a grimace.

He'd started watching more and more of these gruesome films the past couple years. I hear some people get hooked on the adrenaline bumps from horror movies. I had often walked through the room to hear Chor gasp as someone was getting a limb cut off or an eyeball poked out. He seemed to need more and more violence in order to feel anything at all.

But tonight, there was no gasping. He was somber. Lifeless.

There was a hungry void in his eyes, just waiting to be filled. A new presence was taking space inside him—a heavy, insatiable darkness.

I planted myself at home. I was afraid to leave him alone, for fear of where he might run off to or what he might bring back. I missed several days of work, having canceled on good private yoga clients. Money for groceries and bills wore thin.

"Are you going to call your family? Are you going to let them know what's going on?" I asked, raising my voice over the slasher-film screams.

His family had seen him during his last trip to San Diego. They had suspected, he told me. "Are you doing drugs again, son?" He had denied everything to their knowing faces.

"Yeah...I will call them," he uttered.

The screams continued. I glanced at the decrepit zombie on the screen and shuddered at its resemblance to Chor that night—vacant, scraped up, falling apart. *You are what you eat, and you are what you feed your brain,* I thought.

I didn't need any more horror than already existed in the world, so I retreated to my room to further research iboga in peace.

CHAPTER 9
HOW IN THE WORLD?

"With nature's help, humankind can set into creation all that is necessary and life sustaining."
— HILDEBARD VON BINGEN

"Shamanism, to me, is simply the choice and ability to be in direct relationship with the elements that make life happen, to be of service to Life, and to cultivate relationships with all beings."
— AMANDA ELO'ESH JOHNSEN, M.A.

IBOGA SEEMED TO BE effective earth magic, in the right hands at least, but I wanted to know more about *how* it worked.

I followed a trail of clues on the internet, carefully filtering the legitimate information from the sensational and the slanderous. I learned that iboga essentially baptized the brain receptor sites that were locked into a toxic relationship with the drug of choice. In addition, the function of the neurotransmitters were reset to the pre-addictive state. But these actions were only what could be deciphered through our laboratory lenses; I imagined that the medicine must perform many nuanced acts of magic that we as humans cannot measure or comprehend.

I also learned that iboga dramatically increased neuroplasticity. Simply put, the brain remembers its flexibility, and it can be rewired for the better. Iboga helped humans to shed stale old stories and well-worn loops. Negative thinking, conceptual traps, familiar fixes, and senseless fears could be swiftly etched away and replaced with positive paradigms and nourishing strategies.

From a traditional shamanic perspective, iboga was referred to as a plant teacher. It was said to reveal the very roots of suffering, while offering guidance for a healthy and fulfilling path. Iboga refreshed the spirit along with the mind and body. Ordinary life, if it had become lackluster, could become luminous again.

I was curious. Maybe I would experience Iboga, too. I definitely had some healing left on my life's to-do list. But Chor was the starring emergency here. I shelved the thought and read on.

Iboga seemed to have a much higher success rate than rehabs, though it wasn't foolproof. Many apparently found lasting healing, but not everyone made it. *Why not?* I suppose it wouldn't be interesting unless it was somehow participatory. It is called a plant *teacher,* after all. Iboga offered this gift of profound holistic healing and illumination, but from there, I imagined, it was up to the aspirant to walk the new path.

Why is it that this plant cultivated within itself the remedy for addiction? I wondered. Plants often develop sophisticated medicinal, nutritive, or sensual gifts to appease the humans that will help to cultivate and protect it. Iboga's addiction-breaking actions in the brain were far more precise than even a skilled surgeon was capable of. And yet, iboga first manifested before there was ever such a thing as substance abuse.

This medicine has foresight.

Iboga came from the belly of Africa, the womb of the modern human. This medicine coevolved with humans since the beginning of time. It must have been keeping a close watch over us. This medicine was known to grant prophecy to shamans; it must also possess this ability—for its own purposes and for the survival of the planet it is rooted to. Iboga could likely look into our collective future. *Addicted humans equals a dead earth.* This medicine must have predicted the predicaments that its human children would face in the age of addiction.

CHAPTER 10

LONG LOST SUN

"At the bottom of every frozen heart there is a drop or two of love—just enough to feed the birds."
— HENRY MILLER, *TROPIC OF CANCER*

WE KEPT MY SON in the dark about this darkness, at least for the time being. Kyle didn't need any more stress than already came with teenage life, if I could help it. We dismissed Chor's ailments as the flu, and Kyle just kept on watching TV right next to Chor's haunted shell, oblivious to the drama.

Chor's crisis was easy to disguise, as Chor had always been distant with Kyle anyway. Chor had accepted Kyle as a part of this package deal with me, but Chor didn't give him much attention. Chor's chilly presence punctured Kyle. Kyle took it personally. This was an ever-present thorn in my side. I felt Kyle's pain, being so connected to my son. A strand of my heart lives in him.

"You are my stepdad!" Kyle had said with exuberance, one shining day in the early years with Chor.

"No, I'm not. I'm just Chor," came the terse response. I could see Kyle's smile sink as he ingested this subtle rejection into his freshly forming self-esteem. Kyle was still in the developmental phase in which he needed clan approval in order to feel his value in the world.

Kyle had long since deserted seeking meaning-ful interactions with Chor and settled for occasionally annoying him for scraps of negative attention instead. Kyle would steal Chor's cookies and say mean things and challenge him like a baby bull. Yet every so often, Kyle would simply say, "I love you, Chor." Chor never responded, either pretending not to hear him or too busy with more important things.

"He needs too much attention," Chor assessed. "So do you."

Once in a blue moon, Kyle would offer Chor a hug, and Chor would literally keep him at arm's length—unless we both ganged up and trapped him in a human sandwich. I think Chor secretly liked it. He could keep his tough-guy act going while still getting some close contact.

I pleaded with Chor to offer more of himself. "He's not MY son!" Chor yelled within earshot of Kyle. "We just live in the same house, that's all."

"Yeah, we all live in the same house!" I affirmed. "You might not be his biological dad, but we are still a tribe."

"Chor doesn't like me," Kyle would say, defeated. I encouraged Kyle to be patient and compassionate with Chor.

"Chor just isn't as affectionate as my side of the family. We all love in different ways," I'd say. "Try to accept him the way he is."

The daily tensions in our patchwork family were heartbreaking for me sometimes. It wasn't the Brady Bunch. It was more like a nest of Tasmanian devils, but it was our little nest. I loved them both so much.

Despite the cycle of Chor's indifference and Kyle's abrasive antics, the guys would sometimes bond over forbidden scary movies and wrestle each other from across the couch. They settled into a very manly-man kind of mutual tolerance.

Chor and I agreed. We would tell Kyle the whole story of the relapse—after Chor had healed. That might lower the impact. Hopefully.

If Chor lives through this, I thought.

—

"You have a son, too," I reminded Chor of the obvious, in the private sanctuary of our bedroom. His long-lost son. "You wanna see him grow up? You need to show him how to be a man. You need to show him the power that runs in his blood. Just because he's not in your life right now doesn't mean he won't be in the future."

Chor told me when we first got together, "I think I might have a son, but I'm...not sure." How can someone be unsure if they have a son?

Chor had had a fleeting teenage love affair with a girl, Selena. They dated when she was freshly broken up with her boyfriend, Marcos. Soon after she hooked up with Chor, she reunited with Marcos. About nine months later, Selena had a baby boy named Augustin. Word on the street: this boy looked like Chor. Somewhere along the way, Selena and Marcos had married.

Chor's young heart was filled with paternal sentiments and noble intentions. "If this baby is mine, I would be there for you both," he privately expressed to Selena. The young Selena would not, or could not, acknowledge Chor as the father.

The boy was raised as if Marcos was his father. Chor felt shunned. What could he do? He didn't want to rock their boat. So Chor lived with this knowing and gnawing in his heart and respectfully stayed out of the way.

Ten years later and five years into our relationship, Selena found Chor. She couldn't keep the secret locked up anymore. Secrets have a way of eating at you. She could see the truth looking back at her daily.

Selena had grown from an immature teen mom into a strong woman. She'd long since divorced Marcos, though Augustin still lived with him. One day, by chance, she had wandered by a local tattoo shop with spray paint artwork. "I used to date a guy who did stuff like this." They asked who. She said Chor.

"Chor...Boogie? *This* Chor?" they asked. The guys at the tattoo shop pulled up his website and Facebook page. Her heart stopped. She saw her son's face looking back at her. At long last, she reached out and acknowledged the truth.

"Yes! I have a son!" Chor announced to me one afternoon, after he heard from Selena.

"I thought you'd be angry with me, after all this time," Selena had said to Chor. But Chor was the pillar of patience, acceptance, and love.

I saw a photo. This kid, Augustin, was clearly Chor's son. I could see the spirit lineage shining through. My love's fruit. I loved him immediately. They even smiled with the same charming sass. Chor took to referring to him as his "sun" in all communications.

A DNA test was done to confirm what they already knew. Then came the delicate process of telling young Augustin and Marcos, a man of intense machismo. Marcos was furious, though some part of him had apparently suspected. "I always knew this day was coming," he steamed when Selena told him. He banned Augustin from speaking to Chor. He threatened Selena with further legal action unless everyone complied with his dominance.

"I don't understand," I said upon hearing the story. "It's an abundance of dads! An abundance of love and support! It's a great thing! There's a shortage of dads in this world." Then I reflected that Marcos must have been dealing with shattered pride and heartbreak on multiple levels. Though I didn't condone his response, I certainly felt compassion for him.

Chor would covertly send Augustin texts and the occasional gift, in spite of Marcos's threats. Selena arranged for some top-secret visits whenever Chor was visiting San Diego. But it was an awkward situation. Augustin was often unresponsive to Chor's outreach, and I could sense that this was the heartbreaking cherry on top of an already heartbreaking situation for Chor. I imagined that Augustin felt stuck in the middle of everyone's desires. "Give him time," I offered. "He will grow, and he will want to know you."

"Yeah, I need to be there for him," Chor affirmed with dim light in his eyes, in the midst of his hellish withdrawal.

CHAPTER 11
PLAYING WITH FIRE

"The Sacred Medicine is completely willing and able to open the eyes and ears of anyone who expresses a willingness to spend their life continually awakening from the dream of death into the blessed awareness that is our lives and the lives of everything that is Holy and Sacred. But we have to ASK for that help. Every time. That is what prayer is for."
— GEORGE BERTELSTEIN

CHOR STARTED TO GAIN some balance and strength on the fourth day, but he was still poisoned. I could see it. The demon was clawing at his insides. The demon didn't want to let him get too far away.

Chor could string more words together in sentences, but he was terse and aggravated. His face grimaced most of the time, steaming with a constant discomfort. Although he returned to his computer to check on his business, he was still glassy eyed, lost looking, and puffy. My love. *Where are you under there?*

I had been scouring the internet for more information on iboga. I thought I had a good case, and I felt my intuition humming in a positive direction.

As he was capable of thinking again and there was

no time to waste, I went to him, determined to bring up the possibility of this medicine. He sat peering into his computer. His business wouldn't mean shit if he was dead—or the walking dead, I thought. But he gazed intently nonetheless, pretending that he wasn't hanging on by a thread.

Spring light poured into our bedroom. One of his paintings watched over me, two color-streaked mermaid faces, hair and arms intertwined. It was one of his first gifts to me. Sometimes he wanted to sell it or paint over it when his momentum ran away with him, but I would never let him. Our grey kitty, Jasmine, was curled up on our bed, purring lazily. For a moment, I wished our problems could be as simple as hers. I looked at the simple altar adorning my dresser for strength. On it rested the vulture-wing ceremonial fan made by my mother, heirloom drums, a Quan Yin statue, dried cedar, and a fresh rose. It drip-fed my spirit daily. Where was his altar? I glanced at his desk, plastered with stickers depicting cryptic skulls, skater sass, and lewd ladies.

I took a deep breath. "Love."

Now, if only he would listen.

"There is one, well, radical option. Iboga." I pleaded with delicate word steps. "I've been doing my homework, and it sounds pretty miraculous, if taken in the right way. It might be worth exploring."

In my mind, he'd fallen into a frozen lake, and there was but a flash of time I had to be useful. I wanted to lunge at his feet and beg and cry, claw my way up to his shirt, and shake him awake. *Listen to me, love! I might have a key!* But I restrained myself. I knew him too well.

This approach would not be effective for my stubborn lover, especially now as he lay in the intoxicating jaws of this relapse.

"Yeah, I've heard of iboga," Chor said dismissively, "but not good things. That stuff scares me. I don't know if I wanna mess with that." My eyes fell to the ground, and my lungs deflated.

Chor told me the story. A good friend of his, Jake, had struggled with heroin addiction for years. Desperate to recover, he had mail-ordered iboga and self-administered it alone several times. It did not end well.

After Jake's first use of iboga, he did feel physically free of his addiction. But he was a lone psychonaut, without the presence of a masterful guide, the roots of lineage, or the mirror of a tribe to check him. After a while, Jake became lost. His hubris and greed kicked in.

Jake convinced himself that he could indulge and party for a stint and then use the iboga to clear the addiction when it became inconvenient. I understood. He had tried to exploit this master plant. So he went through several cycles like this over the course of a couple years. Each time, the medicine became more severe with him, until the final journey landed him in the emergency room, screaming for his life.

After my own limited yet profound experiences with other kinds of visionary plant medicines, I was shocked that anyone would mail-order such a powerful sacrament online, from God knows where, consume it outside of traditional ceremony, and alone! That seemed ludicrous. Disrespectful. Ignorant at best. Then I remembered, sacred medicine culture is far from being widespread in the industrialized nations. I was fortunate to have had such benevolent and masterful mentors.

I'd first learned about the importance of ceremony through my Native American roots. As a teen, my mother had brought me along to Long Dances, sweat lodges, and pipe ceremonies. Though we had not worked with visionary plant medicines, we had worked with more subtle forms of medicine: the songs, deities, directions, drums, trance, and prayer. I understood that invoking great power and great shamanic healing required a clear intention, strong container, and lineage blessing.

Jake had been playing with a fire of cosmic proportions.

I tried to explain. "He didn't approach it in a good way, love.

"These medicines are held in ceremony for a reason. Ceremony forms a heavy-duty vessel for the immense magic of the medicines. The ceremonies are born from the traditions that have held these medicines for thousands upon thousands of years. The shamans have cultivated a deep intimacy with the medicines over all that time.

"The most potent sacred plants require the presence of an experienced guide, not only for physical and psychological safety, but for the greatest possible healing and illumination." Chor flicked through the internet as I spoke. My words seemed to roll right off him.

My voice and heart pressed on. A story from my own ayahuasca maestra leapt into my mind. "Check it out. A group of teenage boys had heard through the grapevine that my teacher had a rare visionary 'drug' from the Amazon in her basement refrigerator. They broke in and stole it, and they gulped it down just for kicks. The same medicine that had blessed so many others with bliss, peace, and revelations now brought hellfire to these naughty boys. They were chased by demons and saw all kinds of horrors. They ran home to their parents, wailing and weeping. The medicine was, in essence, 'spanking' these naughty boys." Chor seemed unimpressed, or perhaps just distracted. I continued on my soapbox, hoping some words would eventually land in the right place.

"It was a small community. My teacher reached out to the confounded parents. She explained that the boys had stolen a sacred plant medicine and they were simply being taught a lesson. She ensured them with a wink that these boys would never again indulge in mysterious 'drugs' after that. Nor would they ever have the gall to steal again. It was actually a blessing."

I knew intuitively that Jake had disrespected the iboga medicine. I presented my finale. "The medicine schooled Jake."

"Hmm," Chor said, his tone tainted with suspicion. "I don't know if a plant can do *all that.*" Chor didn't understand how a mere plant could have such an adaptogenic intelligence. Still, he understood that it might at least save his life.

"I don't know..." he paused. "Honestly, it scares the shit out of me."

Was he impenetrable?

"Maybe," he said after a pause, finally looking me in the eyes.

Maybe is better than no, I thought.

I kept on the info hunt.

Chor, the devil's advocate, hunted for himself. He sent me a link to an internet forum where someone had reported a devastating experience and psychological damage after taking iboga. "See, this is dangerous!" he almost sounded relieved, but apparently he didn't read past the first line.

I read the thread and showed him: This person had gone to a shady-sounding medical detox facility in Mexico that had since closed down. The patient was given a whole slew of pharmaceutical antianxiety and antinausea meds right along with ibogaine. This person also admitted right there in the post that they had a preexisting, severe mental illness—that came part and parcel with all the symptoms that he was later blaming on the iboga. I pointed out the obvious to Chor: bad place, bad protocol, disturbed person.

My heart urged me to continue the quest for iboga.

I came across a video that quelled many concerns. A medical doctor by the name of Kenneth Alper spoke about his study of all the iboga related deaths over two decades, 19 in total. With deeper investigation, he had discovered that the good majority of the cases, all those with sufficient data, were explained by either preexisting contraindicated medical conditions (cardiac disease in particular), excessive dosage, inexperienced or uninformed providers, unsupervised self-administration, the use of opiates or stimulants during a treatment, or alcohol withdrawal seizures. It seemed that we would be able to navigate the dangers.

"Look at this, loveness." He indulged me. He was starting to look closer.

CHAPTER 12

GETTING WARMER

"When you act from within the wisdom of love, you become the medicine and sustain the circle. It shapes you as you draw it. The wisdom of love is the medicine. This medicine is the serpent swallowing its own tail. Alpha and omega are just pulsations within the coiling."
— RICHARD POWER, *PLANETARY EMERGENCY, PERSONAL EMERGENCE: PATH OF AN EVOLUTIONARY*

"When we heal ourselves, we also heal our ancestors, our grandmothers, our grandfathers, and our children. When we heal ourselves, we also heal mother earth."
— RITA PITKA BLUMENSTEIN

I WOULD HAVE TO LOOK outside of the country for treatment, as iboga was illegal here in the United States. *Why?* I wondered. Yes, it was powerful medicine, but I was learning that it could be safe in the right hands.

Maybe it's illegal because it works too well, I mused. Or maybe because the plant itself can't be patented, as something already so perfect growing straight out of the ground. Or maybe...because of a deeply ingrained puritanical prejudice against visionary medicines and the "heathen" indigenous wisdom traditions that hold them. No matter the reason, we'd have to leave familiar territory.

In my search for a healer, I found a smattering of medical detox facilities in the world that featured ibogaine, rather than iboga.

Ibogaine had clearly helped many people. I understood that certain people would surely feel more at ease with a medical and Western therapeutic approach, but I did not feel called to it for either Chor or myself. I was feeling in the dark on behalf of both our searching spirits.

Finding the right healer, tradition, and medicine is an extremely delicate and intuitive matter, for we are all unique. I felt magnetized to the natural medicine and a traditional shamanic healer. Maybe Chor's ancestors were whispering to me. And mine.

There were very few providers in the world offering drug detox treatment with the natural iboga plant medicine, and even fewer that featured traditional roots. My antennae tingled when I found a website for a retreat center called Iboga House in Costa Rica featuring Moughenda, a 10th generation Bwiti shaman from Gabon, Africa, where the medicine grows.

Moughenda seemed to be a living bridge between two very different worlds. The medicine was literally in his blood. Moughenda was a traditional African shaman, yet he worked at a healing retreat center accessible to the Western world. He had grown up in a tribe in Gabon, yet he spoke fluent English and he had an understanding of American and Western culture. It seemed vital to be able to communicate intimately with one's healer. Moughenda had many years of experience healing drug addiction, and he had a team of medical doctors on call for support if needed.

Hmm. We are getting warmer.

In one video, Moughenda explained that "taking iboga without a qualified guide is like driving a car while blindfolded." In another video, he expressed sadness over the bad press about iboga, for people had reported bad experiences only when they had inadvertently disrespected or misused the medicine.

I watched the many video testimonials on the Iboga House website. Visitors would bare their souls and reveal their most intimate struggles and victories before the camera. Former addicts, trauma survivors, veterans, and people recovering from depression spoke bravely about their miracles with iboga—and with Moughenda. My body shimmered with resonance. My eyes widened and my senses sharpened as I struggled to catch every detail. I leaned forward, my heart reaching. I felt the excitement of possibility and a sensation of inner light. Each testimonial touched me. These people were putting their faces out there for this place. I could feel the palpable frequency of sincerity and genuine healing.

"Look at these, baby." Chor and I curled up with the laptop on our big, cozy, velvet, modern, earth-colored couch. It had been our first big adult purchase together, and it had served as our sweet sanctuary ever since. The couch cradled us as we watched the videos together. Chor was intrigued. Opening. Softening. Listening. His mind opened a sliver more.

Chor did some of his own research in the next few days, though he was still tentative. A good sign, but he was headed in a different direction. He sent me links to some medical detox centers that used ibogaine.

I had to voice my sixth sense on the matter. "Love, I encourage you to experience the natural iboga—with the complete plant spirit and all the alkaloids—in traditional ceremony. It just feels like the right thing...*for you.*"

He balked at my intuition and pagan predilections. "You just think you know everything!" He didn't outwardly display much respect for my take on things. Sometimes expressing my opinions to Chor felt like a subtle battle.

Like a brute lawyer, Chor challenged me on every positive point I brought up regarding Moughenda and the natural medicine. I wondered how much of his aggravated vibe was the demon inside him, resisting banishment. But at least he was still engaged in this conversation, desperate to survive and thrive, and open to possibilities for the medicine.

I showed Chor a video interview I found in which Moughenda spoke about the difference between iboga and ibogaine; he shared his perspective that ibogaine lacked the complete plant spirit. So great was his passionate reverence for the natural plant medicine and Bwiti ceremony, he seemed to beam over the borders of the little screen right into our living room. I could see Chor contemplating; Moughenda's words were simmering and settling within him.

"This is a traditional shaman," I pleaded. "He has thousands of years of experience distilled in him. He is *from* Africa where this medicine grows."

"That doesn't mean anything, being *from* Africa!"

He argued, slinging suspicion. His eyes narrowed into arrows pointing right at me. "Crooked motherfuckers can be anywhere!" He built a bitter fortress with his words. So I retreated for the moment.

Despite his acidic attitude, I still felt drawn to this oasis in Costa Rica, to the plant spirit, to this man, Moughenda.

CHAPTER 13

SEARCHING

"You are willing to die, you coward, but not to live."
— HERMANN HESSE, *STEPPENWOLF*

DESPITE BEING SPIKED with resistance, Chor pursued a phone conversation with a person at an ibogaine facility, and he opened the conversation to speakerphone to let me listen in. We also called a different Bwiti lineage healing facility that was less expensive— and less experienced. In both cases, I simply didn't feel the full-body "yes" that I had learned to detect when making decisions.

Almost every day, we'd watch more videos from Moughenda and Iboga House.

One video featured Moughenda speaking about the medicine and the healing process:

> "After detoxing someone, we put them on a very special spiritual journey where they have to face themselves no matter what. Even if you've been running from your own truth, there's nowhere to run with iboga. That's why a lot of people have

a high success rate—because they receive a lot of good insight from that journey. Becoming your own witness on your journey, that's the best way to resolve the issues you've been dealing with. There's no way you are going to resolve deep issues just by thinking about it or by reading some books or by listening to someone talk. Yes, counseling will help, but it's not enough to just to tell someone how to deal with themselves—until someone faces themselves and has a deep understanding of what's been going on in their lives.

All plants have their unique purpose, every one. Iboga to us is the plant of knowledge and life. We've been using the plant for thousands of years. For generations, it's been our teacher, our guide. It's been everything to us. Iboga heals the physical—and the spiritual. It can take you to a very deep spiritual discovery.

Someone as a provider has to know what to do. It takes skill and knowledge to be able to work with the medicine. It is the spirit of iboga who comes to take you back to see your past and allows you see your own soul, face to face.

That's why it's called *awakening*. It's not a dream. There's no sleeping with iboga. You will be able to see your soul and talk with your own soul. That's what awakening is. You go past your own limited imagining and thinking. In that moment, you become your own witness. I can guarantee you 100% that iboga will take you there if you are ready and you have a good provider.

It's hard for some people to believe that this is actually happening to them. I'm just a guide. The medicine takes you there; then it's you against you.

I love that moment when a person is fighting with themselves and they finally see the real truth about themselves and how they've been sabotaging themselves every day, using excuses and blaming other people for their own mistakes. You have to stop that. You want to be able to face yourself and be able to recognize how badly you fuck up your own self. Just do it and go! It's easy to be able to fix yourself!

It's beautiful to be alive and to be happy. You do not spend a dime to be born. It's just a gift! That's what life is! A gift! Iboga reveals this.

I'm blessed to have been born and raised in that tradition and to continue to do what I'm supposed to do.

Iboga is our teacher. We do not follow people's words or beliefs. There are thousands of beliefs on this planet today, which is really messed up. Be careful what you believe in—whether you believe in your own thoughts or other people's experience with books. That's why people change their beliefs every few years because they are believing in a construct that's not real.

When you are on a very true spiritual path, you do not need to believe, because you are living it. That's the difference between a belief system and the art of knowing."

Chor chuckled. "Yeah, I like that he cussed. He's for real." After all that profound wisdom, it came down to cussing to convince Chor. "This looks good. It does. And it still scares the shit out of me."

We let all the possibilities percolate in our awareness

for a few days.

I thought to inquire with my circle of friends—and friends of friends. I put the word out: Had anyone ever personally partaken of this medicine? If Chor could hear about a real first hand experience, that might help help him to feel more at ease with iboga.

We waited for the universe to answer.

CHAPTER 14

REPORTS FROM THE UNIVERSE

*"Psychedelics are to the study of consciousness
what the telescope is to astronomy."*
— TERRENCE MCKENNA

*"Wisdom requires not only the investigation of many
things, but contemplation of the mystery."*
— JEREMY NARBY,
THE COSMIC SERPENT: *DNA* AND THE ORIGINS OF KNOWLEDGE

ONE THING that had me fretting was the length of
the journey, 24–48 hours. I had a hard time sitting still
for more than 20 minutes. If I partook of the medicine,
would I feel "trapped" in the experience? Would it be
too much?

"Yes, it was a long journey," Sharese confirmed, "but
it was so perfect. I felt such a deep state of surrender,
trust, ease." Her bright, peaceful eyes and the centered
tone of her voice communicated even more than her
words. A deep, calm current of love flowed out from her.

Sharese was a new but instantly adored friend, a
yoga instructor, and a radiant, energetic lady. She shared

generously about her experience. She had participated in a ceremony in Costa Rica several years prior.

"I have also experienced ayahuasca, and they are very different," she said. "Aya is very expansive, up and out into the cosmos. Iboga takes you so deep within...deep, deep down into yourself. Iboga felt more like a father to me. Clear, stern, gentle. Iboga shows you visions, but you cannot 'grab' at the visions with your mind—or they fade away. You just have to watch and receive."

"I'm nervous actually. This medicine seems so intense," I confessed.

"There is nothing to fear," she said with a warm smile and knowing gaze.

—

Jason, an acquaintance and a close friend of a close friend, had experienced the medicine and agreed to speak with us. We didn't know each other well, but we'd had pleasant interactions before. Even though he was a busy entrepreneur, he made time to share his story. Synchronicity would have it that he had actually visited Iboga House and worked with Moughenda! We settled into our phone meeting.

"Did you have a positive experience?" I asked.

"Yes, absolutely. Moughenda was a great guide. I felt so at ease. Many friends of mine had experienced ayahuasca, but no one I knew had experienced iboga. I wanted to understand another perspective, another plant teacher. I came to iboga as a spiritual seeker.

"Though I didn't seek out iboga for addiction, per

se, I had definitely been partying like a rock star for a while before I arrived there. After I left Iboga House, I noticed that my desire to party dropped to almost nothing. It just didn't have the same draw anymore."

"And how have you been doing since?" I asked.

"Really great! I've been working hard at my new business. I feel focused, creative, fulfilled. I'm loving life! I was definitely sorting through some personal issues before I experienced the medicine. I am still dealing with the reverb of it all, but I feel so clear and empowered, better equipped."

"And what was the journey like for you?"

"Intense. Profound. Amazing. I saw myself in all my lifetimes. And I met my higher self, my eternal soul, which was threaded through all those lifetimes. It's wild, but that's what happened. I was in awe. I felt so much love for myself.

"I've had just a few psychedelic experiences that really informed my life and shaped who I am, and that was definitely one of them. I came away from that experience with a deeper respect for life and some pretty deep agreements with myself."

"Did you feel well taken care of there?"

"Absolutely. They were great."

—

I heard from another friend, Dawn. She had experienced iboga a few years prior, and she generously offered to share her intimate experience of healing in our conversation. I knew her as a serene yogini, gifted healer, and artist, but once upon a time, she'd been a wild one. Years earlier as a restless 20-something, she lived a fast-paced life working as a model and fashion designer in London.

Dawn had suffered an early impact. Her brilliant parents had been cold, distant, and severe despite their underlying love. She had emerged from their home severely traumatized, her heart and spirit numb.

Espressos, chain smoking, and partying fueled her life. Despite being a tall, gorgeous vision of feminine beauty, she loathed herself inside. "I felt so much shame because of my inner darkness. I was lost. I was destroying myself. I engaged in all these risky and extreme activities, just so I could feel my life a little," she bravely revealed.

She compulsively traveled the world, endlessly searching for satiation in all the wrong places. She started down an even more treacherous path when she began snorting cocaine and smuggling drugs to finance her globetrotting party girl lifestyle. One day, possessed by drug-induced paranoia, she bolted from her gig in South America and abandoned a fortune of drugs in a suitcase. She wound up on her family's doorstep as a shivering, rail-thin wreck.

"I knew I needed serious healing. I was initially drawn to experience ayahuasca. The ceremonies were grueling at first," Dawn explained. Far from healing, they seemed to throw salt in all her wounds. In retrospect, she felt she had been working with the wrong facilitator. "I finally found an experienced traditional shaman who was also a good fit *for me.*" The medicine finally granted her deep healing and lasting positive changes. Toxic elements fell away from her life. She shifted her deadly trajectory. She reconnected with meditation and yoga.

Then she learned about iboga. The medicine called to her to deepen her spiritual journey, and also to disrupt her smoking. "Cigarettes were my 'best friend' for 20 years. I needed a miracle," she confessed. She was soon invited to a traditional Bwiti iboga ceremony being held in a remote countryside sanctuary in Europe. She had fasted and prayed. She made the long journey.

African Bwiti shamans and several apprentices greeted her as they prepared for the ceremony. She donned her ceremonial attire and stood in line to receive the medicine. But right before she was to receive the sacrament, the shamans pulled her aside.

"The spirits had told them that I wasn't ready. They said I was especially delicate at that time. And they were right. So that was that. I was disappointed, as I had come so far and carefully prepared, but I accepted their guidance.

"The medicine found me again a couple years later. It was the right time, I know in my heart. I was introduced to a man who worked with iboga and ibogaine for detoxes, and he was a very experienced provider. He himself had been freed from heroin addiction with iboga. I was given the natural extract of iboga, with the alkaloids left intact. I had what is known as a 'booster' dose, rather than the more substantial 'flood' dose. My journey only lasted a few hours, unlike the more intense three-day journey with the flood dose. It was perfect for me."

Dawn had been taken deep down into herself. The medicine had felt deeply cleansing—physically, mentally, spiritually. As she lay in bed in a meditative state, she saw thousands of snapshots of her life where she had abandoned herself. She was confronted with her darkness in a firm but loving way. She realized that she'd been wrestling with symptoms that her smoking was a part of, and the medicine showed her what truly needed to be addressed.

It was the longest amount of time that she'd gone without smoking in years, she explained. "Right after my journey, I went straight for a cigarette like a bat out of hell! But it felt different. Things had started to shift. Within a couple months, the smoking completely faded out of my life."

My heart sang like a choir of earth angels. All good signs. Ordinary oracles showing the way.

I conveyed these reports to Chor as they trickled in. He oscillated between apprehension and enthusiasm, suspicion and curiosity, fear and love.

Iboga held the promise of complete healing. And as he wavered, I could feel the demon in him doing everything it could to avoid being evicted.

CHAPTER 15

THE SCANDALOUS AND THE SACRED

"Goddess grant me the serenity to not accept the media-mind, to change the channel, to my own intuitive sensitivity, and the wisdom to know the difference between the guides of my feelings and the distractions of stories."
— EDEN RUMELT

"Be brave and walk through the country of your own wild heart."
— ST. TERESA OF AVILA

WITH MORE DATA scavenging, I found a couple scandalous blurbs about Moughenda on different internet forums. Would this equate to a red light in this direction?

In one post, the writer complained that the temple at Iboga House was not all that they imagined a traditional African temple should be, simply for it being a converted garage. It made sense to me that a covered carport could be transformed into a temple. Why not? How utilitarian. The DIY spirit was more authentically African than any imported jungle materials. The writer went on, noting that the food wasn't spectacular enough. The staff wasn't friendly enough. The ceremony wasn't "shamanic" enough—though I didn't get they impression that they were some kind of expert on Bwiti shamanism. They didn't get their money's worth, apparently. I sensed that this terminally sour person wouldn't have been satisfied or grateful anywhere. It seemed as though they really wanted the Ritz, not radical healing.

Was I to take this report at face value? Spontaneous reflections streamed. Big medicine could stir up a lot of personal shit, literally and figuratively. Sadly, some people stop when they are only half-baked in their healing process. Some people project saviors or demons onto their facilitator. Some people seek impossible miracles. Some people don't want to take any responsibility for their part in the transformation. And some people are just unhappy no matter what.

Then I noticed other posts in embedded deeper in this thread; someone was promoting their iboga for sale via mail order. "Buy iboga real cheap from Dr. Joe. We ship to your door. Don't be taken by this guy Moughenda. You don't need to pay so much for the medicine." Another offered to sell "affordable ibogaine treatment packages" complete with easy home instructions. These merchants were taking the opportunity to benefit from all the mudslinging by dangling the bait of a discount, impelling me to scrutinize the initial accusations.

In another post, the writer claimed that Moughenda had some unhappy clients, and more, he had dared to have romantic relationships, leaving one for another, with a trail of broken hearts and broken promises. And, of course, wherever a medicine man goes, there is medicine in the mix. The posts derailed with dramatic details, laced with spite rather than insight, sounding like a soap opera.

Something didn't feel right. This rant felt tainted.

Random other writers tossed their two cents into these threads who admittedly didn't even have any direct experience with Moughenda, but they did have a chip on their shoulder about shamans or money or sex abuse. Others scoffed at some of the traditional uses and health benefits of iboga that Moughenda extolled on his website, despite having no experience with the medicine. Others left snarky comments touting the cheapest prices one could find for iboga; as if that were all there was to consider when seeking treatment. There were also some posts in defense of Moughenda's good character, written by people who claimed to have actually worked with him. Those seemed genuine, grounded, clear.

Did these posts indicate danger? Or slander?

Had Moughenda had some complicated romantic relationships? Somebody seemed to think so. Were these a matter of two consenting adults, or a true abuse of the powerful role of shaman? There are always two sides to every story, and Moughenda had not posted his for this public show.

Were there some cultural differences at play in these dramas? Likely.

Was Moughenda imperfect according to somebody's standards? Apparently.

I wasn't seeking some universally "perfect" person, for that was an impossible fantasy. And I didn't need to judge his evolving romantic life. I did need to know:

Would Moughenda be the right healer for us?

So I prayed hard and "thought" with my heart.

I considered the many testimonials we'd found that were overwhelmingly positive. The video of Moughenda's bright face and sincere voice replayed in my mind. My hands relaxed, my chest softened, my breath deepened.

The silent guidance whispered: *Look past this tangled web of human drama for your answers.*

CHAPTER 16

A STEP CLOSER

"Real shadow work does not leave us in tact; it is not some neat and tidy process, but rather an inherently messy one, as vital and unpredictably alive as birth."
— ROBERT AUGUSTUS MASTERS, *SPIRITUAL BYPASSING: WHEN SPIRITUALITY DISCONNECTS FROM WHAT REALLY MATTERS*

"Everybody's scandalous flaw is mine."
— RUMI

CHOR BEGAN to seriously flirt with the possibility of iboga. He took the time to fill out the intricate intake form for Iboga House. There were many questions about medical history and the particulars of his addiction.

"So do you want me to go with you?" I asked Chor. "Or do you want to go alone?"

"Yes. I do. I want you to go with me," he said clearly.

I wasn't yet sure if I would partake of the medicine, but I definitely wanted to go with him. Yes, this was his healing journey—but letting him go all alone would have been like letting him walk in and out of heart surgery alone. If he could get himself there, then I wanted to be there by his side. I wanted to walk him to the gates and be the first to welcome him to the other side of this transformation.

The more I learned about iboga, the more the medicine called to me for my own healing. I definitely rode a constant wild ride of dark moods and negative thoughts and frazzled nerves. Yoga and a healthy diet had kept me alive with a reasonable amount of grace, but I knew I had plenty more evolving to do.

I had become completely addicted to caffeine and chocolate. It might sound trite compared to Chor's affliction, but I was enslaved. My adrenals were drained, and I was trapped in a daily cycle of dependence. I wondered what life might be like if I wasn't addicted.

I had survived abuse as a child, and now I carried the heavy, automated armor of post-traumatic stress disorder. I struggled with an aggravated sense of guardedness, stifling fears, and anxiety at times. Other plant medicines and therapy had benefited me, but nothing had entirely relieved me of this daily embodied burden.

I went ahead and filled out the intake form, and I had to confess my own blossoming addiction. I had started drinking more just in the previous couple months, indulging in an evening glass of wine a few times a week when Chor was out of town. Though it was quite light, it was the motivation behind it that was dangerous. I was not drinking to celebrate. I was drinking to numb my thirsty heart. I was missing Chor more and more, even when he was there.

I'd once heard a wise woman say, "There's no such thing as a 'light' addiction. You're on either one train or another. You are headed either up or down. You might not realize it in the moment, but every action in our lives is part of a vast trajectory."

I had to step off that train.

Apparently, Chor and I had both been building up to something. Our hearts and our wounds were inextricably intertwined. Now we both sat at a crossroads.

—

Julia, the director, emailed us back, acknowledging the receipt of our questionnaires. She'd call us soon. We counted the minutes, excited and terrified, wondering aloud and pacing in our living room. Finally, she spoke with us at length and answered all of our logistical and health questions.

And then she quoted us the price. For two journeys in an eight-day retreat, it would cost $6,000 for Chor and $5,000 for me. My heart sank. Chor loathed spending money.

"$6,000!" Chor complained, right on schedule. "I thought it might be $3,000 or $4,000; that's a shitload of money!"

Chor was frugal, to put it politely. He never splurged on much, aside from fancy sneakers and his recent partying stints as a born-again drug addict. How could I convince him to spend the money for this treatment?

"Babe, the cost of rehab centers can be $25,000 to $100,000 per month. And they don't even work most of the time! And, I gotta say it: a decent funeral costs at least as much as this retreat." His face went slack in pensive reflection. The magnitude of the situation seemed to sink in.

"What is this chance worth to you? What is your LIFE worth to you?" I implored.

Chor asked to speak with Moughenda directly and resolved to go if he called him back personally.

A couple days later, Moughenda made time for an in-depth phone conversation with both of us. He spoke with passion, patience, and confidence. The tone of his voice communicated; he understood his medicine, and he understood the nature of addiction. His voice resonated down to my bones, and I felt that silent, mystical "yes."

They had an opening for our visit, just three weeks away.

"OK. Let's do it!" Chor agreed enthusiastically, though still terrified. I was relieved but simultaneously nervous.

"OK! Yes!" I said. I was elated, high on hope. Then suddenly, I plummeted into a wormhole within myself.

I turned away, supposedly to do something mundane like put away a dish. I bit my lip. We would need to buy plane tickets pronto. I *had* to offer my confession, soon. Would he still want me to go when he knew? It was crunch time. I mustered the nerve while we moved forward with logistics.

We had to pass all the tests first.

Iboga required medical clearance. We each had to get a full physical complete with an EKG, a liver test, and a kidney test. Iboga was not recommended for people with certain medical conditions. We felt like we were getting ready to climb Mt. Everest, within ourselves.

"What's all this testing for?" Both of our doctors asked.

We had an answer prepped to avoid and awkward-ness. "We are preparing to train for a triathlon."

They were perky and supportive, as expected. We didn't know how they'd react to our plan to take this exotic medicine that was illegal in the United States—and for a heroin detox. We didn't want them to rain on our parade, much less bring up any legal challenges, so we kept our intentions under wraps.

We passed all the tests. Our physical vessels qualified us for this journey. We sent our test results to Iboga House.

I should be able to relax a little now. Chor had com-mitted to this treatment. He had gone through the toughest few days of withdrawals. I grilled him, and he claimed to be free of cravings. He professed his resolve to heal and stay clean.

But everyone knows that heroin addicts are wild cards, land mines, unpredictable beasts.

I prayed for him to make it through the next three weeks clean. From all my research on iboga, I learned that it was best to be as detoxed as possible before the iboga treatment, as it could be more effective. Heavy detoxes from fresh opiate use could still be grueling, even without the typical withdrawal symptoms. Even more important, taking drugs right after the treatment could be deadly if the impulse prevailed.

Though he claimed that his immediate desire for heroin had dissolved, we knew that he had to clear it from his body, brain, and spirit—once and for all. If he didn't exorcise it completely, it would sneak up on him again and steal his life when he wasn't looking. That's the nature of the demon. I'd read too many headlines:

Some famous person relapses after a lengthy recovery—and dies. Boom. Just like that.

—

I told my mother everything about the relapse, the iboga, my broken heart. "He should go alone," she firmly advised. "This is his journey, not yours."

I let that percolate. I deeply respect my mama. She is a wise being and a shaman in her own right. But she is still my very human mama, protective and biased, of course.

What is MY truth here?

CHAPTER 17
THE LAST SUPPER

"You don't have to be perfect.
You just have to be WILLING."
— MICAH BLACKLIGHT LAEL

"ELIZABETH!" Chor yelped.

"Yes, Mr. Boogie. How can I serve you, sir?" I'd often answer with sardonic sass when he said my name.

"I need to go to Safeway. Gotta get my food."

"What? You wanna take me to Paris? Sure, baby," I teased. I was blowing off steam.

Most of the time I was hearing my name then, it was because he wanted a favor or a ride. He was often effective, though ultimately draining. He didn't seem to feel the mounting effects of unequal energetic exchanges. Mr. Boogie was not a sustainable crop.

"And hey, can I have that wood panel in the garage that you are not using?"

Somewhere along the way, when our relationship became oh so familiar, I nicknamed him "the Hustler." He had become a taker more than a giver. And I accepted him in spite of this flaming flaw. Oh, the beauty of love mixed with strange psychological triggers.

The hustler in him synced well with the martyr-mother that ran in my blood. My grandmothers were strong, so strong, too strong. They were well trained to give and give to their husbands, babies, and churches—until their nerves short-circuited, breasts dried up, and bodies broke down. They were self-effacing to the point of being self-erasing. Their personal passions were always the last priorities in the day-to-day business of family life.

I was aware of this ancestral pattern, and I fought to maintain a healthy sense of self. I cultivated rituals of self-care. I clung to my arts for dear life. I remained committed to my big life to-do list. Still, I would often catch myself giving even when I was on empty. I hadn't yet mastered that balancing act of nurturing self and lover. It was hard for me to say no to my love, even when I really needed to.

I walked over to his desk. He sat hunched over his computer, glowering as he combed over his social media. He'd get so angry about the online politics of followers and likes. He seemed to relish his swear words as he vented, almost foaming at the mouth. He took the game all so personally. His blood pressure and mood depended his numbers on any given day, but it was never enough.

"So...can you take me to Safeway, love?" he said again. "Oh you're so amazing, yes you are," he said, with as much sincerity as a wind-up toy.

He didn't want to own a car, claiming he didn't need one, but he sure loved to ride in everyone else's. He also didn't want to pay the insurance needed to jump behind my wheel; his bad driving record came with a high price. He'd ask me for rides a few times a week when he wasn't traveling. Once in a while would have been fine, but it had become a steady imposition.

I felt cornered into being the chauffeur in the relationship. I ended up driving for all our errands and dates. I longed to melt into the passenger side at times, but paradoxically, some part of me was relieved to stay in control. It was hard for me to trust him with the big stuff.

So I drove. Again.

We perused the isles at Safeway. This was our first outing since the relapse. Chor was out of heavy withdrawals, and it seemed to be a reasonably low-risk mission, but I'd been so shaken. I was a worried ghost, haunted, barely aware of anything except for Chor. I watched him like a hawk out of the corner of my eye. Would he dart off? Would he swallow a bottle of Robitussin when I wasn't looking?

He grabbed his chicken nuggets and chips. I grabbed my organic, vegan eats. Though he had often asked me to cook for him, he loathed having to chip in for communal groceries. He complained that my food was too expensive. Good food was something I wasn't willing to compromise on. "Superfood for superheroes," I liked to say. So we made peace and simplified things. We just bought separate food.

We made it back to the house alive. Chor collapsed on the couch and chomped on his meal in front of the TV. I prayed over my food and ate slowly—at the table. All separate.

Another night of horror flicks and gloom. I escaped to my room.

CHAPTER 18
MONEY HONEY

"Blame keeps the sad game going. It keeps stealing all your wealth—giving it to an imbecile with no financial skills. Dear one, wise up."
— HAFIZ

"If we had the courage to love we would not so value these acts of war."
— JEANETTE WINTERSON, THE PASSION

"BABE, CAN YOU CHIP in for the house sitter while we are away? The cost of this trip and all my missed days of work are weighing on me this month," I asked.

"NO!" he said emphatically. "I didn't ask for the dog or the cats. They just kinda came with the package. I don't need that responsibility. Get rid of 'em!" I was shocked, but I sensed the demon was responsible for his extra callous speech. He had always adored animals.

"Hey, think about the *reason* why I'm going," I said. "And yes, exactly, they came with the package." He grumbled and walked away.

Money is tricky. It's one of those wild worldly things that can be an opportunity for bondage—or for liberation. It's quite a precarious practice to have it without being attached to it, to be generous and yet discerning, and to conquer poverty consciousness without falling into greed. Couples get double jeopardy in this game, and we both struggled.

Chor pinched all his pennies with a vice grip. True, he didn't have regular paychecks. He never knew when the next chunk of change would come. But he probably spent more energy clinging to his cash than it took to make more.

For years, I accommodated his meager "artist budget" as I carried the brunt of our household bills. He justified his humble contributions on the grounds that I had more responsibilities and chose to maintain a certain standard of living. True, being a mama, I didn't want to live in a closet or the corner of an illegal warehouse (like plenty of artists in San Francisco). Had I matched his budget, those would have been our only options. Yeah, I was fancy like that. So the house and car and those luxurious utilities were mostly on me.

Chor had his rare moments of springing for movie tickets or an obligatory birthday dinner, but he didn't seem to understand the thrill of generosity, and he clearly wasn't concerned with creating a balancing act with our resources. My resentment had steadily swollen.

As Chor began to make more money over the years, I noticed that he invested more and more in himself—and only himself: *his* career, *his* fame, *his* future. He regularly took on unpaid painting gigs when they included the right press coverage or social media bragging rights. This meant more travel time away from home—and more money away from home. He could somehow cover his travel costs, professional press releases, and painting supplies for these glory gigs, but wouldn't contribute more to our shared living expenses. And though Chor fantasized about family life, he was never quite ready, fiscally or otherwise, for the babies he said he wanted.

Supposedly it was all for the long-term goals of our family, but I smelled the rot of some self-centric sickness under it all, and the enduring imbalance imposed heavy taxes on our relationship.

I responded like a sparring partner. He was out for himself, so I was out for myself. And I kept our score card etched on my heart with a rusty nail.

I desperately wanted him to give more, but *I* didn't want to give more. What modest material wealth I had would stay mine all mine. Sharing closets was already pushing it. Sharing bank accounts made my skin crawl; I might just disappear in that big, sappy puddle of oneness.

We both instinctively kept our assets strictly separate and shrouded in some mystery. I secretly found solace in our neatly divided empires. We'd be prepared for a clean getaway, in case of emotional emergency. Defense vs. devotion.

We weren't building our castle together, yet we still belonged together. So it went.

CHAPTER 19

ONE SPEC OF DUST AT A TIME

"And now here is my secret, a very simple secret:
It is only with the heart that one can see rightly;
what is essential is invisible to the eye."
— ANTOINE DE SAINT-EXUPÉRY, *THE LITTLE PRINCE*

WHAT KEPT ME there? You might be wondering after reading all this.

Maybe I'd been brainwashed by too many Hollywood movies, and I was waiting for a happy ending that would never come. Maybe I had karma to eat. Maybe tragedy had become ordinary. Maybe I was just acclimating to a desert.

Do you know how it is to fall in love with someone and then see them slowly being covered in dust, one speck at a time, one day at a time? That beloved is still there somewhere—buried.

I'll admit, there were fleeting moments that I fantasized about packing up all his shit and putting it into storage and changing the locks while he was away. I was tired of his ravenous dream and the slow starvation of my heart and the hold he had over me even when he was on the other side of the world. But those moments would vanish like flash paper on fire with his next embrace or deep phone call. Even on his worst days, he was still kind, and his presence in my life—and my heart—was steady and sturdy. I affectionately referred to him as the "redwood tree in the middle of my life."

So I stayed, waiting out a couple years of drought and some epic storms to salvage this love, thanks only to amazing grace and a magical combination of true love, fear of change, stagnation, dedication, hope, attachment, comfort, complacency, and prayer.

Every day I prayed: *Great Spirit, show me the way. Whisper to my heart. Show me how I can best serve all beings. Show me how to be an artist of love. Show me where I need to be.* I listened to that still, small voice of spirit, and I stayed—one day at a time.

CHAPTER 20
NOT ANOTHER SECOND

"Truth embraces love. It is an inextinguishable kiss. They refuse to be separated. Within that embrace, the story of you and the universe arises."
— RICHARD POWER, *HUMANIFESTO: A GUIDE TO PRIMAL REALITY IN AN ERA OF GLOBAL PERIL*

"Daily the wisdom of the human body is ravaged by the mind."
— MARION WOODMAN, *FORWARD, THE SACRED PROSTITUTE: ETERNAL ASPECT OF THE FEMININE*

WE LAY IN BED, on the brink of sleep.

Not another second. I had to confess. Even with all the drama lately.

There's no such thing as a good time to drop a bomb like this. *It's now or never.* I had to come clean. I had to ask him if he still wanted take this journey with me—and if he still wanted to be with me at all.

My body and mind had hardened around the secret over time—like scar tissue around a shard of glass. I feared it would soon manifest as a tumor in my womb if I did not expose it.

My fleeting fantasies about leaving him had not only stemmed from our other battles; they were also sometimes fueled by my secret. It would have been so much easier to run away than to reveal the naked truth. I wouldn't have to be exposed. I wouldn't have to look bad. I wouldn't have to hear him yell. I wouldn't have to hold his breaking heart in my hands or look into his searching chocolate eyes. It almost seemed like I wouldn't really have to face myself—if I didn't have to face him. But I knew I had to go deeper into this relationship, not run away from it, if he would let me.

I sat up in the dark, shivering, weeping.

"What's wrong?" he asked. "Elizabeth, what's wrong? Elizabeth!"

I fell mute for a few moments. Frozen with fear. Finally I broke through, unable to carry the invisible burden a second longer.

"I have to tell you something. And you might want to leave me."

"What IS it?" he pleaded.

I prayed that this revelation would not push him over the edge, yet I knew that it was the right thing to do, the only way.

"You know how I love to be touched. I *need* to be touched," I responded. "I was starving...."

"What IS it?" he asked again with urgency. "What did you do?"

"Please, baby. Just hear me out. OK? Please? I will

tell you everything...."

—

A week after Chor and I had first met, I revealed layers of my colorful past—and my secret gig as a holy whore. *A what?* That's right.

I was a wild young woman and a highly experimental sexual creature. I'd started off as a stripper, and I had relished it. That San Francisco strip club was my urban Goddess Temple—if only in my own mind. I was privy to the underbelly of the collective psyche in that sparkly human petting zoo. When people asked what I did for a living, I liked to say that I took confessions and doled out blessings—in a bikini.

I didn't swallow the patriarchy's prudish attitudes. It seemed crystal clear to me; women's naked bodies were divine, vivifying, beautiful. Most people just didn't know what to do with all the energy that they sparked.

I knew that passion had the potential to be a nourishing force. Our human erotic streak would never go away, not for long at least, as much as ascetic traditions wanted to bleach it away. My sentiment: We may as well just bring it into the light already. I drew inspiration from the ancient temple cultures that had revered erotica and fertile feminine energy. So I danced to the beat of my own drum, in sacred glitter and lingerie.

My penchant for salacious exploration evolved when I found Kamala, an adept tantric yogini from a hidden feminine lineage, one that eludes religious scholars when they aren't privy to its paper trail. She taught yogic technologies to channel sexual energy and offered full-body sensual healing touch, within the container of ritual. She called herself a dakini.

I would come to learn that this sacred word, dakini, could refer to this intimate initiatory service—and so much more. The dakini was ultimately indefinable, uncontainable, and limitless in how she could spark spiritual love in the flesh. The dakini could be a messenger, initiatress, and guardian, manifesting in any domain of human culture or spiritual existence, taking any form that proved effective. I would also come to learn that tantra could encompass sexual yoga—and so much more, for tantra is a path that touches *every* aspect of human life.

Kamala allowed me to apprentice with her. This form of service sparked an ancient memory in me and fulfilled my passionate heart. We were essentially shamanic sex workers—without the sex. Our chosen medium of connection was the magic touch. Intercourse was not on the menu. We preferred to bask in the electrified space of "almost."

Like Kamala, I eventually made my living serving as a sensual priestess in underground realms. My soul guided me to the trenches, where I was most needed: the red-light districts of the internet. I planted myself on various websites amidst a virtual buffet of other sex workers, quite intentionally, for it was one of the only places where the starving knew to look. I was always impressed with the sincere seekers who would choose my esoteric offerings—even with all kinds of fleshy indulgence flashing right there as well.

This work was not only controversial for polite society, it was also shunned by some public tantra educators who, in their well-intentioned zeal, wanted to sanitize the path enough to be palatable for the mainstream. Despite tantra having many courtesans, racy entertainers, religious renegades, and other radical outsiders noted as major players in its official history, any contemporary association with the world of "sex work" was apparently just too touchy. Others dismissed the authenticity and value of our work, without any intimate knowledge or personal experience, based on their own petrified preconceptions about sensual professionals, and mistakenly assumed our work to be nothing more than meretricious cultural appropriation. Yet we endured, outcast, unofficial, and free, true to our heart's calling.

It was a charmed, though clandestine, life. My small and exclusive circle of favored devotees brought lavish offerings to my altar. My days at the office were miraculous, blessing me with awe-inspiring views of souls awakening through the body. My guests were grateful and respectful beings. I knew this work was healing, life giving, and vital to some balance in the universe. Kamala had led me to many others like her, and I loved my covert international coven of fellow priestesses.

Though I could have pursued success in any number of vanilla-flavored vocations, I was most fulfilled in my dakini den. Conveniently, this beautiful work provided me with financial abundance as well as plenty of precious time for my son and my other creative pursuits.

I loved my acolytes (my special word for "client"), like a good doctor loves her patients. It was beautiful work, but just work. I was built for it. It complemented my intensely sensual and caring nature. It quenched my vast capacity for giving and receiving touch. (I theorize that most people have a similar need for touch, but many unconsciously suppress it with alcohol, drugs, ice cream, TV, chocolate, pizza, workaholism, shopping, porn, or all of the above.)

Then I met Chor, and here I had this exceedingly exotic healing arts practice. Would I tell him? And what would I say? I kept my temple extremely private, if only to protect it from the anti-ecstatic, punishing powers that be. Let's just say you couldn't find me in the Yellow Pages.

I knew, there was no way things were going to stay superficial with Chor. I needed to know that he accepted me. So I sat him down on the giant velvet leopard print poof ball that I called furniture, and I told him everything.

"Whoah," he said, jaw agape—never having heard of such things. "Sensual...*healer?*" he asked as if he couldn't imagine that those two words could ever go together in the same sentence. I could see paradigms shifting behind his eyes.

"Are you...naked when you do this?"

"Yes." I answered without hesitation.

"Are there orgasms?"

"Sometimes, but that's not the primary goal. The primary goals are to be present, channel the passionate energy through the yogic practices, and cultivate our *ojas,* vitality. Whatever pleasure that arises is regarded as a devotional offering, rather than personal gratification. Many times, no external release is needed."

"Well," he pondered, taking a few deep breaths as he refocused his swirling eyes on me. "This is my opportunity to practice tolerance and acceptance."

Hmm, I thought, *and an opportunity...to celebrate?* I was proud of my wild journey and my skills and my naked honesty. I'd been so blessed and sensitized by all that I'd learned. He was lucky to have such a seasoned and crafty lover. I adored him for reasons even beyond my own comprehension, so I settled for tolerance and acceptance.

"So what *exactly* do you do?" he probed.

"To strip it down to the basics: I teach breath work and internal tantric yogas, while naked, because more energy is ignited when we are naked. And I touch every part of the body—because every part needs loving touch. This sensual activation also provides a potent opportunity for practice. Essentially, I teach meditation in the fire, baby, and it's quite the alchemy."

"Well, show me."

So I showed him, one candlelit evening in the bedroom, but he proved himself to be a difficult student—feisty and impatient and somewhat detached. He never asked to learn again. So I didn't offer. If he didn't come reverently asking to learn these precious technologies, then I would not push them on him.

Though he didn't seem to take an active interest in my tantric practices, I knew that he must appreciate them on some level, for I was saturated in their reverb. They gave me a certain radiant field and autonomous ecstasy and a mainline to infinite love. He licked the energetic honey off of me, daily.

We were alien from each other in some fundamental ways, yet I was impressed that he was at least accepting of something so radical. Chor struggled a little with the technical details of my profession, he admitted, but he rolled with it, practicing the tolerance he had preached about.

"Well...I just ask that you don't let anyone else touch this," he said soon after I first told him about my secret work, as he gently placed his big panther paw over my pussy like a protective shield. "Your *yoni* is very sacred and precious to me," he crooned in his raspy, macho voice, practicing the poetic new Sanskrit word.

"Yes, my love," I readily agreed. This was a boundary I could honor. There had only ever been a select few acolytes I'd taught to touch me intimately, and I could let that go for him.

Within our first year, my soul spoke for change. I naturally grew to feel that I wanted to focus my passion with Chor and leave my work in the secret temple, but the intricacies involved in a swift professional transition were daunting to my mind at that time. I had a home to maintain in one of the most expensive cities in the world and a son to provide for and a lover who couldn't match me in the bills.

The work still suited me more than anything else, and Chor didn't seem to mind—too much. "Don't quit *because of me,* if that's what you love to do," he liked to say, but I sensed that deep down he was allergic to having any involvement with my financial reality.

So I went on with my work in the secret temple. Reason told me it was the most practical option. My soul's call was dismissed as whimsy. And if I was going to do the work, I resolved, I would do it with love and compassion—and delight.

Our unusual existence flowed peacefully, on the surface at least. And our agreement stayed strong...until the hunger came to haunt me.

—

Slow down, baby. Softer. Feel me. Tease me. Touch me, please. Wait for me to unfold. Wait for me to get wet.

When we first met, Chor's favored mating modus operandi was to roll onto me, pull at my panties, and try to penetrate me, pronto. *Eh hem?* It was an awkward dance sometimes, but it would usually lead us somewhere magical.

Before me, he'd lived off a lot of late-night skin-deep booty calls from booze-lubricated hotties, as well as a few short relationships. At least that's the impression I had from his many fishing tales. For all his wild promiscuity in his younger days, I imagined that he'd have learned how to slowly ripen a woman, but elaborate foreplay was not a survival skill he needed, apparently. He'd gotten plenty of action with his good looks, talent, loud charm, and a certain formidable physical asset. (Such qualities can get a man places, but they won't necessarily take him very deep once he gets there.)

I did my best to ask him for sensual favors with grace, but his pride was pierced and his patience was tested. Sometimes he'd indulge my requests, and for this I was grateful, but it was clear, the slow zone was not his comfort zone. His choreography was often completed with haste in order to get to the main course of intercourse.

Of course, there were elements that I adored about Chor's passionate expression. He seemed almost super-human with his strength of steel and broad bones of iron and Olympian sexual power. When we were in sync, he could literally rock my universe as he coaxed endless waves of pleasure from me. But if he was not listening to my unfolding, he was a devastating force of nature.

I longed to surrender to him all the time, but my requests for slow sex were not only a matter of taste; they could prevent physical pain. Sometimes I could match his primal pace, depending on the stars and the moon and the particular day of the my cycle, but most often, my fruit of pleasure just couldn't be rushed, and any attempt to do so would leave me bruised inside.

I admit, I possess an extreme sensual sensitivity. And I love it. I've honed it even. It's a double-edged sword, for I am only as ecstatic as I am finicky. Most women have the potential for such natural sensitivity, but some might not understand it or honor it. Sadly, many women fake orgasms. It's true. I have inside information on that one. Girls like to talk. And once, long ago, I was among the legions. So trained are women to please that even our own pleasure is not for themselves.

Thanks only to my tantric initiations and a strict vow of sexual authenticity, I had come to know my body especially well. I shared these subtle inner practices in my yoga teachings. I was on a mission to heal, empower, and ignite women—and to educate men. And yet, educating my own man was like swimming upstream. Exhausting. Awkward. Full of heavy sighs.

I longed for more physical affection, sensual adoration, feathery fingertips, deep kisses, and pure closeness. "Oh, you need *so much attention,* don't you?" he often teased me when I came calling for smooches and strokes.

So I teased him back. "And you need *so much hole,* don't you?" I played on his own crass word for the female genitalia, just to push buttons.

I was jealous of the care and detailed attention that he gave to his paintings. Couldn't he see? I was worthy of the same artistry, even though I couldn't be mounted on a museum wall. I was a living, breathing canvas, and our love was the highest art of all—temporal, delicate, precious. Every moment was an opportunity to create a once-in-a-lifetime masterpiece.

"Love is an ART," I'd say.

"Don't even say that," he'd say, as if it were sacrilege.

So it went. A subtle yet unrelenting battle. Two warriors connected with sweet and sticky unseen cords. We knew we were an odd couple, and yet we both felt perfect for each other. Somehow, we balanced each other. Above all, we loved each other. We were drawn to each other like gravity to the earth. There was nowhere else to go but into each other's arms.

Even with all our mismatched sexual idiosyncrasies, we had many nights where we stuck it out and found each other in mutual volcanic eruptions and holy mind-body-spirit melding.

So I accepted him. He accepted me.

He made me stronger. I made him softer.

I navigated our predicament as best as I could, until

his travels seemed to never end, until he became ever more distant, until I couldn't remember the last time he'd given me a true and tender kiss. Then the alcohol returned. The more he drank, the more I starved for his spirit. I ached for deeper connection. Still, I wanted to need only him. My hungry heart and yearning body fought with the promises my mind had made. My desires eventually came to bite me in the ass.

Then I broke my word.

—

I was forward. It was slippery, unintentional, primal. It felt so good, on the surface.

Three times. Over three years. Three different men. Acolytes. I let them touch the forbidden zone. Our private inner sanctum. My pussy. These three times satiated a need that I could no longer suppress.

Each time, they coaxed the ripe Goddess out of me. My moisture reached. I blossomed. Each time, my acolyte revered the opportunity to touch me. Sweet touch for the sake of touch. They brought out the stifled alpha in me. They attended to the many overlooked inches of my body. I was warm honey in their hands.

It was just touch, but I'd crossed a sacred line, the one my love asked me not to.

It felt delicious in the moment, but then immediately afterward I found myself coated in a thick layer of shame. I'd endure months of regret and inner conflict. I had disrespected my king and the boundaries of our relationship, yet I knew I was starved out. I was torn.

I resisted telling him. I talked myself out of it. *He wouldn't want to know anyway*, I rationalized. *And he probably wouldn't really care. I'll just never do it again. I can just forgive myself. That's enough.*

There was a tug of war inside my mind between guilt and cold indifference. I allowed myself to be "in process" with it, but this process felt like a paper cut in my heart that refused to heal.

I hadn't felt sexual shame in a long, long time. I once prided myself on being comfortable with my sexuality. I didn't keep secrets, and I didn't need to. I had harshly judged people who kept secrets from their lovers, but here I was doing just that.

I was terrified of revealing my secret to him. Maybe he would scream, or kick a door in, or worse. I had seen him angry before. During a fierce argument, just once, I screamed "it's over!" He hit my car dashboard with his fist and almost started an earthquake. He was a powerful man and more intimidating than he realized. He never laid a hand on me, and I imagined that he never would, but I still harbored an ancient, irrational fear of being branded or burned or stoned.

I wondered about his own desires, especially due to his frequent travels and his powerful libido. I would verbally check his pulse at least once a year, "Do you still like being *only* with me? Do you ever have desires for an open relationship?"

He'd smile warmly and gather me in his arms. "You are enough for me, loveness," he'd say. "I don't want to put a rift in our design." That was his slogan.

"Well, then, what about a threesome?" I'd probe.

We were well past the honeymoon phase. Such dreams can grow over time.

"Hmm. It might just be *too much* fun," he'd say with an eyebrow raised, both tempted and apprehensive. "I just don't know. Well, no." He knew I was essentially bisexual, but I happened to be in love with him.

"Yeah, it *is* like playing with fire," I'd say, validating his caution. *He's too sensitive to share me,* I thought.

So I was the only freak in the room, apparently. I was the only one struggling with my hunger. So I carried the weight of that shame, and I kept my secret locked up tight.

Eventually, when he'd been out of town for nearly two months straight, I allowed myself to be enchanted. I kissed a beautiful woman. Monica had been a good friend for a long time. The night started innocently enough as we soaked in her hot tub. (Then again, are hot tubs ever really innocent?) I was slowly pulled into her timeless, sultry vortex. I didn't see it coming, or didn't want to. Her silken, seeking, full lips met mine and awakened something buried in me.

I knew I had to tell him. This was *personal.* I had treaded into even more dangerous territory.

I told him about that kiss when he returned home from his trip the next day. He exploded. He tortured me with snide, jealous comments for months afterward. I honestly thought he'd be a little relieved to share the burden of my desires—at least when he was out of town and at least with a woman. He'd still be my main man. But no. He was devastated. He'd have none of it. I felt his pain. I did not want to hurt him. From then on, I bit my lip and wore a psychic chastity belt no matter how much it hurt.

———

"What do you want to tell me, Elizabeth?" he asked again, that night in our bed as I wept, with my confession on the tip of my tongue. His voice shook with worry.

Carrying the secret had finally become more terrible than my fears of coming clean. I confessed everything, between my gasps and tears. The truth was delivered with an exposed belly and a raw heart.

He fell silent.

"I'm sorry. I'm so sorry," I said. "I couldn't keep this inside anymore. I understand if you are angry—and I understand if you need to leave me. I know it's a delicate time for you, but you deserve to know and make your own choice.

"One thing is so clear to me: The inside of me should be for you—and only you. You are the only one who should enter. This is not a dogma. It's just a natural feeling about what is right for us. I violated the sanctity of our agreement. I disrespected you, my king. I had a nutrient missing in my life, yet I should have attended to this need in a more intentional and honest way."

He was silent, yet he simmered. He took long breaths. "I don't know," he said. "This is intense. So... did they touch you like you needed?" He had to ask.

"Yes," I admitted bluntly. My heart was too worn down for any more smoke or mirrors.

"So this is my fault," he said with a jagged edge.

"No. It's not your fault. It was my action. And it was not the right one. I didn't mean to hurt you.... There is a deep need in me that I cannot run from anymore. I need to know that you accept me, as I am. And I need care—somehow, some way."

I cried.

The air was charged and thick with tension, silent except for the reverb of weeping and somber respiration. The future was a throbbing mass of uncertainty.

My heart exhaled. I was stripped, ashamed, and peaceful. In that moment, years of hardened dust were suddenly washed from my spirit.

"I forgive you," he said softly. He held me. I was liquid in his arms.

I was so grateful for this grace of forgiveness, though I hadn't expected it. For the first time in a long time, he made love to me when I was truly naked—flaws and scars and hunger and sins and all. This naked love was worth risking everything for. And I would never trade it for an airbrushed life again.

"Are you sure you want me to go on this journey to Costa Rica with you?" I asked.

"Yes. I want you to come with me." Clear and certain.

We drifted into silence and sleep, peaceful and exhausted.

CHAPTER 21

BACK IN THE DANGER ZONE

"Death has taken everything. I throw myself into love now for love is all that remains. So I hold the precious mystery close, and sing it endless praises."
— MAYA LUNA

"CAN'T YOU JUST cancel this trip to San Diego?" My begging came out as a question.

We were set to depart for Costa Rica in two weeks. Just two weeks. He had another art show and live painting gig planned back in San Diego, the city host to his heroin contacts and debaucherous haunting grounds. Danger. Danger.

"You're not up for this. Let it go, love. This is your *life.* You need to stay close to home right now and take care of yourself." I wished he would just bow to his humanity and honor the self-care that this crisis demanded.

"I *have* to go. I gotta finish this," Chor insisted. His zealous work ethic was prevailing. Seemed to me like he was tempting fate, but he was determined to go.

We had a tight plan. His family would pick him up from the airport, enfold him in their protective clan, and attend his upcoming art show with him. His uncle Douglas promised: he would watch him like a hawk the whole time.

"You've got nothing to worry about, love," Chor said confidently.

He felt about as stable as quicksand to me. But I had nothing to worry about, right? Chor had given his word. His family would be on guard. It would be a swift and purposeful operation. No detours. He would be fine.

—

I drove Chor to the bus station, where he'd catch his ride to the airport. "Goodbye, love." His kiss was swifter than ever. His mind had already caught the flight. "I love you!" he said as he dashed off and slammed the car door. I gripped the steering wheel too hard, trying somehow to steer life. I prayed hard right there on the side of the road.

Despite his bold words, my heart skipped beats when he didn't return my calls within minutes. My mind wandered into tragedy and doom. I was strung tight, about to break.

Chor always called me back eventually. He professed his love, like he always did. All was well, he confirmed daily.

He'd had a few drinks at his art show, he told me, explaining away some slurred sweet speech one night. *He had to be OK. Everyone had eyes on him.* His family would have told me if it was time to have a heart attack.

—

I was scheduled to teach a women's dance and yoga intensive for two days in Los Angeles at the same time he was in San Diego.

My time with the goddesses did me good. Mystical females have a private language. It was a yin oasis: fusion temple dance, yoga, mantra, magic, ritual, lyrical laughter, and jokes that only mermaids get. We anointed each other's hearts, brows, hands, and feet with sacred unguents. We danced our devotion and shared our dreams and offered our wounds to the invisible cauldron in the center of the room.

After hours, I told my soul sister and co-teacher, Aradia Sunseri, about Chor's recent relapse. We held him in our prayers. We chanted the Tara mantra together at midnight: pleading, offering, blessing, and letting go.

Great Spirit, where is this winding journey leading us? What drama are you dreaming for humanity to observe through us?

Maybe not everything has a "reason" that a human brain can perceive, but everything can become a blessing—if we are willing to tango with it.

—

Chor and I had planned to meet up at Disneyland for some rare and much needed frivolity; then we'd drive home together and prepare for our trip to Costa Rica. Nature usually called to me for vacation time, but we needed to feel like kids again for a day, and Disneyland was a nostalgic place for both of us.

As we went over our Disneyland details on the phone the night before we were to meet, I suddenly felt overwhelmed. I almost backed out of our plan. "It seems like such a complex production to just get there and find each other, and it's such a ridiculous indulgence at this time of crisis and expense!"

Chor talked me down. "Come on...a little play will do us good!"

Chapter 22
The Happiest Place on Earth

"Woman can feel Man's dishonesty
When He is not in his true alignment and purpose
She feels Him as a psychic disturbance
M-I-A—Missing in Awareness
She is moved to expressing unrelenting, chaotic insanity—
Ushering Him into Truth—
Back to His True Nature"
— Marja West a.k.a Shriimate

I SAW MY LOVE near the gates of Disneyland. Tired eyes. He looked a bit ragged, but that was to be expected. He'd been working like mad, and he'd been through the ringer recently. I came closer and embraced him. The hairs on the back of my neck stood up. I backed up and scanned him. Silent wondering ensued. *Did you stay clean?*

"Hi, love. How are you?" I probed.

"Good! Good, love! Come on. Let's get in there!" and he rushed off, staying a few giant steps ahead of me.

We bought our tickets and entered the park.

"Just a sec," he said and hastily headed to the restroom.

Five minutes. Seven minutes. Ten minutes. With every passing minute, my heart pounded harder in my chest. I watched the bathroom with eagle eyes, waiting on pins and needles at this point for him to emerge. Ten, 20, 30 other men who had gone in after him had come out already.

What the fuck? Did he OD? Was he hitting brain death right about now? Would they drag out his lifeless body from the toilet here at the happiest place on earth?

Pacing. Praying. Nauseous. Nervous. Biting nails. I was a split second away from calling security.

Finally Chor returned, sauntering with an extra bounce in his step, donning artificially sweetened bedroom eyes. "Yeah baby...let's go!" he said, pumping his hands in the air as if to rev up his excitement.

I looked at him sideways, devastated.

"You used," I said, bewildered. "You used!"

"Ah, come on, baby. Don't be like that right now," he said, his eyes dodging everywhere except for directly at mine. "I didn't use anything! Ah, you are so suspicious now. Your mind is playing tricks on you!" And he wobbled away with his new rhythmic strut, feeling slick as I felt sick.

He wanted to get a special pass that would allow him to jump to the front of the lines. "Come with me, love, I need my white-woman power!" he said. This was one of his favorite wisecracks about racism. Stunned, I slowly followed him into the guest relations office. I sat in a chair against the wall and watched the show.

Chor shifted back and forth on his legs, never quite finding a balanced stance. He had a damp white rag across his forehead to cool him on this hot Southern California day. I could see the poison running through him. This voracious demon was playing inside him, riding his strong body like a roller coaster, and it wanted to ride him right into the grave. It was more powerful this time around. There was less of Chor's spirit looking out from behind his eyes.

"Hi there, young queen. How ya doin'?" he said to the nice elderly lady behind the counter. "Yes now. Do you think I can get one of those special passes to jump the lines? My knee, well, hurts," he said seductively as he decorated his face with fidgety hands. She had to have suspected that he was on drugs—or at least a little crazy.

Then I saw his legs. *Fresh scabs.* On the three inches of skin peeking out from between his long athletic shorts and knee high tube socks. He had been scratching himself again.

Yes, he used.

He scored his pass and grabbed my upper arm on the way out. "Yeah! Here we go! Whoooo!"

We stepped out of the office. I stopped in my tracks. "You are HIGH!" I said emphatically, waiting for some mysterious solution to this drama.

"Why do you gotta be like this right now?" He scowled. "We are at DISNEYLAND. Let's have some FUN! I did not use! Baby, you are imagining things, now come ON."

He walked off. I stayed. My feet felt stuck in cement. I gripped my belly.

He whirled around, realizing I wasn't by his side. "What are you DOING?" he said, looking at how I held myself.

"You are LYING to me! And it feels like I'm being force-fed poison."

"Ah, yeah? How do you know? You are just paranoid."

I didn't want to tell him that I could decipher the scabs on his legs, in fear that he would learn how to hide it.

"I just KNOW," I said firmly. "That's it! I can't take any more of this."

"OK, I did it! Is that what you want to hear? By the way, I was just lying. I didn't actually use, but that's what you want to hear, isn't it? You just have to believe the worst, don't you?"

After a taxing 30 minutes of mind games and futile attempts to make me second-guess myself, I was fed up. "I'm done! This is bullshit. I am leaving. You can call your uncle to come and get you!"

I turned to walk away. He came storming after me. "What are you going to do, then, go let some guy put his fingers up in you?" He said venomously.

I froze for a moment and choked up. He'd stabbed me with his words. I looked ahead, determined, and reignited to my pace. "I'm not gonna let you leave!" he howled. "I'm going to get IN your car and go with you! And you can't stop me!"

I kept walking. *Fuck this. I don't need this.*

Then a whisper came from within: *If you leave him here today, he's going to die.*

I stopped. I looked at Chor. The demon was riding his body like a roller coaster, and it wanted to ride him right into the grave.

Chor caught up and touched me softly. "Look. I did smoke a little a few days ago. OK? There. I admitted it."

I didn't buy it. He had done more than that, just now in the bathroom at Disneyland. He was high. He was a mess. He was a nest of lies.

"Look, why did we even come here today? Don't ruin it! You are such a drag today," he taunted me abrasively. Was he seriously giving me shit for *his* fuck-up?

He lit a cigarette, sucked down a few deep drags, and then tossed it like a used tissue. I knew he smoked when he was out of town, but he usually never smoked around me.

"Come on, we are *here*. Let's just BE HERE and have a good time. OK?" He shook my arm gently, trying to break down my armor. The motion rippled through my whole body. His strong body wavered.

I was lost inside myself. My mind spun. What was I to do with this intoxicated, possessed Goliath?

Part of me wanted to stomp off and ditch him forever. I was already way past my breaking point.

A vision flashed before me. If I left him here, he would go down like wild fire. He would wind up a gutter rat in no time flat.

I just need to make it through this day, I consoled myself in silence. *And get him to Costa Rica.*

"OK, then. Let's just be here," I acquiesced.

—

I was a cardboard cutout of myself there at Disneyland, empty and tired and sad.

We headed for a roller coaster. Chor had muscled his way past the kids to the front of the line. We jumped in and locked ourselves down. He howled in delight through the twists and turns. Kids squealed. The sun shined. Good old-fashioned family fun.

My tummy tingled on the roller coaster as my heart wept in secret. I was a strange cocktail of diversion and doom.

He got off the ride and danced away. "Well, now you know what it's like to have sex with you," I joked without the strength to smile. He chuckled. *Maybe we'll make it through this surreal maze today.*

I wasn't making a scene. I wasn't frowning, but I wasn't happy. I was just there, along for his toxic joy ride. Surviving. Yet, it wasn't enough for him.

"You are being such a downer, E.," he whined. "This is ridiculous. You are just *so sad.* You are ruining everything."

"Me? Ruining everything?" I lit up. "That's it! For real! I'm out of here." His salvation was beyond me. I took off ahead of him. I dialed his uncle on my cell. I would let him sweep up this tragedy. He could handle him better than I could anyway. Chor raced after me, speed walking with his zombie strut.

"Douglas, he used," I whispered into the phone, a few paces ahead of Chor. "I know it," I spoke swiftly and softly, not wanting to draw attention. "He's lying about it and giving me shit. I can't handle him. This is a nightmare."

"Really? Are you sure?" said Douglas, shocked. "I watched him every second!"

"Yes. He did. And I have proof. I'll tell you about it later. I don't know what to do. He's walking all over me. He's popping off with drama. I have to get out of here...now."

"Can you at least bring him here to my house?" Douglas asked.

Pregnant pause.

"OK."

"You can't leave me here!" Chor exclaimed from behind me. "This was stupid. We shouldn't have even come," Chor grumbled.

"You think?" I fired back.

We made it to the car with brisk, forlorn, silent steps.

<hr>

We drove an hour in silence, jaws clenched and looking out of opposite windows. We made it to Douglas's condo. I took my first deep breath since Chor and I locked eyes earlier that day.

Douglas came out and quickly ushered us into his

place, avoiding a scene for the neighbors. "OK, kids, let's take it inside."

Chor immediately retreated to the balcony to nurse a cigarette. I took Douglas aside for a moment and whispered, "First, I could sense it. Then I saw it. The evidence is on his legs. He's covered in new scabs. He scratches himself when he's high." He nodded, glancing at Chor's legs. "He used in the bathroom at Disneyland, too. I know it. He was in there forever and teetered out with black hole eyes."

We all sat down, inhabiting different corners of the sectional sofa like boxers about to launch into a match. Chor looked down intently like he was trying to burrow a hole in the floor with his gaze.

"He used. And he lied to me about it."

"So what? Fuck! Why did you have to make such a big deal about it? And at fucking Disneyland of all places?" said the demon that posed as my lover.

Exasperated, I threw my arms in the air. "See what I am dealing with?"

"Chor! You fucked up, man!" Douglas laid into him, man to man. "What are you doing?! What do you mean, 'so what?' You used. You can't expect her to go along for this ride. You are playing with your LIFE, man! And you can't put her through this shit!"

Chor bowed his head. Douglas was the elder alpha here. Sullen, Chor received the scolding in silence.

"Douglas, I'm scared. I can't bring him home like this. I am a mother. This is getting crazy. Too crazy. I need to keep our home safe," I expressed.

"Look, I won't bring this home," Chor said.

"I can't believe anything you say at this point. Your words don't mean anything anymore. It's just hot air coming out of your mouth. *You've got nothing to worry about.* 'Sound familiar?"

I remembered when his words were as good as gold. I had never met a more reliable man. I loved that about him. I quietly mourned the clear, powerful, focused love warrior that he was before his soul got sick.

"Chor, is that what you want? You're gonna get left behind man. You wanna go home?" Douglas asked.

"Yes, I want to go home," Chor said clearly as he looked at his folded hands.

"I don't know..." I said, shaking my head. "I just don't know what's right."

We all paused. Quiet. Wheels turning.

"There HAVE to be some ground rules," I said finally. "No more drugs. And you don't have any privacy at all. I will go through your stuff at any time. Any violations—and you are out."

"OK?" Douglas checked Chor. Chor nodded.

"I need to hear you. Clearly." I demanded.

"OK!" Chor barked as he jumped up to hit the balcony for another cigarette.

I turned to Douglas. "I need your support, Doug. I don't want to leave him here, but I have to think about my son. If I take him home, I need to know that you will be my backup. You've got to take him immediately if he goes down."

"OK. I understand," he said solidly.

Chor returned to the couch. "And no visitors," I added. "Not now."

"Fuck that! I'll do whatever I want! I'm a grown-ass man! I'm not gonna be a prisoner." His voice spewed fire at me. Douglas shot him a fierce look.

"That's it! I cannot deal with him like this! It's like I'm not even talking *to him*. I'm just talking to the drugs. I need some air. You two talk."

I left and walked along the neat sidewalks through the condo complex, contemplating with every step. Exhausted. Sullen. The sun went down. The moon rose. After some time in the quaint courtyard and a little silent conversation with the moon, I returned.

Our awkward council reconvened. "You gotta do what she says if you are going home," Douglas enforced the terms.

"All right. I'm cool," Chor surrendered.

"I went through all his stuff with a fine-tooth comb," Douglas said. "I took out the last of it."

"OK," I said. "Let's go."

"I need another cigarette first," said Chor.

"Thank you, Douglas. I couldn't have managed this without you."

"Anytime. You guys wanna stay here tonight?" Douglas asked.

"Thanks anyway. We need to get on the road. We'll stop at a motel halfway," I said.

CHAPTER 23
THE LONG ROAD

"The mentality and behavior of drug addicts and alcoholics is wholly irrational until you understand that they are completely powerless over their addiction and unless they have structured help, they have no hope."
— RUSSELL BRAND

"I saw the best minds of my generation destroyed by madness, starving hysterical naked, dragging themselves through the negro streets at dawn looking for an angry fix angelheaded hipsters burning for the ancient heavenly connection to the starry dynamo in the machinery of the night...."
—ALLEN GINSBERG, *HOWL AND OTHER POEMS*

WE DROVE NORTH in silence. Chor's feisty attitude faded into a passive vacancy. We stopped at a Best Western after a few hours, both sleepy and sapped of life force.

Chor went into the bathroom. He tried several times to shut the door, and then fumbled with the lock. I walked in and examined the door. "Yeah, it's broken." He'd have to use the bathroom with the door cracked.

We swiftly slipped into bed. We were drawn into a

vortex of desperate kisses, but I could not let him inside me again yet. "No. Go to sleep, love. Get better."

In the morning, Chor went to the bathroom. I slipped in through the broken door to grab my toothbrush. He suddenly looked up from his seat on the toilet, his eyes as wide as saucers. His legs locked together. "Yeah? What?" he said, alarmed. He was up to something. I went over to him, suspicious.

"WHAT are you DOING in here?" I demanded.

"Nothing, Elizabeth. Nothing!" He sounded frantic.

I could see a swatch of fabric that didn't match his shorts peeking out from deep between his legs. "WHAT do you have there? WHAT are you hiding?"

"Nothing! Nothing! Come ON, Elizabeth. Please!" he pleaded.

"Give it to me!" I held out my hand. "NOW!" I was a terrified commander.

"Please!" he tried once more.

"I'm leaving your ass here unless you show me what you have!"

He didn't have the strength to fight or flee.

He sighed and handed me a Lycra sports cap. I opened it to reveal a capped needle and a prescription bottle filled with clear liquid.

"What IS this?" I demanded.

"It's just methadone, Elizabeth! It will ease the withdrawals!"

My adrenaline pumped as fear and rage ravaged me

from within. I ripped the top off the bottle and hastily poured the liquid down the drain. "*Just* methadone?" I repeated with an acrid taste in my mouth.

He flushed the fresh needle down the toilet. "I'm sorry. Fuck. I was just going to use the needle to squirt it in my mouth," he said, as if that would somehow absolve the flagrant violation.

"Jesus, Chor! It's still drugs! Besides, I don't believe anything you say. You are LOST." We paused, panting.

"Do you have anything else? You better hand it over now!" I wailed.

He'd already crossed the line I set, but I couldn't really just leave him here in the middle of nowhere. Or could I?

"No, I don't have anything else. That's it."

I reminded him what we had learned on the Iboga House website. "You know about methadone, Chor! Methadone is even harder to detox than heroin. You wanna let this medicine work? You wanna heal? You HAVE to be as clean as possible upon arrival."

I went through all his things, shaking and shocked, while I silently thanked the angel that had broken our bathroom door handle.

I gathered myself. *I will do everything in my power to get him to Costa Rica,* I swore. *And that's where my part as his personal prison warden and nurse ends. It's up to him after that.*

I wasn't even sure if our love would survive this, but I hoped that he would, at least.

Our drive back to San Francisco was charged with tension. The slightest spark might lead either of us to exploding. My every human limit had been shattered. I felt lost, except for the forward momentum of the car. *Just keep heading north.*

I played an audio book called *The Brain That Changes Itself* by Normal Doige, to fill up the silence, hoping that brain's limitless capacity to heal itself would sink into Chor's awareness as he faded in and out.

He devolved into the various stages of withdrawal, but it was worse this time. First he was empty, then irritable, then downright nasty. He cussed and grimaced. The demon had its claws around his neck; it was choking him out.

Once home, I nursed him through the torture all over again, but he was not so grateful for my care this round. He pouted contemptuously with every offering. The demon did not want my healing potions.

I was on guard 24/7. I jumped up and burst in every time he went to the bathroom. I rifled through his backpack and bathroom drawers every chance I could. I had never been a snoop before, but I had become obsessed. I fought for our life together—by digging through his stuff like a bare-knuckle boxer.

"Do you have anything else?" I asked him several times, with fire in my voice, despite my total lack of faith in his words. My interrogation was irrational. Each time he would say no, but ultimately it was up to me to observe him.

The next morning after we returned home, he actually handed me a couple pharmaceutical pills. "It's called Norco. It helps with the withdrawals. Go ahead. Take it. I don't want anything. There. You have everything." My bitter hostility softened a bit with his offering, though I remained suspicious.

I canceled work that day. Again. *Shit.* Bills were staring at me.

He'd been stalling on his deposit for Iboga House, too busy. *Right.*

"What's more important than this? What good is anything if you're dead? You wanna stay in this house? You do the deposit *today.*" I pushed.

"OK!" he snapped. We drove to the bank. He was unshaven and shabby.

"I need to do a wire transfer to Costa Rica," Chor said to a banker with a frown as we sat down in his cubicle.

The man was robotically polite. "Ah, Costa Rrrrica. Pura Vida, eh? You know, 'Pura Vida?' Are you going on a nice vacation? You lucky folks!" The banker began typing on this computer.

Chor slumped over the desk and propped his head on his hand. He looked up at the banker with dark, distant eyes. He tapped a pen on the desk like he was sending a furious telegram. I sat next to him and silently screamed at him with my eyes. *Normal. Please just act normal.*

I worried whether he'd even make it through the transaction. He was acting so shady, I imagined they'd call the police.

"We are in a hurry. Thank you," I said.

"And I need three thousand cash," Chor told the banker. That was balance of the treatment cost that would be due upon our arrival.

"Chor, don't you want to wait until a bit closer to our departure date?" I said softly to him, fretting. What would a jonesing heroin addict do with three grand cash and a couple weeks to kill?

"No. Let's just get it now." He said firmly.

"Right away. Just a moment." The banker left his desk to fetch the cash.

"Then I'll handle that cash. You understand?" I whispered. "Just hand it over to me for safekeeping. You won't need it until we get there anyway."

When the banker returned, he counted out 30 hundred-dollar bills on the desk, placed them neatly in an envelope, and handed the small fortune to Chor. "Thank you," I said to the banker, on behalf of my terse lover.

We walked toward the car. Chor handed me the money. As soon as we got home, I promptly hid it where he'd never find it.

I remembered an important point on an email from Iboga House. "Chor, they requested updates on drug usage so they could be properly prepared for the detox. You MUST tell them about this second relapse. It could affect their treatment protocol," I emphasized.

Chor sighed and typed out his update. He relayed their response later that day. "They suggested staying a few extra days for an additional medicine journey—and an added $1,500. Plus we'd have to change our flights and miss more work to stay longer. There's no way, Elizabeth.

I can't pay any more," he said. And neither could I.

"Did you tell them that you can't do it?"

"Yes," he said. "They'll do their best to work with the time we'd planned for."

"No more, Chor. *No more.*" I said through clenched jaws.

"I KNOW." He grumbled.

Make-or-break time.

He settled in for a horror film. I did the dishes and the laundry, in between checking his bags again and again.

CHAPTER 24
BACK IN THE SADDLE

"There is nothing you must do to make me love you. There is nothing you can do to make me not love you. I simply love you."

— ARIEL SPILSBURY, *GREAT MOTHER TRANSMISSION*

I HAD TO GET BACK to work soon, but I agonized about Chor being alone. I had yoga students scheduled in the coming days and bills nipping at my heels. I couldn't imagine guiding others to inner peace with this going on in my own home, but I had to carry on somehow.

I prepared to go to work the next morning: I showered, dressed, and packed up my lunch. I clung to my routine, high strung and resentful.

I walked up to him in the living room. "I need to know that you are going to be OK. Or I'm gonna have panic attacks at work. Are you going to be OK? Be straight with me, for God's sake. If you are struggling, we'll figure something out."

"Yeah," he said sedately. "I'll be OK."

I went back to the bathroom to put the final touches on my mascara and mask of normalcy. He came in behind me a moment later.

"Hey...actually, I'm feeling kinda...jumpy. Could you...stay?"

I knew him so well. It was not like him to admit any vulnerability. This was serious.

"Alright. I'll cancel my day."

I was relieved and bitter all at once. I didn't know how I would have functioned anyway, had I gone to work. I was compulsively drawn to keep a close watch on him.

"You know...you are starting to look like a Tenderloin ghost," I said coldly. I hit a nerve, precisely on target.

Whenever we drove through the Tenderloin neighborhood of San Francisco, I observed the way Chor watched all the lost souls: junkies, street hookers, pimps, dealers. They bickered and snarled and walked straight into oncoming traffic like euphoric zombies. I could almost see the subtle shiver running down his spine, as he contemplated the fate he'd averted many years ago when he cleaned up.

"Na, I don't look like that...I'm not that bad. I had it under control. You're overreacting," he said, not quite believing himself.

I just scoffed. "Oh yes, you DO look like that. And you are not in any kind of control. You're dancing on deadly thin ice. Two more minutes, and you would have been trolling Hyde Street selling your life for junk. Get humble, man." I walked briskly off into my own corners of the house.

I reminisced about the first night we met, bittersweet from this vantage point. *A different lifetime, a different person even.*

I'd seen his art the night before at a small gathering at Hotel Des Arts in San Francisco. John, a refugee of the corporate world and Chor's aspiring agent, told me Chor's story as we explored his paintings in the hallway gallery. Chor had brazenly abandoned his job in San Diego as a hotel janitor to pursue his dream full time when John offered him a corner in his warehouse, a few art gigs, and some PR services. His art was clearly the love child of a wild mind. "He's totally sober," John said with pride and wonder, as he sipped his cocktail. "Amazing, huh? He used to be an addict way, way back, and then he totally cleaned up. His art is amazing, isn't it?" And it was *amazing.*

I had plans to meet up with Kira, a mutual friend of John and mine, the next evening at Rock the Bells, a big hip-hop concert. They hooked me up with a ticket. I wasn't generally a party girl, but I could be lured out with free entrance and great company. I waved to John on my way in and slipped passed the throbbing masses toward the backstage area, looking for Kira.

Suddenly a chiseled, golden man barreled past me, holding an enormous painting of Rage Against the Machine, one of the bands playing that night.

It was not love at first sight, for me. I had too thick of a fortress over my heart to recognize it, anyway. I smiled in passing. Chor carried his painting high and proud like an advertisement. He flashed a toothy smile my way. *Oh no,* I thought, *not another strikingly handsome, plenty talented, cocky, young artist.* They were a dime a dozen in San Francisco, and they all thought they were the next big thing. *Surely he's made of nothing but frosting,* I thought, and strode onward after exchanging pleasantries. He wouldn't let me go so easily.

"Wait up!" He pursued me with an old-world attention span that night.

"I'm looking for a friend," I responded with a reserved smile. He was gorgeous and magnetic, but I was quite cozy being sovereign, and I wasn't about to flirt for kicks. After a couple devastating long-term relationships, I had taken a good chunk of time for intentional celibacy to cleanse my field. My prayer went something like this: *Great Spirit, please don't send any lovers my way—unless they completely ROCK my WORLD and BLOW my MIND with their love. Otherwise I would be happy to spend the rest of my life alone with my piano, thank you very much.* I wasn't hopeful, to say the least.

Chor could see that I was peeking at a restricted area backstage as I searched for Kira. "You wanna get back there? Come with me! Hold the other end of this... let's see if we can work you in."

I grabbed one side of the painting's frame and held on as he shuffled swiftly through the gate. Security nabbed me as they meticulously checked everyone for VIP access badges. "Sorry, we just can't let you past here without the right ID." Though we didn't succeed, I was touched by his valiant effort.

"It's all right," I smiled. "Go ahead."

"I'll be right back! Stay here!" Chor dropped off the painting with the band and left the celebrities and the paparazzi to find me again.

We went through the regular "what do you do?" banter, and I discovered that this was the artist whose work I'd viewed the night before. "I love your creations," I said.

Honey poured from his kingly eyes. He was deeper than I guessed at first glance. I gave him five minutes, and my card.

"I've been wanting to learn yoga," he said when he saw my card.

"Maybe we can trade yoga for art sometime," I said, warming up.

I didn't stay long. I'd had enough of the volume and the mall fashion show and the ravenous meat market. "I'm heading out," I told Chor. "I have to go walk my dog."

"Can I come? Can I...*walk your dog* with you?" he asked, making that simple question sound so very naughty. I was taken aback. Did this swagger work for him often, I wondered?

"No, you can't come with me!" I scoffed. "We just met! Walking my dog is more like a third date thing... maybe!" I started walking away.

"Can I at least walk you out?" he asked.

"It's a ways to the gate. Don't you have famous people waiting for you?" I asked in earnest.

"Yeah, but they can wait," he smiled warmly as he strutted right alongside me. *Impressive.* I gave him a warm hug as we said our goodbyes. "I'll call you," he promised.

And he did call me, that night at midnight. Nice. No waiting games. No downplaying his enthusiasm.

We chatted for a long time. "Are you a queen?" he asked point blank in the midst of our conversation. I knew what he meant. He was not inferring arrogance or high-maintenance ways. He was asking about my self-respect and self-love.

"Yes." I said, more impressed.

For our first date, I took him to a teahouse, the best festive place for sober people. Over oolong and aloe vera nectar, we talked philosophy. "Do you *know* who you are?" he asked me, intently.

"Yes!" I replied, amused by the question. "I am a drop of God."

"Hmmm," he responded with deep reflection, equally amused.

We shared prayers and poetry.

His sparkling eyes, sass, and scent drew me into a sweet remembrance.

I dropped him off after tea, and he seemed surprised I wasn't taking him right back to my place. "Not yet, mister," I smirked. We kissed passionately, and I played with his tender nipples until they were as hard as diamonds and about to pop. Hmm, he was fun to play with. "Sweet dreams!" I said as I drove back to my enclave of peace.

I shared with that Chor I had an eight-year-old son. In the first few days of our new courtship, I found myself in his neighborhood and offered to stop by with Kyle. Chor excitedly welcomed us to his studio/crash pad. He threw the respirator on Kyle and handed him his fancy spray cans to play with. Kyle officially collaborated on what would later become a famous portrait of Hugh Hefner. *A man who can play with a kid. So hot!* It started off full of color and harmony.

We went on a few dates before I let my shell crack and my legs part. That first night that we made love, spirit spoke to my heart: it was time to share myself, with this man. I had become too comfortable in my hermitage.

I broke open. My body blossomed.

I was hardly a virgin when we met, but Chor was the first man that I ever gushed over, literally. Tantric practice had long since awakened in me the buried birth right of female ejaculation, yet I had only been able to trigger it with touch up until that point. For some mysterious reason, my body had never before released the dam during intercourse. But Chor would penetrate me, and I'd burst with hot holy water. Very auspicious indeed.

Our fragrances mixed into a beautiful potion. "We make LOVE perfume together, baby!" I said, feeling the earthy intelligence of our chemistry.

When we showered together, I washed his every filthy crevice with sweet strokes. "Yup, you're a keeper," he said. Ah, the fresh fire we had.

After our third date, he never left my side except to work. He even wanted to do laundry with me. *Laundry.* From the very beginning, it felt so natural to be with him, as if he'd just returned home after a long journey.

There was no fear, no demands, no games of hide and seek. We were just together. My heart felt at ease.

It was clear: our love was holy.

It wasn't long before I overheard him refer to me as his girlfriend during a phone conversation, and I smiled.

One day in our first few months, someone I'd previously dated was coming to town, and I'd long ago promised to put him up at my yoga studio. I explained to Chor, "Look, I want you to know, I'm just giving him a place to crash. I am not interested in dating him anymore—or anyone else but you." I did not ask him for anything in return. I was simply affirming a commitment I was making to *myself* that just felt right.

"Really? You feel that way?" Chor asked tenderly. Then he confessed, "I feel the same way." And that was that. We were two little lovebirds, sitting in a tree.

How did we wind up so far from paradise?

———

We settled into another day of withdrawals. He watched movies, dazed and distant. I did computer work and futzed around the house.

"Maybe this all happened for a reason," he said that evening, his eyes still on the movie. "Maybe this is all happened to get me somewhere that I need to be."

I felt a shiver of resonance, but also rage: "I don't think your relapse happened for any 'divine reason.' This whole drama is fucked. What a tragic detour! And do you realize how hard this is on me? I can't hear that right now. Maybe you needed to go where you're headed, but maybe you could have found a better way to get there." I was incensed.

"I do know one thing," I conceded. "This demon

entered you because there was space for it. You've got some renovating to do."

Thick silence. Wisdom pushed through his foggy mind. Words emerged. "I stopped praying," he acknowledged.

"And you were working yourself to death."

I went into a sermon. "When I first met you, you told me about cultivating 'positive addiction.' Remember? You taught me...there is no lasting escape from addictions; we can only create positive ones. This way, addiction can become devotion.

"This idea goes way back. Legend goes that Shiva, the first yogi and the symbol of infinite consciousness, went from being addicted to wine and gambling to being addicted to annihilating the fear of all beings. The Śiva Mahimnah Stōtram, a hymn to Shiva, uses the Sanskrit word for *addicted*. Shiva created a *positive addiction.*"

"Yeah, positive addiction," he said softly, remembering his own gem from another era.

Chapter 25
Storm Shelter

"Secrets are hidden in darkness
And difficult nights.
You awaken into a pang of aloneness,
A howl of separation.

This is the call of the Dark One,
The roar of life seeking its source.
The union you long for is within reach...."

— Lorin Roche, *The Radiance Sutras:*
112 Gateways to the Yoga of Wonder and Delight

THAT NIGHT IN BED, next to Chor's sleeping body, I started to tremble and weep like a summer storm. It seemed to come out of nowhere. It blew in and shattered my bones. I was breaking down. The burden was just too heavy. Instinctively, I held myself tightly; I was the only one I could count on anymore. Tears carved rivers through me. I tried to keep quiet and pushed my face into the pillow.

Chor stirred. "Elizabeth, what's going on? Why are you crying?"

I couldn't respond for a few long seconds. I was

choking on my grief.

"What do you think?" I shot back at him. "It's like I have two kids right now. I was already needing you to step up more. Now I'm afraid for your life! And you ARE my life! I'm terrified to go back to work, and bills are just piling up. I can't...I can't do this. It's too much."

He wrapped his strong, sick arms around me and drew me close. He just held me and stroked my face until the storm passed and we drifted back into sleep.

—

We carried on with life, having survived a second set of withdrawals. He didn't dart off into the street to refill the needle, but I was always on edge, watching and worrying. It became a daily routine for me to anxiously rifle through his belongings.

We kept his demon well dressed for the most part. We didn't want our neighbors to know. Kyle still didn't know. We didn't tell our friends, except for just a very few. We both did our best to pull off the show without a hitch, but there were close calls and excuses.

—

Chor had always been a blunt type of man. Now, with the drugs ripped from his system a second time, he was an abrasive brute. He snapped at me over everything. I responded in kind. I was a stern shrew, if only to keep him alive. He was a pushy ingrate, snarling at my strict rules and my every attempt to protect him. I tried not to take anything personally, but I still suffered.

I counted the days until Costa Rica, exasperated.

Chor continued to pick at my heart's stitches, in a hushed voice reserved for lovers' secrets, after dark and alone in our bedroom. "It's like you think I should just get over this immediately," he said, referring to my recent sordid confession.

"No," I responded. "I don't think that. Feel what you feel. Express what you need. Do whatever you need. Go if you must. I love you, love, and I'm so so sorry. I feel terrible about my actions, but I don't regret confessing."

I set him free and offered myself fully. He stayed another day. So did I.

"Hopefully we'll still be together after all this," he said one evening in the living room.

My heart fell into my belly. "What?"

My knees buckled a little. I held onto the couch like a crutch. I was making this great journey, and I understood that there were no guarantees. Maybe our relationship would be so tattered that we'd simply fall apart by the time we made it across this fire. "I understand. We both have a lot to heal. Wherever we end up, we'll be right where we need to be."

"It's just that...*things might come out,*" he added.

"What do you mean, 'Things might come out?'"

"I don't know. We'll be taking this strong medicine. I might say things. Bad things."

"Like what?" I pressed.

"I don't know," he insisted.

We'll make it to Costa Rica. At least.

CHAPTER 26
FEEDING DEMONS

"When the darkness is hidden rather than valued and processed, it can easily fester and grow into internal monsters that haunt us and manifest as physical and mental illness. Our work is to find the balance of darkness and light because both are meant to be present in every human being."
— ANANDHA RAY

I PICKED UP my old practice of feeding demons.

It's not as morose as it sounds. *Feeding Demons* is a simplified version of an elaborate tantric Tibetan Buddhist practice called Chöd, taught by Tsultrim Allione, a great feminine voice of wisdom and renowned Buddhist teacher.

When inner demons appear in our lives, we are generally so consumed with battling the demon that we often never ask why it came in the first place. Through this intricate meditation, a demon is revealed, questioned, and finally "fed" the pure essence of what it truly needs to be healed.

This practice could be done on behalf of others, so I gave it a go for Chor. I settled into a quiet place in our back yard. Closing my eyes, I tapped into my deep love for Chor and felt the familiar sweet warmth pour through me. I focused my burning desire to benefit all beings. The initial breath practice followed, clearing out any cobwebs.

I summoned Chor's heroin demon into my awareness. Emerging from darkness, I saw a devilish reptilian creature with jet-black, cold, slick skin and dark, vacuous eyes. Its long, slender body slowly writhed and taloned little hands curled, readying to penetrate soft flesh or porous minds. It was powerful, determined, stealth, and insatiable.

I asked him silently, "What do you *want* from Chor?"

He said, "I want to devour his life. I want to suck him down into the abyss of my endless belly." Yikes.

The questioning went deeper. "And what do you *need* from Chor?"

"I need him to...rest." Wow. Rest. What a villain.

"What will you feel if he rests?" I asked.

"I will feel balanced and peaceful," responded the demon.

I visualized feeding this demon the flavor of peace that arises from a balanced life; it flowed as nectar from my some inexhaustible source within my heart. I watched as this dark, parasitic demon transformed into a benevolent white serpent, which then settled affectionately on Chor's neck, gently decorating and protecting him, like Shiva's famous jewelry. This serpent adorning the neck was an age-old symbol of mastered kundalini.

I translated my vision for Chor: He could transform

this heroin demon by mastering the monumental force of his kundalini, in essence, his creative and passionate energy. This could mean living a more balanced life, complete with good breakfasts, a sane work schedule, and practices to harness this inner rocket fuel. "Kundalini can light up your life—or it can burn you alive if allowed to run rampant," I warned.

I knew that he could still paint prolifically and tap into greater abundance—all while enjoying a healthy and sustainable rhythm. For just the length of a breath, I wondered what unrealized visionary art he had laying dormant in him, waiting to be activated by a wiser way. "Take it all with a grain of salt, love. It's just an invitation, if it resonates," I offered softly.

Chor listened with listless eyes, but I didn't know if it really sank in. He may have just been too battle weary to bark back. I was grateful he didn't fight me like a lawyer, at least.

CHAPTER 27
FINAL COUNTDOWN

*"The spiritual path is a warrior's path. It is not a path of
escapism or sugar coating reality with lofty ideals.
It is about burning again and again in the fires
of your own unfolding."*
— MIRIAM ELYSE

FIVE DAYS LEFT before takeoff. Chor and I were
driving in the car, somewhere between the grocery store
and FedEx, when, quite unexpectedly, I became an
oracle for a moment. My lips parted, and an ancient,
beneficent being spoke to Chor through me: "You will
be crowned again as king of your Self. You will guide
others to healing. You will be able to speak to those who
no one else can reach. You will illuminate many."

Gasp. Where did that come from?

The words carried a solid confidence that I didn't
possess at that moment. I had been filled with fear and
cynicism, yet I was proceeding forward with our plans
anyway. I couldn't take any credit for being brave. In
truth, I was just backed into a corner. Nowhere else to
go, nothing else to do.

"We'll see," said Chor, likely harboring the same
desperate, dismal attitude as I.

—

The house sitter was all lined up. Check. Kyle would be with his dad. Check. Our email auto-reply and voice-mail greeting changed: "We're on retreat for the month," to put it nicely. Suitcases packed. Plants watered one more time. Passports ready. Check.

I pulled the remaining money for my treatment out of emergency savings. Well, this is an emergency.

One last email confirmation came from Iboga House with instructions for our preparation: "Bring light clothing, sunscreen, personal care products, and a notebook for journaling. Write down personal questions. You can ask the medicine anything in your journey."

I responded: "Anything?"

"Yes, anything," Julia replied. "Think about any spiritual matters that you desire guidance on. It will come to you direct from your higher self, through the medicine."

"How many questions?" I replied.

"As many as you want."

Well, what would you ask God if you had a tea date?

—

Chor and I didn't speak much during those last couple days. Like soldiers heading into a secret mission, we focused all our energy on the journey ahead.

There were still unspoken shards of fear. Would we make it back alive? Was this place all that it was cracked up to be? Zillions of doubts and dark thoughts, but we moved through them, coaxed by spirit, toward our destination.

Taxi scheduled to arrive before dawn. Check.

CHAPTER 28

TAKING FLIGHT

"Remember that just because you hit bottom doesn't mean you have to stay there."
— ROBERT DOWNEY JR.

"If you never fail, that means you never tried to do something impossible."
— POLLY WHITTAKER, *POLLY: SEX CULTURE REVOLUTIONARY*

WE WOKE in darkness, silent and somber. Any traces of affection had vanished. We were in survival mode.

Chor wore a festive Hawaiian shirt and bright shorts. With his hardened expression and shady demeanor, he looked like an escaped prisoner posing as a tacky American tourist.

The taxi brought us to the bus station. Chor was immersed in his music, his smartphone, his virtual world. His enormous headphones served as an iron shield that isolated him from the rest of the world—and from me.

Every time I had to mention a logistical detail or ask him a question, he'd flip his headphones off one ear dramatically and suck his teeth, irritated and inconvenienced. I trimmed down our interactions to the bare minimum. *Just get there.*

At the airport, he pushed past a couple people, muttering under his breath, "Get the fuck out of the way." Offended or confused looks would follow from people who almost heard him.

"Chor, take it easy, baby."

Past security. Bathroom break. Five minutes...seven minutes. *Fuck! Not again!*

Ten minutes. Heart pounding. Breath shallow.

That's it. I'm calling airport security.

Finally, Chor walked out, with a clear and even stride.

"What the fuck?" I gasped. "Ten minutes? Did you DO anything?"

"I took a BIG SHIT! And I was looking at my phone while I did it. Get off my back. I'm not doing any drugs. Let's go," he said sourly and strode off ahead of me.

Your words don't mean anything.

My heart wouldn't take this panicked pace much longer.

Just get there.

On the plane, I leaned onto his shoulder. I reached for his hand. I was met with dead weight. He was unresponsive. Eyes closed. Music blasting. Alive, but not there.

Don't take it personally, I advised myself. *He's just making it one breath to another.*

Just get there.

—

"What am I gonna ask?" Chor asked softly on the plane.

"What?" I asked, just slipping into sleep.

"I'm just thinking about what in the world I should ask...the Most High."

He's engaging. He's going to give it a shot. Grateful, I silently celebrated.

"Yeah, I was wondering the same thing. What in the world do you ask the Supreme?"

While he contemplated, I turned away, hunched over my journal, and unleashed a torrent of words. "Are you writing about me?" he probed. "What are you writing?"

"I'm in a process. It's not for you yet."

Everything started to pour out. Our story. Our sickness. It was my first peaceful moment of self-reflection in a long time.

Venting into my journal cleansed my mind. I could feel fresh space for the cosmic questions to form.

—

We left the plane travel weary, anxious, hopeful, and desperate.

We walked up to the customs desk. Chor whipped off one side of the headphones so he could hear, looking like an asymmetrical alien. "What brings you to Costa Rica?" the man behind the customs desk asked us politely, as he scanned us from head to toe. Chor barely passed as a functional human.

"Vacation?"

"Yeah," Chor said, rough and robotic.

Salvation, I wanted to say.

Julia had told us that our shuttle driver would be waiting for us with a sign that read Iboga House. After exiting the baggage claim area, we looked around. No sign.

We went outside into the tropical night air, searching.

"Chor, you HAVE to tell them if you took any more," I whispered, vowing to make that question the last act of the warden in me.

Chor didn't answer me. "God, I hope that ends after we do this medicine," he whispered spitefully.

"Yeah, me too! Seriously!" I screamed under my breath.

Where was our sign?

Then I saw Chor walking purposefully forward. He outstretched his hand. There was Moughenda himself, the shaman, in a baseball cap, polo shirt, and cargo shorts, smiling kindly at us. No pomp. No entourage. No sign.

They shook hands. Chor actually seemed enthusiastic. "Hey Moughenda! It's you, in the flesh! Good to meetcha. Good to meetcha."

"Yeah, so good to meet you! Welcome!" Moughenda responded warmly.

I wouldn't have thought the head honcho of the

retreat center would be our driver, but I'd soon learn why he had to be there.

"You...READY?" Moughenda asked us, excitedly. His words seemed loaded and multilayered: Ready to go? Ready for life? Ready for miracles?

We packed up the SUV and headed out into the night, through 30 minutes of jungle roads and small towns. We conversed with Moughenda about the medicine, drugs, and detox. Chor opened up to him immediately. I hadn't heard him engage in such lively conversation in weeks.

"So, you ready to be free of your addiction?" Moughenda asked Chor point-blank.

"Yeah. I'm ready!" Chor said, solid.

"When you're addicted, you are a slave, man," Moughenda said as he glanced over at Chor. I'd never heard it worded just so, but that was the raw truth.

"Yeah, that is true." Chor said, contemplative.

We brought up Chor's friend Jake and his less than ideal experience. "Yes, it's SO important to have a guide with iboga...a true guide, who knows this medicine," Moughenda affirmed, live and in person.

"So, you have a 70% success rate for addicts in recovery?" I asked, probing for the current stats.

"Actually it's about an 80% success rate without relapse so far. The deciding factor is if people really *want* to heal. The 20% that relapse were pressured to come here by loved ones. They weren't ready. A lot of kids are pushed here by their parents. Sometimes people wake up when they are here, but ultimately someone has to do this *for themselves*. Then basically it's 100% successful."

"So...am I going to shit myself on this medicine?" Chor asked, and then exploded with a rowdy laugh. Moughenda laughed right along with him.

"No, man, you won't shit yourself. You'll see."

"So, you don't have a driver?" I asked.

"Not this time. I needed to check you out personally. I've been scanning you since the airport."

"Scanning us?" Chor asked, fascinated. I'd never heard him listen to anyone so intently, ever.

"Yes, I needed to see how much medicine to give you. The medicine tells me. Sometimes, for severe detoxes, when people are on a tight schedule of using, we have to start giving the medicine immediately, like right off the plane. You are both good for tonight. Get some rest. You will start your first journey tomorrow night at 7 o'clock," he said confidently.

A proud old-world ranch gate welcomed us, and we drove along a short road up to a modest Mediterranean-style mansion.

CHAPTER 29

WELCOME

"How we treat the vulnerable is how we
define ourselves as a species."
— RUSSELL BRAND

A LARGE, ELEGANTLY carved wooden door donning a horse greeted us and opened into an expansive,
welcoming, minimalist living room. High ceilings and
vast windows created plenty of space to contemplate.
A jubilant, slender man buzzed out to greet us. "OK,
guys," said Moughenda, "Have a good sleep. Michael is
the house manager. He will take good care of you! I'll
see you tomorrow!" Moughenda left to go to his nearby
apartment.

Michael was like a wild bird in human form.
"Welcome! Welcome!" he said, warm as summer sun,
flitting about the living room. "You made it!" he
exclaimed, sounding relieved. I wondered how often
people didn't make it. "Wonderful! This is going to be
AMAZING! This is the BEST medicine. You are so
lucky to be here with Moughenda. He's the real deal!"
Michael's eyes sparkled.

Mountains of fresh tropical fruit salad waited for
us in the kitchen: papaya, watermelon, pineapple. The

house was charming, clean, safe, and homey. Yes, the door hinges needed a little lubrication. The landscaping looked a little wild. It wasn't the Ritz. But we didn't need the Ritz. We needed good medicine. And good care.

"It's my duty to go over the house policies with you. I know you must be tired. It'll only take a minute." Michael went to get his laptop.

We sat on the sofa and began to flip through the photo albums. They were filled with images of the traditional rite of passage and the Bwiti initiation ceremony that was offered with Moughenda's tribe in Gabon, Africa. The eyes of the men in the photos pierced me. *These are the eyes of men who know themselves.* One strong elder graced the cover of one album. "That's Moughenda's grandfather. He was the bigwig shaman of his tribe and the surrounding tribes. Moughenda began studying with him when he was 12 years old. Moughenda has been through five initiations with the medicine, doses beyond what we could believe." Michael nodded passionately.

"Here we go. Just a formality, really. You guys will be great, I know! So no drugs or alcohol in the house, of course." Big smile. "Gotta do a bag check before you settle in. I'm sure you understand," he said with a wink. "Please don't leave the grounds. Let us know if you need anything. No inappropriate sexual behavior with other guests or staff, et cetera. Oh, and no electronics or internet or phones the day after ceremonies." *Yes!* I smirked with joy. *Finally, Chor will get to be off the matrix for more than a minute!*

"We have a great week planned for you. After your first ceremony, we'll visit a volcanic clay spa where you can soak and enjoy the mud baths and massages. And it's Costa Rica, after all, so you can enjoy a horseback ride through the jungle."

Horses? *Drats.* "Oh, it all sounds lovely, but no horseback riding for me," I said. "It's just not my thing. Horse trauma. Chor likes it."

A friend in my third grade class had been encased in a full body cast for weeks, after being thrown from a horse. That image of her always sat like a thorn in my psyche. I had tried to give horseback riding a chance as a teen, but the horse had run away with me. It was terrifying, like being on a derailed train. Another rider had to chase the big beast down. Supposedly just a gentle trail horse. Yeah, no thanks.

"They sure are pretty, though," I added. "Gorgeous animals. I'd be happy to just look at 'em while you all ride."

"Oh yeah?" Michael asked curiously. "That's fine. As you like."

We entered our private suite. No TV. No radio. No computer. No internet, at least in this main house. Nothing but our journals, each other, and the sounds of nature.

"OK, kids. Bag check." Chor complied with ease and laid out his bags on the bed. Michael was meticulous with his search, keeping polite conversation about our flight and our journey the whole time. "Everything looks good! Sweet dreams!"

We barely slept that night, excited and crammed into the double-sized bed. We were accustomed to our king bed at home, but I'd soon discover that sleep would be almost obsolete over the next eight days. The bed would be merely a place for horizontal meditation.

From what we understood, sometimes the place could be filled with up to 10 guests at a time. We happened to be the only ones there that week, except for the two apprentices, Michael and Ann-Marie. We felt lucky, and stranded. We were at the mercy of these good people, out here in the middle of rural Costa Rica.

—

We awoke the next morning and drew open the curtains to reveal a breathtaking view. We sat atop the highest point for miles around. We stepped out onto our generous balcony that stretched around the most of the stately house. We truly were out in the middle of nowhere. Nothing but epic rural tropical land, fruit trees, wandering bulls out to pasture. Once a day or so, we'd get traffic: a lone caballero striding through a neighboring field.

We had breakfast with Michael. Before we prayed over the food he explained, "The Bwiti have one prayer. ONE," he emphasized, holding up a finger. "'Thank you for this day.' That's it! There's no asking for things or self-deprecation. There's just gratitude. So...thank you for this day!" And we feasted.

"So, how did you first meet Moughenda?" I asked, curious.

Michael told the tale of his auspicious meeting and apprenticeship with Moughenda. He proved to be a tenacious storyteller, animated and excited. He'd been a theater actor, he shared. His training as a thespian was clearly being put to good use.

"Here's a story of what I like now to call, 'A Gathering of Co-Inside-Essences.'"

He went on to tell the story that began with a warm summer evening in Toronto, around five years before, where a few people had gathered for a South American Incan healing ceremony that he was assisting and learning to offer. One of the participants, Sarah, had mentioned that she'd met an African shaman a couple weeks prior. She had participated in a ceremony he offered; a sacred medicine was administered that cures addictions.

"I raised an eyebrow," Michael said. "With a lifetime of believing that addiction was an incurable disease that could only be arrested through recovery programs, I was certainly skeptical. Considering I was raised within 12-step recovery programs, as my father eternally identified as a recovering alcoholic, it was no wonder I didn't take it too seriously. I was focused on other spiritual paths and, quite frankly, I dismissed it and continued with the Incan ceremony."

Michael had been running a small organic seed and sprout shop that also sold wildcrafted teas and other herbs. A couple days after his conversation with Sarah, he was clearing a bulletin board in the front of the shop when he noticed a flier for a talk featuring a Bwiti shaman from Africa that had been held the week prior. He immediately thought this must have been the man that Sarah was talking about. Michael had considered attending when he originally saw the flier; however, he'd been sidetracked and had forgotten about it.

"I chuckled to myself at the 'co-inside-essence,'" he said again, giggling. "Get it? Coincidence!" More giggles. Michael was thoroughly amused with his own story, as were we.

Michael went on to explain that despite his beliefs, he was intrigued by the possibility of a plant medicine capable of curing addictions. He had all kind of thoughts and ideas about what that meant—but ultimately he had more questions than answers.

He took big mouthfuls of his omelet between his spirited sentences. Michael was pure wind and motion. I could almost see his wings.

Michael continued his story. The following day after seeing the flier, he noticed Sarah sitting in a restaurant a few doors down, across from his shop. He peered in to say hello, and she was sitting with a guy with a hip-hop style. They invited Michael to join them.

"Sarah proceeded to tell me that this hip-hop dude was the shaman she'd spoken of, Moughenda. I remembered the photo from the flier; he was decked out in traditional Bwiti gear and tribal makeup. I blurted out, 'Oh, *you're* the shaman?' with a slightly puzzled look, I guess. Moughenda smiled and looked around as if to check for any other shamans in the room, and then shrugged his shoulders with his hands turned up. He replied with a matter-of-fact, 'Yeah.' We all laughed. It was a pretty humorous exchange, yet we had also spoken seriously about addictions and mental health.

"When Moughenda told me that iboga assists in spiritual awakening and brings someone to meet their own soul, I immediately replied, 'Oh, you mean it can bring you to the beginning of Creation.' He responded with a resounding, 'Yes, exactly!'"

Michael had spent many years practicing meditation and studying various Tao and Zen traditions. What
Moughenda spoke of resonated with some of his own
perspectives, yet he still had some big questions.

"How could something this simple do something
so quickly for a problem that everyone says takes years
and maybe lifetimes to deal with?" Michael replayed his
thoughts. "It honestly sounded a bit too good to be true."

Michael's questions would have to wait for answers.
He had stayed away from his shop too long already, and
he had to return quickly. Michael invited Moughenda
to attend the Incan rites he was offering the following
weekend. Moughenda agreed and attended the ceremony. After the ceremony, Moughenda asked if Michael
would be interested in joining him in Costa Rica to
learn more about his medicine, iboga. "Frankly, I was
intrigued," said Michael, "but, I thought, I have this
store, ceremonies, and traditions here in Canada. How
could I take time off work? What would it accomplish?
So, I blew it off at that time, despite my interest."

Michael's voice settled into a more serious baritone.
A few months after first meeting Moughenda, Michael
developed a serious illness. He thought it was the swine
flu that had been going around. He was so sick that
he couldn't get out of bed for days. None of his herbs
worked. He finally broke down and went to the hospital.

"On my walk down, my phone rings and I answer
with a sputter and cough, 'Hello.' Lo and behold, it's
Moughenda. He then says, 'I'm calling from Costa
Rica. Man you sound like shit. What's up? You OK?'"

Michael proceeded to tell Moughenda about his

predicament and that he was on his way to the hospital to get medical care. "He tells me straight up that the doctors won't be able to do anything for me and I'll just be wasting my time. He told me to just go home and that he would take care of my sickness when he arrived in a week. I thanked him, but I thought it was all pretty bold. I told him that I'd see him when he got here. I hung up and then continued right on my way to the hospital anyway. Ha!" Sure enough, Michael spent seven hours in the emergency room only to have the doctors tell him that they weren't even sure what he had, but they'd be happy to prescribe him an antibiotic all the same. He declined and headed back home.

When Moughenda arrived, Michael attended his first Bwiti ceremony. The first night, iboga cleared up 90% of his sickness. Not only that, he had a psycho-spiritual journey where he met his own soul and found answers to many questions he'd had about his life, who he really was, and much more.

"The first place I saw my soul was in Africa at Moughenda's village. Then he asked that I go to his clinic in Costa Rica. He said, 'Do not ask how you are gonna get there, just go.' I found myself standing in the field just outside the house. I walked up the driveway, looked at the cactuses, archways, and then the intricate carving of a horse on the door." After the ceremony, Michael knew that he wanted to go and train with Moughenda.

After another three months, Michael finally flew down to his clinic in Costa Rica. "When I stepped out of the car, my jaw dropped in complete astonishment. Everything was exactly as it had been in my vision: the cactus, the carving on the door, everything! Moughenda laughed and laughed and said, 'What? You still don't believe you were really here in that ceremony? Hahaha, you Westerners! You'll learn.' Let's just say, he's patient!"

The day rolled on like a turtle race. Time moved slower out here. We eventually made our way to the balcony with our notebooks. I streamed out a few more questions for God, and Chor started his own with earnest attention.

Later that afternoon, Chor wandered next door to the guesthouse to chat with Michael and Moughenda.

I had surrendered the snooping entirely. I let Michael take over. He was a pro. But completely by accident, I saw Chor's questions as I was getting into my suitcase. He boldly, or carelessly, left them lying out, stark naked, on the shelves in our bedroom. His handwriting jumped out at me.

Does Elizabeth love me?

Do I really love Elizabeth?

Will Elizabeth and I have children?

Do I love me?

I turned away suddenly, shocked and ashamed, an accidental thief. There were clearly a multitude of other questions on the page, but I would not read them.

Chor had first asked that question almost seven years earlier. We were curled up in my living room, just a month deep into each other. We had become enmeshed so swiftly; we hadn't yet had the time to form concepts or contracts around our connection. That night, he finally gave words to the ineffable. "Do you LOVE me? Are you IN LOVE with me?" He asked, looking into me. My heart had jumped. I was speechless. He implored again, taking me gently by the shoulders and penetrating my eyes ever deeper with his.

Lightning passed through my body. My chest was pierced by flowered arrows. All that came out of my mouth was a full, unbounded laugh. My head fell back as I looked up into the heavens that I envisioned above our roof. My eyes blinked slowly, enchanted, then finally returned to earth to refocus on Chor.

He looked confused. I realized how this laughter might have come across in the wrong way.

"Oh, darling..." I held his face in my hands and dove equally into his eyes. "Do you even have to ask? You *know*."

He stood up and held out his hand for me like a princess. I rose to meet him and he picked me up, cradling me in both of his powerful arms. I felt like a languid feather. It was a miracle...because I am an amazon, so to speak. I am 5 foot 9 and 140 pounds of strength and curve. No man had ever been able to pick me up like that, so solid and sure, much less walk with me.

He carried me to the bedroom. Candles were lit. Music was put on. We stripped each other in a slow ritual. We crawled to each other on the bed and met on our knees. Heart to heart. Sex to sex. Face to face. "I LOVE YOU," I said firmly. "My heart is yours. You are my temple. I've never been so deep. You are heaven on earth, baby." I spoke in a honeyed rhythm.

"And I...LOVE...YOU." He answered, smiling like the sunrise.

There is something about words: declarations and

prose, incantations and prayer. They are something so human. Communion through communication. Audible art. Written reflection. Translation of raw reality. Intellectual intimacy. So we professed our love with words for the first time, and often after that.

Chor entered me and made my heart rain and rain and rain. He planted himself in my soul. My body unfurled for him, petal by petal. The ancient feminine sentiment washed through me like a silent tidal wave: *I wanna make you live forever.* My body-mind-spirit knew how deep to go with him. My unfolding was in alignment with nature.

Here we were, all these years later...asking the same questions all over again. Do you love me? Do I love you? We were asking with new bodies. New cells. New challenges. In a new era. And I was curious to know his fresh answers.

The kitchen staff, all motherly local ladies, fed us fresh comidas tipicas de Costa Rica, typical food of Costa Rica: Casada, meaning married, referred to rice and beans, along with steamed vegetables, and salad with fresh herbs. The big bowl of fresh-cut local fruit was continually abundant. Aguas frescas were cool nectars of freshly blended fruits. This was my kind of food. Vegan, whole, simple food. They made fried chicken for Chor. He indulged.

Moughenda joined us for lunch, and I took the opportunity to indulge my curiosity. "Would you tell us about your grandfather?" I asked. He smiled with his eyes.

"Oh yeah, he was a tough man! He knew about so many plants. And my grandmother was with him always, helping him. He would feed me all kinds of medicinal plants to see how I'd take it. Sometimes I didn't even know what he was giving me!" He laughed. "One time he loaded me with some crazy plants and left me in the jungle overnight!" He chortled, barely containing all the amusement that was popping off inside him. "Well, I did kind of wander off, but he just left me out there!

"He was strict, but I was a rascal. Oh, I was trouble! Once I wandered into another village to steal some eggs with friends. When we were caught, I just told them who my grandfather was and they let me off the hook! He really was the big shaman for miles around. But, boy, did he give it to me later!" I thought Moughenda's belly was going to burst from laughing.

I shuffled the food around on my plate. "I am so excited for our first healing ceremony. Tropical butterflies are fluttering in my belly! I could easily eat only fruit today."

"Eat! And eat good!" Moughenda insisted. "You will need your strength," he encouraged us, as if we were preparing to climb a formidable mountain. So we feasted, and then stopped eating at 4 p.m., as our guides had advised.

Just after 4 p.m., Michael tapped on our door as we lay holding each other. "We are going to look at another house real quick. You guys want to come along? It's right on the beach. You'll be able to see more of Costa Rica," he tempted with a grin.

Moughenda had received a call back about a new place for rent. Iboga House needed to expand, to meet the growing demand for treatments while being able to lower the price. They were looking at larger mansions and small hotels.

I was still tired from jet lag and felt to conserve my energy for the evening's journey. Chor leapt up. "Yeah, I'll go!" Ever the adventurer.

I'm sure they would keep a good eye on him. And Chor's commitment to the experience was so solid at this point; I felt it in my gut. Indeed, Moughenda seemed to have eyes in the back of his head. He would likely keep multiple eyes on Chor from multiple angles in time and space. So I rested.

5 p.m. passed. 6 p.m. passed. 7 p.m. The sun went down.

Relax, Elizabeth.

Worry ate at my belly a bit, like a persistent little ferret.

7:30 p.m. *Ay dios mio!*

Where *are* they?

CHAPTER 30
THE DOORWAY

"You have to die a few times before you can really live."
— CHARLES BUKOWSKI

8 P.M. The trio of men finally rolled in. They were in good spirits and did not seem concerned or even aware about the hourlong delay. "That was beautiful!" said Chor, expressing genuine joy for the first time in ages. They greeted me and went to the kitchen for refreshments. Tropical timing was clearly organic.

I was so very tired of worrying. *Please God, take my worries.*

Moughenda and Michael relished a full dinner, meat and all. "Are you guys taking the medicine?" I asked, shocked by the extent of their feast. It had been my understanding that they were also partaking of a little iboga in order to guide our journey. Moughenda had said as much on the ride from the airport.

"Oh yeah! We will take some medicine. We are just more used to it," Moughenda said, looking at Michael with a knowing grin.

Chor looked at their full plates longingly. The guys noticed his begging puppy eyes.

"Eh, it's OK! Have a little food. You don't want to be starving." Chor sat down and gobbled down some dinner. Even more chicken.

I'd taken ayahuasca before, also an intense internal cleanser and purgative. I couldn't imagine eating such heavy food right before taking that medicine. It's like placing a pile of cement bricks in front of a snow truck. It's just more junk that the medicine has to push around before getting to the deeper layers. But I intuitively trusted Moughenda's offering.

Chor ate enough to be lightly sated, and we relaxed in our room for another hour. Finally, we were summoned by Michael. He knocked lightly and then poked his head in. He spoke with a gentle, firm voice. "OK guys, it's time. Join us at the fire ceremony in about 15 minutes."

We gathered our questions and walked slowly over to the ceremony site near the guesthouse. The gusts of sweet air and the orchestra of jungle creatures serenaded us.

We sat in chairs in front of the temple.

They had indeed transformed the covered garage at the guesthouse into a Bwiti temple. As we learned, the structure of the garage was identical to the humble temples in Africa, with three walls and one open wall. The open wall expressed the Bwiti philosophy: anyone is free to enter, and anyone is free to leave. The walls were covered in woven reeds. Two mattresses lay out, covered in white sheets, beckoning miracles.

Michael slowly stacked wood for the fire in a complex tower with great care; it was his work of art. We settled into our chairs. Moughenda was sitting across the fire pit from us. Our modern shaman was dressed simply in his athletic shorts and a T-shirt.

"Welcome, Elizabeth and Chor. Tonight," he paused, "you are taking 'the red pill,' as they say in your American movie, *The Matrix*." We all laughed, and our bodies relaxed a few notches.

"Ah, I love working with couples," He smiled glee-fully and placed his hand thoughtfully under his chin, like Rodin's statue *The Thinker.*

"Couples, you can bring each other up. Or you can bring each other down. There's usually no in-between. Sometimes with addiction, one partner pulls the other into the poison and then you have two addicts. So...you two want to have a healthy, beautiful relationship." We nodded in agreement.

"In order to have a good relationship, you first have to heal yourself. So in this journey, you heal yourself—for yourself. So tonight, you are divorced, in the sense that you are totally on your own. It's just you facing you. In the morning, you can be together again."

Chor and I glanced at each other for a moment, bathed in the amber light, and nodded in mutual understanding.

"Your wife will become the most important woman to you," Moughenda streamed toward Chor. "I couldn't believe it when my father first told me that one day: my wife would be more important than even my mother or my sister. I said, 'Na, Dad, no way. I can't imagine. I love my mom so much.' But it's true. Because...a good wife will be there for you anytime, day or night, if you really need her. Your sister will be making love to her own husband at 2 a.m. when you call with an emergency." He chuckled. "Maybe you are sick as a dog. You think she's gonna take your call? Probably not. Your mom might be getting older. She might be far away. It's a good wife who's gonna be there for you." He paused.

"A good woman will know you, inside and out. You need to listen to her," Moughenda schooled Chor, "because she knows you better than you know yourself, man." Moughenda laughed abundantly.

Chor stood at attention. Only a warrior can speak to a warrior sometimes. And this warrior was telling him to listen to his woman.

"She's your best friend, man. So many women today are actually competing with their men," he said, turning to me. "This causes a lot of problems. Just be *his* woman," Moughenda emphasized. "Make that a priority in your life. So many beautiful things can come out of that."

"Of course," he continued, "you both need time on your own and time with your friends. Women need to go be with the women sometimes. And men need to go be with the men sometimes. Of course, too much going out is just too much. But you also can't be together every second, for that will suffocate the relationship. So...you give each other some space...to breathe."

He folded his hands in his lap and paused. "Study each other. *Learn* each other."

With a silent yes, we acknowledged the transmission.

"Iboga was discovered by people long ago, thousands of years ago. A Pygmy man was walking home. He was hunting and caught a porcupine on the trail. It had been eating the roots of a bush along the way, which turned out to be the iboga bush. 'Mm! That will make a nice dinner. I will bring that home to my wife to cook!' He felt blessed and packed up the porcupine. He came home and gave it to his wife, who cooked it up for him. But he liked palm wine, oh yeah...just like I love me some palm wine in Africa!" His full belly laugh shook the tension off our bodies.

"Well this man fell asleep, from all that palm wine. So the man's wife went ahead and ate the porcupine all by herself. And she began to have visions. So many visions. She saw her ancestors, and they spoke to her and taught her. She saw so many things that did not exist in the material world. She thought maybe she was dying, but she did not.

"When her husband awoke in the morning, she told him what happened, but he did not believe her. So she went straight to the chief of the village and told him. The chief demanded that the husband take him to where he found the porcupine. Right next to that place, he saw that the roots of the bush had been dug up and chewed on. So they took the plant, and the chief asked his wife to eat it—because he was too scared!" Moughenda and Michael exploded with laughter.

"The chief's wife agreed, and the rest is history. Male and female shamans have studied iboga ever since.

"Long ago, humans also asked many questions. 'Where do we come from? What is the purpose of life? Is God in the sky? Or is God in the earth?' Iboga revealed to us that it had been watching humans for a long time. All plants on the earth have a purpose, and this plant had come to answer our questions. This is called the godfather of all sacred plant medicines in the world. From iboga comes all other medicines. It is both male and female energies in one plant. Sometimes the father side comes out to be fierce and stern, and sometimes the mother side comes out to be gentle and nurturing.

"The Pygmies first studied this plant and later passed on their knowledge to the Bantu tribes who were living in the south of Gabon, our people. This is known as the Bwiti tradition, the study of life."

Moughenda spoke more slowly, emphasizing each word like a gentle drum. "We hold no 'beliefs' in the Bwiti. *Believing* is different from *knowing*. A belief is an artificial creation. It is not the same as reality. There is ONE reality. And it exists whether we 'believe' in it or not. It's actually very dangerous when humans create beliefs. People kill each other over beliefs. Then you have some people, like scientists, who believe one thing for a while—until they discovery something else. And religious people believe one thing for a while...then change it. Beliefs can come and go."

Michael finally lit the stacked firewood, casting a glow around the circle. Moughenda's silhouette slowly lit up to reveal his bright, animated eyes and exuberant smile.

"In the Bwiti, no one will ever tell you what to believe or what you should do with your own life. There are no gurus. Even shamans are not bosses. Shamans just lead you to find your own truth. *You have to find the truth for yourself.* That is what Bwiti is all about. We come together in ceremony, but we don't try to tell people what to do. This is an oral tradition. Nothing is written down in official books. You cannot find the ultimate truth in books. You have to find that for yourself.

"Let me ask you," Moughenda uncrossed his legs

and leaned in closer, speaking earnestly. *"What is life?"*

"Life is...a beautiful thing," Chor answered. Moughenda nodded in agreement.

I tossed in my two cents. "Life is the opportunity to give love and to receive love, and to awaken. Ultimately, life is a gift!" These answers had hit me like lightning while in medicine ceremonies and deep states of meditation.

"Yes!" Moughenda said as his pointer finger leapt up into the night air.

Michael clapped his hands and giggled, "All right!" He was the perfect sidekick. I felt like I'd won a round in a cosmic game show.

"Life IS a GIFT! Think about it. You don't pay any money to be born. Sure, you might pay for some things eventually, but you don't actually pay even a cent to get here. Life is just a great gift. When you know that, you appreciate life. Let me ask you: What makes humans different than all the other creatures on Earth?"

After a pensive silence, Moughenda answered his own question with gusto. "Creativity. We can create anything!"

Suddenly, a light bulb went on over my head and a mysterious old proverb held new meaning for me. "That's why it is said that we are created 'in God's image!' Not because of our physical form, but because of our ability to create!"

"Yes! Humans can create whole worlds. Humans can create so many things! Humans can create happiness. Humans can even create misery. And how can you create happiness?"

We were on the edge of our seats, silent, curious about his take on this one.

"With *happy* thoughts!"

So simple.

"Think about it," Moughenda continued, "How do you feel with negative thoughts? Negative thoughts take you down. Negative thoughts steal your energy. Depression and addiction start with negative thoughts. And...negative thoughts are just NOT true! When people say they are stupid, it's NOT true! *Everyone* has some kind of intelligence."

I pondered this for a moment. What unconscious negative thought was absolutely true? I did a rapid inventory. Nope. None were really true. Negative thoughts were just brain vomit, nothing more than the nonsensical churning of the mind when it was left running on autopilot for too long.

Negative thoughts were an annoying battle. In yoga, I'd learned to *observe* my mind, but then I'd just *observe* myself having negative thoughts—and they'd still push me around and poison my world and drive me bananas. My mantra practice would lighten the burden *for a while,* but negative thoughts would still return to pester me while I was out in the daily grind. I'd not yet found a very potent or long-lasting solution.

"So how do you find freedom from negative thoughts? It's difficult. They just go and go." I inquired.

"Of course, sometimes negative thoughts happen. It's when they are allowed to go on and on that they grow right into your reality. So I have a 10-second rule. I notice the negative thought approaching and I stop it within 10 seconds. Now, I can feel them coming a mile away and stop them before they even take shape."

"How do you stop them?" I dug deeper.

"When you have a negative thought, you just say to your mind, 'STOP!' And say it *like you mean it!* Like a warrior!" His powerful laughter filled the night sky. Chor sat up straight, attentive.

"You can't just say '*stop*' all weak and soft! No!" Moughenda demonstrated with wishy-washy words.

"Some people actually *love* their negative thoughts! Yeah! They hold onto them and stroke them!" Moughenda acted this out for us, stroking some invisible precious pet in his lap. "They say 'oh, stop' but they don't really mean it and they are not really letting go."

Michael and Moughenda giggled, thoroughly amused by the monkey mind.

"So you say 'STOP!' And then...immediately you say the truth. *Your truth.* Remember, you are the artist of your own mind. You practice thinking happy thoughts. True thoughts. Grateful thoughts."

Moughenda had a distinct strength. It came from the fertile jungle of Africa. He was a spiritual warrior, and a literal warrior. Life or death. Now or never. Happy thoughts. He delivered his words with a playful yet solid punch that I hadn't heard from windy-voiced spiritual teachers before.

"Tonight is the detox. You have to be clean to enter the spirit world, and that is the destination of the next journey. I am here to serve you, but I will need you to do whatever I ask. Nothing crazy. I might ask you to drink a little water or to travel somewhere in your mind. Just participate, and work with my guidance. OK?"

He waited for our nod of acknowledgement.

Moughenda slowly walked over to us and ceremoniously gave us our capsule filled with his hand-prepared, natural, total alkaloid iboga extract. We would learn that each capsule was equivalent to five teaspoons of dried iboga bark powder, on average. Each capsule was a bit personalized, as the medicine would tell him how much to give us.

Here we go, down the ultimate rabbit hole. My heart of hearts led me here, so I'm diving in.

"You will have so many thoughts. Thousands and thousands of thoughts. This is just the medicine, cleansing your mind. Do not attach to any of these thoughts. Just remain in your center," advised Moughenda.

"Tonight, I will take you on the life review. This is one way that we work with the medicine. Iboga opens the door, but you have to walk through it. It will be you facing yourself. There is nowhere to run. No one to fight. You have to be *110% honest* with yourself. You will see the truth about yourself. The truth can hurt like a knife, but it will set you free.

"Chor, you might not 'launch' tonight. It's OK. You are in a heavy detox. Elizabeth, you might launch." He smiled.

"You might feel warm. You might shake a little. You might feel your heart beating a little fast. You might feel sick or purge. It's all OK. Just relax. It's just the medicine working on you. You might not be able to walk very well. It can play with your balance a little. We will help you up if you need to go to the bathroom."

We were led to our beds. Long, white candles were lit a few feet behind each of our beds. They placed loose blindfolds over us, to better support the visions. They started playing recorded traditional Bwiti music from Gabon. We relaxed for some time, feeling the warmth slowly spreading over us.

CHAPTER 31

IN THE EYE
OF THE HURRICANE

"A spirituality that does not embrace the shadow is a feeble, stunted thing. Walk with one foot in the light and the other in the dark; you will need both to journey into the wilderness of truth and beauty."
— RICHARD POWER, *USER'S GUIDE TO HUMAN INCARNATION; THE YOGA OF PRIMAL REALITY*

I BECAME WARM, warmer. Just a subtle shift at first. A softening flowed over me. I slowly liquified into a river of gentle tremors.

The complex rhythms of the Bwiti music were beginning to work on my mind. I was unraveling and opening. I sensed it was just the first glimpse, the dawning of something vast.

I shivered, but with heat instead of cold. A current of electricity ran though my body.

After some time, the pace of my heart quickened a little. Fully aware, I deepened and slowed my breath. These yogic skills had become a part of me. My heart relaxed its excited pace a notch.

"Do you feel the medicine yet?" asked Moughenda.

"A little," I answered.

He sat down near me and began to guide me.

"Now, go to your house, back home. Don't ask how you are gonna get there. Just go."

The medicine seemed to bring mobility and Technicolor to my consciousness.

I floated in. I was in our home. I saw our house sitter curled up on the couch, sad. Her boyfriend had just broken up with her. I wanted to stop and somehow console her, but my mission awaited.

"Now go upstairs to your bedroom. Are you there?"

I floated upstairs.

Back in the material world, I could hear Chor shifting around next to me on his mattress. The medicine was churning in him. Such a deep cleaning would not be easy. Was he OK?

"I'm worried about Chor. Is Chor OK?" I asked Moughenda.

Then, without a word and in a split second, he answered me in silence. *Remember, this is your journey. Let Chor have his own journey. The medicine is working on him in the way he needs.*

I had derailed from my own journey, preoccupied with Chor's experience. My vision faded. It was delicate, like a movie showing on a screen of vapor. "I've lost it. It's black."

"OK. Go outside, in your vision. Look at the moon."

The vision rekindled as I saw the moon.

"Now go straight to the moon. Don't ask how. Just go."

And in a flash, I flew to the moon.

"Look around. What do you see?"

"A glowing landscape."

"Go all over the moon," Moughenda instructed. "Do you see any beings?"

Off in the distance, I saw murky figures of iridescent light, moving slowly.

"Who is there on the moon?" asked Moughenda.

I flew closer to the figures. My dear grandmother emerged, Mary. The image of her clarified. She had died of cancer 14 years before. She had adored me. She was a gentle soul, but not a peaceful one. She had been afraid to die and no doubt passed away with many unanswered questions and unfulfilled dreams.

"Ask her, 'Grandmother, what is the nature of God?'"

Moughenda was now reading from the questions I had written down.

"Ask it out loud," Moughenda instructed.

"Grandmother, what is the nature of God?" I asked.

My grandmother smiled and replied through my lips, "Oh, honey, I don't know. I was hoping you could tell me!" She giggled. "I'm just looking over you. That's all I know."

"Ask your grandmother to bring you to the moon spirit."

"Grandmother, will you bring me to the moon spirit?" I asked.

"Yes," she spoke through me.

Then suddenly, there she was, the moon spirit, rising in the night sky before me. I floated in space, enchanted. She was so beautiful and lustrous, whiter than white. Her gossamer form was a voluptuous, feminine design, two-dimensional, like a woodcut. She was naked and pure. She danced her eternal dance with sinuous grace. Her long hair swirled against the backdrop of stars. Her large eyes gleamed. Her bee-stung lips smiled, demure and playful.

"Ask the moon spirit, 'What is the nature of God?'" Moughenda tried again.

"What is the nature of God?" I repeated.

And suddenly everything disappeared and I saw light. Only light. The brightest light. Life-giving, self-generating, pure, eternal light. I understand this to be her wordless answer; then the moon spirit and her star-studded stage returned to my vision.

"Light," I answered.

"Now ask, 'What is the purpose of life?'" Moughenda continued with my next question.

Again, the moon spirit answered me without words. She simply parted her legs against the night sky and gave birth, in ecstasy. A luminous little spirit baby emerged from her yoni and flew into the cosmos.

"She didn't say anything. She just showed me. I just saw her give birth. The purpose of life is to give the gift of life, and to receive the gift of life."

"Ask, 'How can I be a better mother?'"

"How can I be a better mother?" I inquired ardently, perhaps trying too hard to do the journey 'right.' The image suddenly faded. It was a fragile channel.

"It's gone again. It's all black."

Moughenda guided with confidence, "See the moon spirit again. Just summon her before you."

And violà! There she was. Consciousness could be quite an unlimited spacecraft, apparently. We can go anywhere faster than the speed of light.

"How can I be a better mother?" I asked again, and waited some breaths.

Moughenda coaxed, "Let the answers come quickly."

I realized that my intellect had been trying to take over the process; it slipped in the door when I lingered too long. Answering swiftly seemed to bypass the intellect entirely, drawing from some deeper source.

"Patience," answered the moon spirit. "Be less reactive."

The questions continued to pour through my lips, and the answers immediately echoed back through them.

"Ask, 'How can I control my rage and fear?'"

"Mastery of the mind."

"Ask, 'What is the nature of sacred marriage?'"

"You make each other your religion."

Yes, of course.

The potency and brevity of the rapid-fire answers pummeled me like comets. With each answer, energy shimmered through my being and my spine subtly undulated with the aftershocks.

"Ask, 'How can I best serve beings while providing for my family at this point in my life? What is my dharma now?'"

"Plant medicine and...chocolate. Just make chocolate. Lots of chocolate. And dance. Just keep dancing. Perform every chance you get."

I understood, psychically reading between the lines. These things might pay the bills—or they might not. It wasn't my business either way. These were simply divine prompts, and they would lead me to where I needed to be.

"Ask, 'What kind of plant medicine?'" This was Moughenda's question, not mine, but it felt poignant.

"Iboga...and medicinal essential oils." *Did I say that just because iboga was in my field at this moment?* I wondered, asking my own question within. *All would be revealed in time,* came the silent answer.

"Ask, 'How can I cultivate more natural energy and vitality?'"

"Rest more." Of course.

The profound wisdom of the medicine was startling simple.

"Ask, 'How can I let go after I've had my heart broken?'"

"Follow the love. Direct attention to where love

lives, not where it's missing."

"Ask, 'How can I have a more graceful relationship with time?'"

"Do less."

I almost laughed at the candor of the cosmic common sense.

"And now ask your mystery question #64."

Ah, yes. Moughenda understood that people might want to keep certain matters private. He had suggested that we create a code number for private questions, and the code would serve to summon it in our mind.

I silently asked my mystery question.

What is the nature of the Sacred Prostitute?

I was curious to know the medicine's perspective on this archetype that had captivated my devotion. What was her deeper nature? Where was her true place in human society? Was there inherent goodness in this path, in spite of all the shaming ascetics over time?

Then I saw *Her.* I saw *them*...long ago in ancient times, at the dawn of Sumeria, regal priestesses in lofty temples; anointing and guiding initiates, enchanting the royalty, dancing for the people. They held the secrets of sexual yogas, esoteric rituals, and devotional arts. They blessed the land with beauty, fertility, shakti. Their skillful magic brought peace to passion, and passion to peace.

I read the thoughts of their enchanted audience: "You make me want to live," the same phrase I had once heard fresh from the lips of an ecstatic acolyte.

Then I saw these majestic women travel through

time, morphing as they incarnated into ever-new bodies. I saw them slowly invaded and degraded with the rise of the patriarchal systems. They became harem girls, harlots, servants, street entertainers. Desired, yet defiled. They flashed between fake smiles and tears. They cowered in fear and prowled dark alleys. They escaped beatings and sometimes took them; belts, whips, willows, fists, brands, and stones sought their tender skin. Some were elegant courtesans drenched in jewels and finery; they were exquisite, but they wore the hopeless expressions of slaves. All the gold that dripped from their fertile forms served as lavish shackles. Screams ripped through my vision as some were tortured and burned alive for being witches.

Her forms kept flowing through this visual timeline into the modern era: these women became porn stars, strippers, even scantily clad hip-swaggering pop stars. They were gaudy and garish with loud costume jewelry and racy lingerie and layers of mask-like makeup. I saw them robotically manipulating the cocks of wanton pig-like men. These feminine beings, reincarnating again and again before me, finally turned to look ahead.

I saw the future. The women rose up and out of this energetic gutter. They began to awaken. As they remembered their power, their oppressors transformed into devotees. Priests, politicians, pimps, and prudes all learned how to channel the fiery energy within themselves that this erotic archetype perpetually ignited.

Temples grew out of the cityscape like weeds bursting through cement sidewalks, and the women returned to them in abounding waves—the self-chosen ones, propelled by free will. They stood straight and tall, proud and polished, shameless and serene. Opulent gowns, crystal-encrusted crowns, and magical amulets adorned their luscious bodies. The priestesses expressed themselves in countless flavors—bawdy, bold, subtle, slick. They all shared one thing in common; they had reclaimed their nobility.

Gathering in the heart of the temples, the women played musical instruments and danced and painted and spouted mystical poetry. They entranced and inspired. They brought heaven on earth, these full-body philosophers.

I sensed it was a grand 10,000-year show of revealing and concealing and again revealing her sacred nature, like a dancer playing with her veil, all to produce a global realization....

Was she sacred or profane? I understood: It's all in the eye of the beholder.

The Sacred Prostitute was an ever-present thread within the human drama, whether tattered or revered. It was clear: She isn't going anywhere, for she's a fundamental aspect of humanity. She simply reflects the collective state of our eros. It's up to us if she is in the gutter—or the temple.

"Did you receive an answer to your question?" asked Moughenda.

"Oh yes, I received an answer," I said, awestruck. It had only been a few earthly moments, but it felt like I'd just lived thousands of lifetimes.

"Now see the moon spirit again. Ask her for her name," asked Moughenda.

That was not one of my questions, but I was game

to ask.

The moon spirit reappeared before me. "What is your name?"

Once again, she did not answer in words. She blithely took her finger to her lush lips and shushed me, expressing in silence: *I am ineffable, silly girl. You cannot comprehend my name with your mortal mind.*

I blushed; I had dared to ask her with my bawdy brain, instead of speaking from the realm wonder. I hadn't even said "please." She was playing with me.

"She wouldn't say," I relayed. "She just...shushed me like this." And I demonstrated from under my blindfold, bringing my pointer finger to my lips.

Moughenda and Michael chuckled as if watching the funny antics of an old friend. "Yeah, that's her."

I could hear Chor churning in his bed, breathing heavily and groaning softly, like someone with a high fever. Oh, my love. I reminded myself to remain at ease. We were in good hands, I knew.

"Now," Moughenda continued, "Go go back to the house where you were as a little baby, maybe eight months old. Don't ask how you are gonna get there. Just go."

The vision was more vivid now. I could see my crib, like a cage, and the stark walls of the humble home. "Find yourself there," said Moughenda. "Do you see yourself?"

There I was, little me, holding onto the bars of the crib, a forsaken, helpless, innocent prisoner. The medicine was stronger now; I struggled a bit to respond with words. "Yes."

I wanted to hold on to my daddy's fingers, but he was nowhere around. Mother had been gone so long; I worried that she ceased to exist. I had no understanding of time. My little heart panicked, and I wondered if I had been left for the vultures.

I realized that everything experienced in infancy was infinitely more intense. Events pressed themselves into the tender flesh and budding brains like a brand.

"What's happening there?" Moughenda asked.

"I'm crying alone in my crib. I feel like I might be there forever. I am afraid that I've been forgotten. I cry a lot because my tummy hurts. My dad doesn't know how to make me feel better. He gets overwhelmed and just leaves me there. My mom is gone. She's working and worried about me at home. She knows my dad can't care for me, but she has to work anyway. She has to pay the bills. She is worried about money."

"Now hold that little girl. Tell her you love her." I cradled my little self in my spirit arms and felt her frantic crying settle into sweet coos. I looked at her and admired her purity and perfection. She was not left in the crib because she was too much; she was left in her crib because her father was not enough—back then at least. He was just fragile. I felt compassion, both for myself and for my young, war-torn, amateur father.

"Now find yourself as a girl, maybe eight years old. Where is she?" asked Moughenda.

"She's in her room, in our house." And there I was, angry and misunderstood, shut away in my own self-created solitary confinement.

"How is she doing?"

"She's crying. She cried a lot. Dad yelled so much then. I never felt heard by the big people, so I talked into my tape recorder and typed poems and letters."

"What does she want to do?" asked Moughenda.

"She wants to meditate."

"But what action does she want in her life? It's not time to meditate. It's time for action."

"She doesn't feel like she fits into normal human civilization. She wants to live in nature. She feels wild. She wants to make forts in the fields by her house. She wants to write and make art and see the world."

"So let her do all those things," Moughenda said. I saw my young self set free from all the fences and rules and schedules. I saw her taste delight.

"Now find yourself when you were a young woman, about 20 years old. Where is she?"

"She's in her apartment, alone." I saw my self in my modern high-rise apartment in San Francisco. I was a brand new stripper, and a baby woman. This was before I had delved deep into yoga and tantra. Before I truly loved myself. I was fascinated with feminine allure. I didn't feel truly beautiful then, but I thought I could fake it pretty well. Bleached blond hair, thick artsy makeup, sexy costuming, and flattering light were theatrical elements I utilized to hide the flawed, ugly, and pained self underneath. I feigned sexual prowess, but in truth I couldn't feel much authentic pleasure. I was numb and clueless about my young body, just scratching the surface of the volcano.

"How is she doing?" asked Moughenda.

"She's lonely. She doesn't let anyone too close to her, because she doesn't feel beautiful under all the layers of paint."

Moughenda said, "Have her look into the mirror, to see how beautiful she really is."

I saw her go to the bathroom mirror, but it wasn't the ordinary form looking back. This was *the real* magic mirror. "I see...fire, in the shape of a woman." My transparent skin was filled with sparkling tongues of flame. I was looking at my spirit, my power. *So beautiful.* My attachment to outer beauty dissolved at the sight of my inner beauty. My breath deepened as I marveled.

"Now let the medicine take you where it will." I surrendered. I was flooded with heat, though I still wanted the comfort of a sheet covering me. My skin felt as though it was steaming. Noxious beauty products and perfumes I'd used many years earlier were being sweated out through my pores. Even my organs were sweating, it seemed.

I had become like Chor, turning endlessly in my bed. I couldn't get comfortable. I was being scrubbed with hot water and pressure cleaned inside by the Divine. And the Divine was thorough. I was overcome with a wave of nausea. I was transformation itself.

Without Moughenda's guidance, my visions evaporated. Everything became a dark amorphous mass.

I heard Moughenda approach Chor. "OK, do you feel the medicine?" he asked.

"Yes," said Chor. "I definitely feel it."

"OK, now go to your house. Don't ask how you are gonna get there. Just go. Do you see it?"

"Yes, but it's faint," said Chor.

"Look around. What do you see?" Moughenda inquired.

Chor paused. "It...faded. It's just black. I feel the medicine...I just don't see anything."

"OK," said Moughenda. "You are still detoxing. Just be."

Chor returned to his arduous breathing and relentless shifting.

Time went by. Thoughts came, but they weren't just mental banter. I could see them. They were visual thoughts. They began to flow at lightning speed. Normally the mind likes to analyze every thought that arises, ever the scientist, but there was no time to linger or figure them out. *Nothing to hold on to.* I had to let go completely.

I remembered: remain in my center—the very center of my being, the core of my awareness, my spiritual heart, the eye of this embodied hurricane. This was the Olympics of meditation. As I was planted in this rushing river of thoughts, I just watched as they poured through me.

Then the horror began. Every monster that lived in the mud of my mind came to the surface to be viewed. Terrible demonic faces perpetually morphed in front of my eyes. It was a whirlpool of fangs, red eyes, long talons, boar snouts, huge jaws—all ferocious, grotesque human animals that nature would never even dare to dream up. My subconscious was being excavated. As this show unfolded, I knew that my task was to look straight at every fear and every attachment.

Even in this dark storm, I knew that my mind was cleansing right along with my body. Things were rising up from their burial grounds to be burned up under the light of awareness. Again and again, I returned to my breath and to the one prayer of the Bwiti, "Thank you for this day."

I was never fearful in a true and primal way. I knew it was just a gnarly mental obstacle course. All the while, I felt held by the powerful drumming and confident, joyous singing.

After what felt like an eternity of the nightmarish show, I pulled off the blindfold and sat up straight to gaze at the tended fire. The fire spirit danced—transforming, transmuting, warming, and illuminating. I offered my heart and mind to the fire. I offered my pain and fear to the fire. I offered the faces of my so-called enemies to the fire. I offered my love to the fire. And the fire ate them all with equal zeal. I felt like the wood—sparkling, burning, changing every moment, and becoming something new.

Nature called. I looked around for help. Before words came out of my mouth, Michael, my trusty telepathic steward, jumped right up to assist me. He held my elbow as I took uncertain steps with shaky limbs through the candlelight toward the bathroom. "Good job. Right this way," he whispered. Even my eyes trembled lightly right along with my body.

Michael waited and helped me back to my bed. The medicine was drawing out all the toxins. My stomach turned. I was dizzy, sick, drowning in full-body nausea. I felt grateful that ayahuasca ceremony had taught me how to purge. There was an art to it. I opened to the medicine. I breathed into the discomfort. I moved with the nausea, instead of contracting against it, and allowed myself to release completely. I sat up with urgency and grabbed the bucket next to my bed. *Let it go.*

"Good, good," said Michael. "It's just the medicine cleansing you of negative thoughts and negative emotions." Yeah. Get 'em out. The geckos sped across the walls and chirped throughout the night. They seemed to enjoy watching the bizarre humans.

After my belly was emptied, I returned to resting. My blindfold was replaced. Someone walked past me, either Moughenda or Michael, with a natural cigarette. I understood that many shamans use tobacco to ground themselves in ceremony and communicate with the spirits, but it was not my medicine. The smoke wafted over me. I sputtered out a cough. Normally I could tolerate smoke if it was outdoors or in a well-ventilated space. With the iboga, I felt the smoke in magnified detail. Thousands of acid-dipped little needles assaulted my tender, pink lungs.

How could anyone just casually smoke? I wondered. I envisioned streams of people, speeding down city streets, sucking down cigarettes without even a thought to pray with the tobacco or offer thanks to the earth. Reverence for the ancient tobacco medicine was a lost art in the modern world. The people were exploiting the tobacco spirit, and as a natural consequence, they suffered addiction and all the ailments that come with it.

"Could you please take the cigarette outside?" I asked from beneath my blindfold, and the mystery smoker kindly obliged.

The myriad of horrific thoughts continued to flow at full speed. Multiple hours must have passed. *When will this end?*

Just remain in the center.

My soul watched from a distance as my own mortal head cut was off with the single swipe of a large curved blade. I saw the body of my executioner emerge out of the abyss, the great goddess Kali. She held my severed head firmly by the hair in one hand and the blade in the other. She laughed like a ghoul and danced as the blood of my body dripped. Her blue-black skin scintillated; her form was the essence of midnight. Her long, wild tendrils flowed into all that is. She had cut off my ego when she cut off my head.

I purged four more times that night. It seemed to never end. Every time I puked, I felt the poison of my dark, neurotic, unconscious patterns being expelled from my body. During one bathroom visit, I puked and shit at the same time. My belly emptied. I shit several more times and released matter that I didn't even know was in there.

The show rolled on. I saw a fierce yogini appear from out of the chaos, wearing only leaves and vines. She had shimmering, dark-emerald skin and a strong, sleek body. She was my reflection from another dimension, my life as a supernatural forest cave dweller. She approached me and slapped my chest again and again, challenging me like a tough-love sensei.

"See who you are!? See who you are!?" She repeated.

She was telepathically transmitting: *Wake up! You are powerful! You are beautiful! You are divine!*

As I heard Chor stir throughout the night, my worry would rear its head over and over. *Was he OK? Was he frightened by this intense medicine?* I would find comfort in his audible breath, occasional utterances, and shuffling to the bathroom. He was OK; he was just going through it. Each time I became distracted by my concerns, I would take a deep breath and return to my own journey.

At a point in the wee hours of the morning, I could hear Chor's soft animal sounds of sleep. I envied his rest. I had no such luck. Sleep was impossible for me. The onslaught of dreadful images continued. It was like being in haunted house on hyper-drive.

The morning crept in. The visions finally quelled. I could hear the tropical creatures waking, chattering, singing. I was physically and mentally exhausted. I removed my blindfold and gazed through the open temple wall at the azure sky and the gently swaying palm tree. *Ahhh. Finally.*

I thought of the second journey that we were supposed to take. The medicine had been more intense than I ever imagined. I didn't want to go through that hell again. *Maybe there is some way I can get out of that second journey, I thought. I could make up some excuse....*

No, I resolved. *I am here to do this. I am here to receive all that this medicine has to offer.*

I looked over at Chor, snoring away, and wondered who he would be when he awoke.

CHAPTER 32

A NEW DAWN, A NEW DAY

*"These are the sort of things people ought to look at.
Things without pretensions,
satisfied to be merely themselves."*
— ALDOUS HUXLEY,
THE DOORS OF PERCEPTION & HEAVEN AND HELL

"Celebrate your suffering & elevate your bliss."
— SHAMANA MA SHARENE

I CLOSED MY EYES again and rested more. The medicine was still strong in me even though the most vibrant visions had subsided. Chor's snoring was strangely comforting; I could sense his presence there next to me even with my eyes closed. I felt a wave of gratitude for my love's life, for his sleep, and even for his snoring.

When I opened my eyes again, I looked up to see Michael next to the remnants of the fire, smiling and moving about in what looked like a playful hybrid of tai chi and bird flight. Michael had stayed up all night to attend to us. This was part of his training. He had to be on his toes even through his desire to sleep. "Good morning!" he said with whispered exuberance. "Wow, I thought Moughenda snored bad! He's the new champion!" Michael nodded toward Chor and giggled. Always an opportunity for laughter here, and, in truth, everywhere. Here we were facing a life-and-death struggle, and Michael had me cracking up.

Chor finally stirred. He took deep breaths and unfurled his strong limbs, stretching like a waking panther in his bed. His eyes fluttered open, and he looked out at the sky through reborn eyes. "Whoah," he said. I cracked open my cocoon of blankets and sat up. Moughenda emerged from the guesthouse. He'd taken a short rest in the predawn hours. He stood observing Chor with a curious smile.

Despite the rigorous night, I emerged feeling profoundly exhilarated, content, and satiated. All was clear and luminous. My looking glass of perception seemed to have been dusted off, revealing the sparkling natural magic of the earth that had been there all along.

Chor moved to stand up. "You good, man?" asked Michael.

"Yes, yes. Thank you, brother." He rose, explored his balance, and slowly walked out of the temple into the dawn light. He looked upward and opened up his powerful arms as if to encompass the sky. He took the deepest breath, drinking in the beauty. His gaze traversed the pristine tropical landscape. "Thank you for this day!" he exclaimed.

Chor turned toward Moughenda and Michael, who greeted him with the warm, knowing smiles of proud parents watching their child take their first steps. "I feel...AMAZING! I feel...so...much...LOVE!" Chor

exclaimed, and then burst with a broad smile and joyous laugh. How I'd missed his authentic expressions of
elation.

"Thank you there, Moughenda! You beautiful
African man! Thank you, Michael!" Chor hugged the
men with plenty of slaps on the back, warrior style.

Chor looked over at me with bright, clear eyes. I
could see his spirit behind his eyes again! I realized just
how deeply it had been buried under the pollution. I
struggled to rise. Michael sprinted to my aid. "OK, take
it easy. How ya doing?"

"Good! Good!" I said. I stood and grounded myself
for a moment, and then latched firmly on to Michael's
elbow. "Just a little wobbly still. Oh my god, that was
intense!"

"Yeah, amazing, huh?!" Michael affirmed with a
little bounce. *Amazing is an understatement.*

I reached out for Chor with my free hand, and he
came over to me. "Baby, how are you?" I asked, gently
holding his face.

"Good! Yes there, loveness, I feel SO GOOD!" He
replied in a warm, grounded voice. "But I feel like I've
been through a war!" He grinned.

"Yeah, me too," I sighed.

"All right, gang," said Michael. "Are you ready to
make the journey back to your room?" We nodded and
smiled. The three of us walked across the jungle lawn
back toward the main house together. Traversing the
lawn felt as epic and arduous as crossing a whole country. My vision shimmered. The earth danced under me.

We headed up the stairs. The floor turned to liquid underneath my feet on the stairs. I swayed and grasped the railing, and my two strong companions steadied me. "Ha!" Michael laughed, amused. "The stairs always get 'em."

Chor and I tumbled into our bed. Michael left us with two water bottles. "OK, guys," he brought his voice down to a reverent tone. "Enjoy your time. Rest. Take it easy. Remember no electronics today. If you really must communicate with the outside world, we will do it for you. Journaling is great! We'll be by every hour. Just leave the curtain open a tad so we can keep an eye on you." He was a divine flight attendant.

Chor and I cradled each other. I felt him as if for the first time. His golden skin was deliciously smooth. I traced the warm, strong, sculpted muscles of his arms, back, thighs. Wondrous glory. This living miracle. His powerful hands enveloped me and explored my limbs, holding and stroking my electrified body. I wrapped my legs around his and kissed his bare skin with my wet yoni lips. We were tangled, sticky starfish. We kissed as new lovers, hungry and curious, exploring with our lips. Magnetized to each other, an ocean couldn't have kept us apart. My heart was quenched, all the more so for having survived a desert.

"Wow, baby, you feel amazing," Chor said, and we drifted into rest. He was able to sleep a little more. I wasn't. Sleep was elusive even though I was exhausted. I settled for deep relaxation.

Chor awoke and excitedly piped up about his experience, like a kid showing off his Christmas presents. "Wow, love. Yeah, I definitely feel cleansed! There were some fleeting visions, but it was mostly a physical and spiritual cleanse. I was scared. I went in there with fear. I went in there with negative thoughts, self-hatred, so much hatred. But I was also thinking of being more open-minded—and other good stuff—all at the same time."

He gazed upward as his words flowed in a lucid stream. His hands softly accented his words like a symphony conductor as he caressed me. "When the medicine kicked in, I started shaking a little bit. When they brought us into the temple and put a blindfold on us I thought, 'What the hell is going on here? This is crrrazy.' I didn't know what to think, you know. I was feeling this medicine, and I just went with it. I was thinking about you, wondering if you were gonna be all right," he said as he clung to me tightly. "But then ultimately I had to go in there for myself. Once I was laying down, I started feeling so cold."

"Wow, really? I was so hot! Roasting!" I said. "It was cooking the toxins out of me," I exclaimed, amazed at how different the medicine could be for each of us.

"Yeah, I was *cold*. Mainly in my heart. My stomach was cold, too. The medicine was going through my body, warming and detoxing everything.

When Moughenda came and did that life review session with you, it was kinda distracting to me. I just wasn't going through my door. I was kinda being jealous, too," Chor confessed.

"Jealous?" I was surprised. "What, because the guys were there?"

He had never become carried away with jealousy in our relationship. Though he experienced a dash here and there, he'd always kept his cool and poked fun at the primal emotion.

"Yeah," Chor continued. "I don't know. I was stuck in my head...with all kinds of crazy, strange thoughts. I was just dealing with my mind. When Moughenda came to me and asked me to go to our house, I started seeing it! I saw the house! And, you know, the vision is kinda faint. There's a fogginess to it, like a dream state. But I imagine that if you practice with the medicine longer, the visions can become more clear.

"So he gets me there and I go into the house. I really opened the door. Everything seemed to happen really fast. I'm zipping through, like *zip zip zip*." His hands reenacted his speed through space. "And then Moughenda said to find myself in my room. I found myself for a little bit, but then..." He waved his hand about, dissolving the imaginary scene.

"You lost the channel?" I asked.

"Yeah. We had to be honest and real. That's me naturally. So I told him: 'No, I lost it. It's just dark.' Moughenda said I was still detoxing. That's when Moughenda stopped guiding me and said, 'Just go with the medicine. Just be. Breathe. Breathe.'"

He continued with his play-by-play. He then saw a vast darkness. Shadowy, ominous faces melted together, twisting endlessly like storm clouds, sometimes devouring each other. "That darkness was my pain, my ego, my pride—all my negativity, right in front of my eyes." We paused to just look into each other and paw at each other. Beloveds, reborn.

Chor continued. "Apparently I walked through a

door, but it wasn't *the* door to the spirit world. This was a different door that I needed to walk through. This door was just showing me all my darkness.

"It was more physical than visionary," he explained. "I felt like I had this swarm of iboga killer bees going through my body, detoxing me and healing me. I could see my body from the inside, like I'm a little speck inside myself! I saw this medicine healing everything, even my blood and my veins. It was attacking these pain spots, like *zzzz*," he said as he touched his alleviated places: kidneys, back, knees, and hands.

"Then *I learned how to move the swarm with my mind.* This medicine gives you that control. You are using a large percentage of your brain when you are on this medicine. So I had it go to other places where I needed it: my stomach lining, my heart, my brain. A swarm, *in my body!*" he reiterated.

"Yeah, this medicine is definitely interactive," I concurred.

"Yeah!" Chor chimed, enthusiastically. "And then I started hearing these voices: 'Chor! Chill! Just RELAX man, RELAX.' It was my higher self talking to myself, because I was fighting it at times. These voices were correcting me in my life. I'd remember, 'Think happy thoughts! Think happy thoughts!'

"And I was told, 'This is already in your DNA,' like in my lineage or my bloodline. I kinda felt like, 'I've been here before. *I remember this.*'

"I remembered the medicine, and I also remembered a lot of the stuff that Moughenda was saying. I've heard it before in my family, through my dad and my grandfather. It may have something to do with my African roots."

"Wow," I said. "I didn't have that feeling exactly. That was something unique for you." I shivered with resonance. This was a homecoming for Chor, centuries in the making.

"When I was clean, I applied a lot of those teachings in my life until I went back into lesson. I won't say that I fucked up. I just went back into lesson. Now I'm reapplying those teachings again."

He returned to his epic tale. "Toward the end, *I could feel the medicine rewiring me.* I almost heard stuff snapping back into place like *chkchkchkchk.*" We laughed and laughed at his sound effects. Giggles came bursting and bubbling up; we were fresh soda cans of energy being cracked open.

"Then it felt like it was cleaning me like a vacuum, *schschsch*, sucking out everything that was impure. It was just sucking everything to the core of where the medicine was at." His hands drew to his belly. "It was not only detoxifying the drugs! It healed my heart, mind, body, and soul!

"I see how people gotta purge. People can throw up, shit, or piss—or throw up and shit at the same time, like you did!" He had heard it all. We laughed.

"Yeah, it felt *beautiful* to throw up and shit—at the same time! So refreshing!" I exclaimed shamelessly.

"I didn't throw up or shit at all, which was interesting. All I had to do was piss. Piss piss piss. I pissed so many times. It seemed like every time you threw up, I had to go take a piss."

"Cosmic!" I joked about the messy mirrored healing of our twin souls. More giggles and bubbles and jiggling bellies. We gripped each other tight, as if we'd dissolve into laughter unless we held on for dear life.

"And I was conscious! Fully conscious the whole time. I was up 'til 6 in the morning while this medicine was working on me.

"Then, I took the blindfold off for a little while and everything seemed so illuminated! I looked at the fire. That fire, it just burns up all the negativity. That's why they keep it burning all night.

"I went to sleep for little bit in the morning, because it was just so physically intense. When I woke up, I felt *amazing*. I felt rejuvenated, real, honest. I felt that...life is just a beautiful thing! I thought, 'I never wanna disrespect myself...I will *never* disrespect my heart, mind, body, soul—again.'"

"Oh, love...I am so grateful for your life, your precious life," I gushed. He held me as I relayed my bizarre journey and colorful reflections. "At first, it seemed like I was having a zillion more thoughts than usual, but now that I think about it, the thoughts were just *louder* than usual, and more visual. Tons of thoughts are always there, just running on and on, like background noise, but many are subconscious or semiconscious, barely noticeable. The medicine shined a spotlight on all my thoughts. I had to face all that was really going on in my head.

"I was able to see the nature of mind—actually *see* it. It's nature is to create, ceaselessly and abundantly. The mind is such a powerful creator. Unless we direct it, it creates tons of poppycock!" More laughter. More kisses.

"It reminded me so much of the bardo, as it's described in the *Tibetan Book of the Dead,* with so many demons and fears and various scenarios flowing super fast," I said. "It was terrifying and confusing. It is said in the *Tibetan Book of the Dead* that the mind moves faster in the spirit world, nine times faster. As yogis, we practice remaining aware during this crazy journey. We don't grasp at things out of attachment and we don't run away from things in fear, for the motivation behind our mental movement determines our rebirth. I'm actually glad that I read that book before experiencing iboga. It was like my guidebook!"

I sighed and stroked my love's body, earthly frosting for a gorgeous soul. Every hair on his body was a fresh miracle. His skin cast a warm glow. His nipples reached out for my fingertips. Every part of him was even more compelling and fascinating, though I hadn't imagined that was possible.

"I sensed that there was a purpose to all the madness," I continued. "My mind was purging, as well as my body. I feel so light and clean now. A weight left me, the fictitious burdens created by negative thoughts. I'd been chasing my own tail of bitterness for years— because I was afraid to look up to the horizon and dream my dreams."

Sweet deep breaths filled our bodies. Our eyes glimmered with fresh love. *This is so good,* I thought. *So good, too good. Will this last?* I caught my grasping mind in the act, and I swiftly returned to the moment, to truth, to gratitude.

Worrying is a waste of time.

We melted into each other for a few more hours, until the primal itch to move prevailed. The sun beckoned. We meandered onto the deck and took in the expansive view.

I studied Chor in the sunlight. My love was radiant again! He was polished and powerful and bright, like the first day I met him. He looked out onto the land with reverence and then bowed slowly, bringing his palms together at his heart. After a thoughtful pause, he flung his arms open, as if to spread his wings and reflect all his love back out to the world. "The earth...is so...beautiful!"

"Yeah, I've been telling you!" I laughed. The sick Chor had never looked at nature much. He marveled, with his fresh vision, and I adored watching his raw wonder.

He turned around and gazed at me. The sun crowned him with a halo. "How do you feel now?" I asked.

"I feel SO GOOD! I feel no craving. No desire for dope. No desire for anything that would be bad for me." I had never in my life witnessed such a swift and comprehensive transformation. It was a miracle. I wouldn't have believed it had I not seen it with my own eyes. He went from dark to light, death to life. He was completely purified and freed of his addiction, it was so clear to me. I knew, the future was still an evolving horizon of choices, but in that moment, he had a clean slate. He was a new man. Iboga was the grace of the universe and earth magic of the highest caliber, and Chor had stepped up to receive it in a good way.

He embraced me, and his magnanimous hands poured warmth into my core. Peering deep into me with his new, light-filled eyes, he expressed, "Thank you, love! I love my life! Thank you!" His words struck a bell in my heart. His tone reminded me of long ago, when he used to speak to me with tenderness and respect—long before I had become like old socks.

We curled up on the outdoor sofa. His fingertips played sweet, silent jazz all over my skin. I could feel him *feeling me*. He was truly listening to me with his hands. The touch. My God, the touch. This was the touch I'd been longing for. Sensual, venerating, receptive, hungry and giving—all at once. We stayed there for an eternity, just taking in the panoramic paradisiacal view and delighting in all the many ways we could make contact.

Eventually we migrated a few feet to the hammock and laid across from each other for what seemed like years, sometimes talking, sometimes resting in tranquil silence. We listened to the symphony of tropical creatures with rapt attention, captivated. We tasted timelessness for a time.

CHAPTER 33

WONDER AND WARNINGS

"To love oneself is the beginning of a lifelong romance."
— OSCAR WILDE

AFTER SOME immeasurable epoch on the deck, we sauntered down to the kitchen, having fully regained our balance. The ladies of the kitchen staff had begun to know our preferences. "Buenos dias, Dominga!" I said.

"Buenos dias, Elisa! ¿Quiere papaya?" asked Dominga with grandmotherly sweetness.

"Sí!"

"Chor, ¿quiere piña y sandia?"

"Yes! Hola, Dominga! Grrracias! Grrracias!"

Chor decided to go by a Spanish variation of his birth name, which he had always preferred. "Joaquin! Call me Jwakeeen! Jwakeeen!"

All the ladies repeated in chorus, laughing, "Ok, Juakeeeeen!" He set free that jovial laugh again, the laugh that lit up my sky as much as this Costa Rican sun.

We brought our bowls of fruit back up to the deck

and settled onto the sofa. The fruit tasted all the sweeter because of our sensitized taste buds and empty bellies and adoring strokes. The other iboga apprentice, Ann-Marie, joined us. "How are you two doing?" she smiled and asked with her gentle Norwegian accent.

"Good!" we both chimed in. "My journey was so intense!" I confessed. "I feel fantastic, but, wow, it was wild. I am curious: Is every journey really different? Or all they all similar for you?"

"Every journey has been really different, yes. It depends on what I'm going through. The medicine always gives you exactly what you need." She smiled.

I nodded, contemplating. *What did this medicine have in store for me for the next ceremony?* I wondered. I was resolved to receive.

We ate our fruit in peace and watched the cattle as they scattered across the land. We melted into more melting—on the sofa, the hammock, the bed. Talking or snuggling or just being. Luxurious.

"Oh, love," Chor smiled. "You care about everything so much. You care about everything 200%. Not just 100%, but 200%." It's true. I was a zealot and a preacher, and I loved my righteous anger too much sometimes.

"Yeah," I heartily agreed, laughing at myself. "It's true. I get neurotic sometimes. I just wanna take such good care of everyone. It all comes from love, though."

"I know, I know," he chuckled.

Michael bounced out to the deck to check on us. "How's it going?" He smiled knowingly.

Chor took some time with the men folk over at the guesthouse. I indulged in some time to myself on the deck with my journal. Writing had always helped me to fully digest my experiences. I emptied the night's rich contents onto the pages.

When Chor returned, he briefly peeked at me as I scribbled away in my journal, and then retreated to the deck on the other side of the house. After a while, I walked over to where he was. "Watcha doin'?" I asked, as he sat on another sofa.

"I am...looking at this tree here." Amazing. Chor would have never just looked at a tree for so long. I loved watching my lover bloom. I sat next to him.

"This looks like a tree from Africa," he said. Indeed it did. It was an enormous, proud, symmetrical tree. Its branches looked like veins.

"What was your mystery question?" he asked.

"I wanted to get iboga's take on something. I asked, 'What is the nature of the Sacred Prostitute?'" I relayed my whole vision for him.

"Hmm," he said. And we sat in a deep silence for a long time. "Why do you keep that part of your life such a secret?" he asked. "Are you ashamed of it?"

"No! Not at all," I replied, a bit frustrated, as he'd asked this in the past and I'd answered him. It seemed so hard for him to understand. "It's just very delicate information. I just wasn't ready to explain this part of my life to Moughenda or Michael just yet. I like to get to know people more before I share all that, you know."

"Hmm," he said thoughtfully, and went back to looking at the tree.

The afternoon rolled around, and Chor and I took a short stroll along the jungle road of the property. The birds sang to us. Chor looked at every bug and rock and flower and butterfly, fascinated like a five-year-old. We searched for the legendary iguanas that supposedly inhabited the tunnel under the long driveway, and sure enough, they scurried around for us upon our approach.

Chor and I had a leisurely dinner with Michael. I had no appetite, and I was enjoying feeling light, but I made the effort to consume a small meal since Moughenda had stressed the importance of eating the day after a ceremony. Chor wolfed down his chicken; I couldn't imagine how he could eat like that just now.

"Tell me about that 5-gram-a-day guy," Chor inquired with Michael. He was curious about the man in one of the video testimonials.

"Oh yeah, that's Jeff," said Michael.

"Seriously, 5 grams a day? That's crazy." Chor was in disbelief that such a person could be salvageable at all. "At my worst, I was maybe at 1 or 2 grams a day, but that was always as much as I could get my hands on."

"Yeah, he was pretty bad. That was the most intense detox I've ever seen. He flew in, and we started feeding him the medicine right after he got off the plane. He couldn't do anything. He just crashed on that couch in the hallway upstairs. For five days, we kept feeding him medicine, and he didn't move. Finally, on the fifth day, he was ready to come out of it.

"His dad was here with him and did the medicine,

too, but just for a psycho-spiritual program, not for drug detox. Gary, a great guy. They both went on to do the iboga provider training, and Gary eventually started up another iboga healing retreat here in Costa Rica."

"Whoah," said Chor.

"Yeah, Jeff was a tough case," Michael continued. "He stayed clean for about eight months. He was one of the few who relapsed."

"Wow. So I guess it's not a magic bullet," Chor reflected.

"No, it's not. The medicine requires participation. The medicine cleanses and teaches. From there, a person has to make their own choices. It's all about choices. That is how we grow." We reflected and drank in the truth with a deep breath.

"Moughenda had foreseen Jeff's crossroads," said Michael ominously. "Moughenda told him simply, 'Sell your motorcycle.' Moughenda knew that his motorcycle was some kind of gateway to his old life, old crew, old patterns. But he didn't listen," Michael chuckled, seeing the humor even in the tragedy.

Michael elaborated. Jeff had returned home to the States for a visit and went out for a night on the town with his motorcycle buddies. It started off with just one beer, his first intoxicant in eight months.

Jeff and his friends ended up getting totally wasted. He skidded out on his motorcycle and was chased by police through three towns. He eventually collided with a moving vehicle and wound up in the hospital with terrible injuries, loaded up on heavy painkillers. Jeff wanted to go right back to Costa Rica to continue his training, but he had charges and court dates and potential jail time to deal with. One thing led to another. Those painkillers plus depression and the wrong company triggered a relapse.

We listened to the warning tale with rapt attention. "Well Jeff came back to Moughenda with his tail between his legs. Jeff knew how Moughenda felt about relapses. Moughenda does not like it when people waste the medicine," Michael shook his head sorrowfully.

Moughenda treated Jeff, Michael explained, but only because he was Gary's son. Gary had become family by then. And Jeff was so ashamed. Moughenda took pity.

It took another five whole days, but Jeff couldn't walk through the door that time—the door to the spirit world. The medicine cleaned up his body but blocked him out of the spirit world. He had no visions, no gifts. Worst of all, he went through all of the withdrawal symptoms that the medicine is generally known to alleviate.

Iboga gave Jeff a very clear message: Iboga is not there to help him every time he got in trouble. It is a living spirit and a teacher to be honored.

"Jeff stayed on the path and proved himself after that," Michael concluded. "He even went back home to rescue a few friends who were still using. He stayed with them while they tapered down their usage to 1 gram a day, for an easier detox. He watched them shoot up and everything, but he didn't touch it. He was by then completely through with the poison." Michael smiled proudly.

"Wow," said Chor, amazed at Jeff's discipline.

Michael continued, "Jeff brought back those friends to be healed, and he carried on with the work. He's a great iboga provider now." Chor digested the story along with our dinner. Iboga was clearly not a cure-all. It was a force to be reckoned with. We would have to step up and honor its gifts.

Michael lightened up the heavy conversation. "You know," he said with a smirk as he leaned over, "you can actually travel into other people's bodies with this medicine!" He waited a moment for the ensuing wows, and then continued. "Yeah, you can actually enter someone's body and heal different ailments they have going on. It's a real *inside job*," he winked. "I tried that once, but I got myself into a bit of trouble. I learned: You gotta ask first!"

Michael shared the story: One day, while in vision with the medicine, Michael decided to fly over to visit his Zen teacher. She was meditating at her altar. He zipped inside her body and started doing healing work on her. But she knew he was there! She was a bit angry and tersely asked Michael what he was doing there.

Michael, surprised that he'd been discovered, explained to her that he was just giving her some healing work.

She advised him to at least get permission first. That made sense to Michael, to have good esoteric manners. So he asked for her permission and she gave it. Michael returned to his healing work inside her, and then he glimpsed a vortex beyond her altar. He started to peek over her shoulder as she meditated.

Suddenly she jumped up like a warrior, grabbed a

staff, and faced Michael. "You can't go in there!" she said.

So Michael asked, "Why not? What's in there? What is that?" Michael reenacted his part in the scene, bouncing around as he peeked, curious and rambunctious like a big kid.

"Moughenda then jumped into my vision all of a sudden, in his full ceremonial regalia, and said 'Come on. You don't need to go there. Let's go. Come with me.' I guess was getting distracted!" Michael laughed with wide toothy grin.

———

I'd always had a sunset fantasy. Doesn't everyone? It's the quintessential lover's date, and I'd never actually had one. Chor was always busy. So busy. Sitting still didn't interest him, unless it was for a movie. But here, the sunset was the inescapable main attraction and Chor had been seasoned to slow down.

Chor and I made our way to the deck and curled up together. We sat in sweet silence, breathing as one, and watched God paint a one-of-a-kind masterpiece in the sky. After the sun went down, our nighttime entertainment commenced: flickering fireflies, abundant stars, and stealth bats. We bantered about the bountiful beauty.

In all of our six-plus years together, I couldn't remember a single full day without the modern matrix of electronic existence. Amazing! Even though it was just because of their house policy, it was still a revelatory experience. I looked over at Chor's peaceful face. I could almost see his brain taking a deep breath. "Isn't this lovely, babe? To be 'unplugged' just for a little while?"

"Yeah! It is, actually."

"Your body and mind can be refreshed from little breaks. Retreats, in balance with action, can help you to create truly visionary work," I lectured, sweetly. I prayed that he'd have more electronic continence after this. I was delighted to witness his new ability to appreciate the simple beauty of nature, silence, and awareness.

We retired to our bedroom love nest. We undressed. In the soft light, we anointed each other with the purest frankincense. We wove our bodies together in artful carnal worship. He penetrated me and paused for a moment, trembling with bliss. He was a lightning rod of vital energy. He was sensitized, more present than ever before. His whole body was reading me, even as he was enjoying me.

He picked me up in his sturdy arms and held me as I encircled his waist with my legs. I surrendered to his power and rode his magnificence. We softly howled, hummed, purred. All the dust I'd gathered was shaken away. I was Venus, on honeymoon: pollinated, sated, loved, alive, cherished with wide-open eyes. I'd been waiting years for this paradisiacal day, eternally intuiting its existence. It had been so worth waiting for, and I yet I knew: I'd never live without this again.

CHAPTER 34

ROOTED

"The point of beginning is the breath. It is that divine moment when we say 'Yes' to embracing and embodying our journey here in this realm, in this form, in this story."
— SHAMANA MA SHARENE

"The attempt to escape from pain, is what creates more pain."
— GABOR MATÉ

EVER SINCE I was a teen, I had a tendency to bolt when relationships became intense. That's the only way I knew: LEAVE.

Mom and dad were divorced twice—from each other. Three times, really, if you count the last breakup. I was just five years old when they divorced the first time. I didn't understand. My little mind and my little world cracked. Yet they soon reunited; then there was a constant torrent of drama leading up to their second divorce a few years later.

After they parted ways again, the house was suddenly peaceful. No yelling. No frantic tears. No doors slamming. No parents getting sucked into vortices called "talks." I remember feeling relieved. The kids finally received all the care and attention that they needed. My parents were healthier than I had ever seen them: fulfilled, creative, and immersed in their own academic and professional goals.

Therapists, family, and friends all offered their consolation when my parents divorced the second time. "Are you kidding?" I asked as a tween. "I am so happy! They need to stay away from each other."

Then they started dating again. I cringed. Maybe it would work this time. The third time was the charm, right? No. They slipped into old habits and triggered the worst in each other. Though they ended things, I felt proud of my parents for at least breaking free of the old script when it just wasn't serving them. But I'd become hardwired with a twisted wisdom. The little me learned well.

When the going gets tough...just get outta there. GO.

As a young woman, I never thought I would be married. Marriage, as I understood it, seemed as sticky and treacherous as quicksand. Yuck. Besides, I was just too freaky. I wasn't good "wife" material. My thinking was too far outside the picket fence. I balked at that line in the old marriage vows about female obedience. No man could ever tell me what to do. Ever. I was an indomitable tigress, happy to live life free and on my own terms.

Most men, I thought, were only able to pigeon-hole women into two categories: virgin or whore. (But wasn't I pigeonholing men right there?) I would surely land in the whore bucket. Though I embodied both the virgin and the whore and every archetype between, no man would ever be able to relate to the terrifyingly vast spectrum of my whole being.

Besides, most men turned into squealing mice and scurried away in the face of my PMS anyway. Silly boys. Who needs them?

So there I am, steeped in all those beliefs. Then Chor comes into my life ... and he just stays. I tell him about my racy past. He stays. I get feisty. He stays. I get raging PMS and cry. He stays. We fight about sex. He stays. Chor, my all-weather earth angel with big muscles.

Chor had the balls to dance with me. After our tussles, he'd come up and hold me tightly, even as I pretended to claw and hiss, and he'd say, "I LOVE YOU. Yes, I do! You are beautiful! Yes you are!" He'd melt my fight or flight, over and over.

Chor inspired me to reconsider marriage: *I fit here, with this man. All of me. Talons and red lipstick and halo and all.*

Chor would stay rooted all those times that I was ready to bolt. My love warrior. I had always affectionately called him my "redwood tree." Solid. Humble. Loyal. He brought me back to love, always.

This rough relapse roller coaster would have been the perfect excuse for me to escape. I didn't. *I became the redwood tree.*

CHAPTER 35
THE FIELD TRIP

"Love your life, dear one. It is more precious than you can possibly know. Everything past is braided into this moment. Yet, we promise you, with each breath, you are born anew. This moment is the only one you have. This place, right here, where you live in your body, is where power shines. Relax into the miracle of it. Breathe into the sacred now. Feast on your life. Enjoy!"

— SAMANTHA SWEETWATER

I LAY NEXT TO Chor as he slept, meditating on his breath and basking in our woven warmth.

He awoke and we bounded out of bed, bright-eyed and bushy-tailed, as they say. Chor went straight to the deck. Again, he marveled and complimented the earth. He stood there for a long while, just taking in the view.

We made our way downstairs for breakfast. "Buenos dias, stars!" Chor said to the ladies in the kitchen staff.

"Buenos dias, Juakeeeeeen!" They chirped, giggling.

"Yes! Yes! Juakeeeeeen!" he repeated with flair, smiling back.

As we feasted on a wholesome breakfast, Michael explained our itinerary. "We'll leave at about 10 a.m.

We'll be going zip lining through the jungle!"

"Yeah! I love it!" Chor sparkled.

Wow. What a fun 'detox' program, I thought. 100% natural thrills seemed like the perfect thing right at that moment.

"We will go horseback riding, but of course you can pass on that if you like, Elizabeth," he smiled kindly. "Then we will go to the volcanic clay spa. They have hot springs to soak in. You can cover your whole body in the wet clay. It helps to detox the body."

"Do we get to be naked?" I asked.

"They are pretty modest here in Costa Rica. You gotta wear a swimsuit." Michael explained.

"How does that work, getting covered in wet clay in your swimsuit?" I asked. It seemed so natural to be au naturel in such a setting. I wanted to feel the wet earth all over my naked skin.

Michael shrugged. "Yeah, I know, but it can work. It still feels amazing! And you can get a massage there if you like."

"Be sure to get one of those massages," said Ann-Marie. "Oh, those ladies are so good! You can get four hands at once!" Yummy.

—

Chor and I laid lazily together on the deck while we waited to leave for our excursion. "So, why didn't you ever teach me about what you know? The tantric arts?" Chor asked. My jaw dropped.

"Well, love, you never asked."

"I did ask!" Chor protested.

"Well, you asked just once...a very long time ago. You seemed so resistant to any kind of guidance. And I certainly didn't want to push it on you. Then you never asked again." I replied, my defenses rising.

"Well, do I have to ask over and over?" he asked.

"Yes, of course. Frankly, you didn't seem that into it. It kills the magic if you don't *really* want it. As a dakini, like any good guide, I need to feel your openness—and your gratitude. These sacred practices, just like the medicine, must be received with respect to be effective. But the more important thing here is that I just accepted you, even though you didn't seem to be into all the same things."

"I...I want to understand you. Yeah, I want to learn. I want to give you what you need," he confessed. The static in the air between us dissipated with his expression.

"Then I need you to ask for it, again and again. Make time and space for these treasures. And receive them as a sincere apprentice."

"OK. I'll work on it." He drew me to his heart and held me tight.

We relished a slow pace, off the clock. We were moving in jungle time. Michael finally came to knock on our door well past 10, but somehow it was the perfect moment. "All right, everybody! Here we go!"

Moughenda drove the whole little clan, including Michael and Ann-Marie, out to the first stop: horseback riding. We took the transit time to rap with Moughenda. Chor asked, "So, what about marijuana? Or the opium poppy plant? Are they sacred plants, too?"

Moughenda lit up. Apparently we had cracked open a favorite subject. "Yes! Marijuana is a medicine plant, a sacred plant. I use it to heal people, but it is not taken as smoke. It's a beautiful plant! A generous, strong plant! But people abuse it. When people abuse a plant, they become a slave. Same thing with the poppy plant. What a wonderful gift of the earth! This sacred plant gives us pain relief and rest—when we really need it. But when people abuse it, they become a slave, or worse, they die."

I offered, "We need to respect the plants and *listen* to the plants. People can get greedy and start taking too much, taking more than the plant is quietly offering. When people abuse plants, the plants abuse them back!"

"Yes, exactly!" said Moughenda. He laughed heartily. No matter what subject Moughenda spoke about, his voice was filled with some kind of indomitable humor. "Attachment leads to addiction. We cannot even be attached to iboga!" We contemplated this wild inner freedom. "All plants are on this earth for a purpose. Not all plants are for human medicine, but every plant has a purpose. All plants are sacred," Moughenda concluded.

When we arrived at the equestrian center, I jumped out. Michael coaxed me. "Hey, Elizabeth," he smiled and spoke softly, as if taming a wild horse. "Would you like to just come and see the horses? They sure are beautiful."

"Sure, I'll take a peek. Indeed, they are beautiful creatures." And I meant it, even though they terrified me.

We walked over to the corral. Chor had already jumped in and was stroking and patting all the horses. He spoke to them in a playful, affectionate tone. He had a way with animals.

I admired the lovely, majestic beings. They flirted, batting the long lashes on their soulful eyes. "Hey, Elizabeth," Michael said gently, "If you want to try, you could have the cowboy lead your horse for you. Maybe that would make you feel more comfortable. They are really gentle trail horses. They do this every day, with all kinds of people."

Should I? "OK. I'll try it," I was shocked at the words coming out of my mouth. Apparently, some part of me was game.

I entered the corral. The cowboy led me to my horse. The mahogany beauty was smaller and meeker than the other horses. I walked up next to her and connected with her eyes. Suddenly I saw an individual being, instead of my own fear. I looked into her. "Hi there, sweetheart. How ya doin'? I would love to ride you today." I stroked her long, graceful neck and shoulders.

My horse was brought up next to a little platform of stairs, making it easier for an inexperienced tourist like me to mount her. I slipped on. Something felt different. The cowboy, riding his own horse, took my horse's rope and led us to the trailhead.

Chor was right next to me on his horse. I saw the kid in him, excited and silly. He hammed it up for some photos. He looked like an emperor posing for the court painter: looking up toward the sky, firmly gripping the reins, and puffing up his chest.

The facilitator, a young Costa Rican lady, came to the front and gave us the ABCs of horseback riding. My heart fluttered a little.

When we began to ascend the trail, I felt my horse. My stiff body relaxed. Her rhythm rippled through me as I harmonized with her movements. I tuned into her nuanced responses. We were merging.

I was amazed. How did these giant beings have such sure footing? The trail was thin and rocky. My fear was tested, but the old buttons didn't set off the panic alarm. Over and over, I returned my full attention to the connection with my horse. The medicine had shifted something within me. The yoke of past trauma had been broken away from the present moment.

Even though the guide had instructed us to keep a gentle walking pace, Chor provoked a full gallop in his horse with a light kick and rode ahead of the lead cowboy all the way to the top. "Yeah! Whoooh!" He said triumphantly as we arrived at the end of the trail. Classic Chor. Full speed ahead, whatever the direction might be.

We dismounted, and we were led to the first platform for zip lining. The crew latched us onto the line with nimble hands, and we went flying over the jungle. It was exhilarating. Of course, Chor opted to zip line while hanging upside down—a few times. Daredevil.

The volcanic spa awaited us. I changed into my swimsuit. We painted each other from head to toe in the warm, wet, dark-green clay.

The clay slowly began to dry. Our eyes peered out

from the cracking earthy mask. We looked like ancient humans. The tranquil jungle river and large moss-covered boulders evoked prehistory. Chor scampered over the boulders ahead of me, on all fours. I made my way slowly, cautiously. I looked up to see him perched on another boulder across the river. He crouched down and stared at me like a nervous wild animal.

I remember you. We've been together since the beginning of time.

I laughed and gestured to him, curling my fingers seductively toward my heart. *Come to me, my darling.* We met on a boulder and embraced, two muddy children of the earth. The clay drew out the last drops of poison as it dried.

Carefully, lovingly, we rinsed each other off in the outdoor shower. We migrated to the natural stone pool. A large, boisterous herd of American tourists trailed in behind us. They ordered piña coladas and other exotic drinks at the bar next to the pool. It somehow seemed so unappealing. I was plenty delighted with the raw experience.

I made my way to the open air massage hut. The massage was indeed incredible. These women were masters. What a glorious thing, four strong hands vigorously rubbing my body all at once. Chor joined me after a while, and one of the women went to him. "¿Fuerte?" She asked.

"She's asking if you want it strong," I translated.

"Yes!" said Chor.

"Sí, gracias."

His moans vented both pleasure and pain. "Is that too hard, baby?"

"No! It's awesome! Wow, this little lady is really strong!" He needed it. He tended to ignore his body until it was breaking down. When my massage was finished, both ladies worked on him together. I loved the thought of my king being so pampered. Every couple should be massaged together at times. Coming back to each other is all the sweeter, with both lovers feeling royal and rejuvenated.

We were fed a tasty lunch of organic comidas tipicas. Sated, we soaked in the sun and admired the tropical flowers; they were lush and immodest, nature's showgirls.

Moughenda picked us up and we continued to feast our eyes on the lush tropical land all the way back to the retreat center. We settled into our bed after dinner. Snuggling, I complimented Chor. "Love, I am so proud of you for coming here, for doing this work, for opening to new possibilities." I petted his broad, bare chest. "You have such a beautiful heart."

He stared off into space, suddenly grim and pensive as he stroked my shoulders. His brow furrowed, as if pricked by a needle. "You really feel that way?" he asked.

"Love, what is it?" I asked.

"No..." his voice trailed off. "I've put you through too much already," he said.

"What IS it?" I pressed.

Heavy silence.

"OK, then," I said, surrendered. "Tell me if you want to. I think you do."

CHAPTER 36
DIAMOND HEART

*"Beings are bound by passion and are released
by utilizing passion."*
— THE HEVAJRA TANTRA

I LAY ONTO his shoulder. My hand found his heart. His breath deepened and slowed.

"I have to tell you...I *have* to," he began. "Moughenda talked about being 110% honest with myself, and that means being honest with you, too. We have to be clean to enter the spirit world. I feel like if this is really going to work, I have to be honest with you."

I sat up and leaned over him, waiting for this bomb to drop. "What is it?" I implored again, unsure if I could take it.

He sat up and choked out the words, "I was... *with*...other women...when I traveled."

I felt a lump in my throat, like a rock I couldn't swallow. My breath stopped. "What?! What do you mean? You had *sex* with other women?"

"Yes." A knife in my heart. A blow to my stomach. Struck. Sick. Not only had I longed to be with him when he traveled, not only had I been tortured by guilt just for having been touched, but I had also been so neglected. My mind screamed even as my mouth was a gaping, silent, void.

"Just *how many women?*" I asked, mouth agape, breathless.

"It doesn't matter now. I did it. And I'm sorry. I'm so sorry, love."

Doesn't matter now?

We sat up and faced each other. Grave eyes and sunken hearts.

"It was only in the past three years. It started when I started drinking. It would happen when I was drunk.

I didn't do anything in the first few years, when I was sober—even when it was thrown in my face. I always loved you, baby," he gushed. "I was still in love with you, only you, even through all of that. I felt so terrible, but it kept happening. It was another addiction. When the heroin started again, I finally stopped feeling the pain. I stopped caring."

I recalled how I could never have sex with him when he was drunk. I couldn't bring myself to fuck his demons. They felt so foreign, so different from his spirit. His demons must have gotten pretty lonely.

Drunken one-night stands with numb and eager women probably sated his sensual impatience. Perfect fast food for his ego, said my cynicism.

Apparently his thick tattooed wedding ring didn't make a speck of difference.

My head spun with scenarios. I wanted details.

Details, so I could map the source of the deceit and figure it out and crush it. Why? When? How? Who? How many times? My belly turned with nausea. My love, sliding his cock into strange bodies. All this treachery, between our nightly phone dates.

I thought of the many times that I'd dutifully schlepped him to and from the airport—and what must have been to and from other women. "Who were these women? Where did you meet them?"

I paused, generating the question, "Were they sex workers?" I had to know—everything. I was a primal detective.

He wasn't answering.

"So, were they sex workers?" I demanded again, seeking all the covert chapters of his life that I'd missed.

"It doesn't matter!" he howled.

"It does matter! I want to know! I feel so in the dark. I at least deserve some answers!"

"Yeah, OK? A hooker in Tijuana..."

I sat, frozen, looking down, slapped by the truth.

I had served as a sensual priestess for acolytes who complained, conflicted and desperate, that they hadn't been touched by their lover in ages, for various reasons. But no, my man was not one of those neglected souls. He'd been loved and worshipped whenever I could get my hands on him. So why? *Why?*

It occurred to me: Our relationship was indeed being uprooted by his excessive travel and workaholic ways. He'd ignored his human needs, all of them, until they screamed for satiation.

He continued confessing. "And art shows. Women at art shows. Some women, I was working on projects with. Groupies. Yeah, I actually have some groupies... *bitches everywhere!*" he howled. "They were ALL whores to me," he said with acidic disdain.

His words were a sledgehammer, leaving me breathless, speechless.

I love whores. Nothing wrong with whores at all. I just mourned the heavy masks people feel they have to wear to worship them—and the misplaced loathing flowing outward from tidal, terrifying, untempered desires.

Did he not realize, after all these years, that he was talking to a proud sensual healer, sex worker rights advocate, and sexual freedom cheerleader? I had long since reclaimed the old slang word to crown free beings making conscious choices to share their bodies. Whores, whether professional sensual artisans or sexually liberated women, held divine status in my eyes as Earth angels. He was slandering my sisters, and he was spitting on me. My heart broke, not only for my sham of a relationship, but for all the women he had disrespected— even as he devoured them.

How could my very own man harbor such attitudes?

I felt the same blow of sadness that I had experienced when people disrespected plant medicines. Indeed, sex is another form of sacred medicine; somewhere between excess and censure exists a realm of potent healing.

I suddenly resented the sexual lockdown he'd had me on—all while he plundered. "Why didn't you ever tell me? I asked if you wanted to see other people. You said no."

"This wasn't 'seeing' other people. There were no relationships, OK? It's not like we kept in touch."

"As if that made it any better?" I gasped. "'Seeing,' 'fucking,' 'being' with other people...whatever! That's a cheap technicality! It's all the same thing! You got naked and had sex with other women.

"I was open to the idea of an open relationship. I TOLD you about Monica. You could have come clean then, but instead you tortured me about it for months! For a *kiss!* And my guilt for just getting some touch was literally making me sick!" I was incensed. I stood up and paced like a caged animal.

Yeah, I had been naughty, but not nearly THAT naughty, said the little judge in my head.

"I was starving myself sensually, doing my best to honor this so-called relationship agreement, waiting for you and wanting you," I choked up. I had realized the night prior, after all that fresh passion, just how starved I'd really been. He'd been sating himself sexually with numerous stray women, while I panted and clutched his dirty T-shirt at night. "I was saving my lovemaking just for you, at least."

I'm such a sucker.

I flashed back to a moment when he'd chastised me for inquiring about a foreign feminine scent on him. "Hmm. What is that, baby?" I asked one night, sniffing his neck. "You smell pretty," I teased. I figured it was some perfumed product he'd used while traveling. From all his proclamations about me being the only one, I hadn't imagined that it was from another woman. He erupted, furious. "It's just my sister's soap! That's all! Stop being paranoid." I laughed. I sniffed him again, pressing his button. He had yelled at me. Loud. "Seriously, Elizabeth. Stop it!" Perhaps there'd been a psychic scent on him, too.

"How many women?" I pressed.

"A lot," he said bluntly. "I don't even know. I'm sorry, baby. I was being greedy. I was. And I didn't want to share you. I didn't want to change what we had. I didn't want to change our home. I didn't want to hurt you. Sometimes I wondered where I'd go if I did go...."

His eyes, desperate and distraught, implored mercy. "I love you. Please forgive me. *Please don't leave me.* I love you. I want to marry you."

I couldn't even think of marriage or happiness or the fairy tale at that moment. My world crashed down around me, and it seemed as fake and feeble as a Hollywood stage set.

"Did you use protection?" I asked, frantically.

"Yes, I did!" He'd always been so meticulous about using protection the first few months we were dating. Then he paused. "I...think...so?" he said, wavering. He'd been drunk, I reflected. "But we were just tested for everything. It's over!" he assured me.

"I know I made my mistakes," I responded, "but sex is just so intimate. It's so much more than touch. You were *inside* other women."

I shivered, contemplating: Beyond the STD danger zone, sex is another level of sharing essence, even when

covered in rubber. Creative juices and sweat and phero-
mones are shared. Bodily fluids carry the frequency of a
person. They can be flavored with adrenaline, cortisol,
alcohol, drugs, nicotine, grasping, fear, shame, jealousy,
rage. Or they can be flavored with oxytocin, oxygen,
green juice, yoga, altruism, worship, generosity, vitality,
creativity, liberation...love.

When people have sex, they share their poison—or
their liquid wisdom, as the tantrikas say. Lovers take
on each other's karma, in a physical and energetic way.
It was no small thing. So here he was, coated in an
unknown number of other women's karma.

I tossed one more confession in, since we were on
a roll. May as well be good and thorough. "Remember
that terrible argument we had, back in San Diego when
we were visiting your grandmother for Christmas, that
night when I asked you to turn off your cell phone for
bedtime? You had refused, so I was going to sleep on the
couch. Then you screamed at me like a crazy man and
threatened to throw me out in the night, with my son.
You really blew a fuse on me. Remember?" He nodded
his head, looking down into his hands. "I was so furious. I doubted our relationship. It was the weakest it
had ever been for me. I had put you on probation in my
mind. When I traveled to Chicago for a work trip just
after that, I let a client there take me to dinner. I hadn't
been so intensely attracted to another man since meeting you, and I know it was because I was so crushed and
confused and deprived during that time."

"Did you tell him about me?" Chor asked.

"Yes. I told him all about you. It was really nice to
just to talk openly to someone about all of it. He just

listened. We kissed goodnight. A real kiss. A hot kiss like I hadn't had in months. And I never told you. It felt good...too good. But then it felt bad, and I never saw him again. I wanted him. Oh I did. He was intoxicating. But I just buried it. There. Now you know everything."

We just sat next to each other on the edge of the bed for a pause, our heads hanging low as we both stared at the floor. "That's another thing," he said. "I didn't know for sure what you were up to—if you were having sex with other people—because of your sensual healing work," he said. "I didn't know what it was all about it. I didn't know how far you took things. I wondered sometimes, but I just loved you anyway. It was hard for me, but that didn't make it right. I was rationalizing my behavior, I know."

"I TOLD you," I emphasized, with my spikes up, fighting for my rightness. "Even when I was doing my sensual healing work, I never had sex with them."

Well, I guess I wasn't entirely honest either. I scolded myself internally. He could probably smell a lie on me, too, psychically at least.

Still, he had numbed his not knowing in all the wrong places, in all the wrong pussies. I fumed. "If you had those questions, why didn't you just ask me about my work? Maybe that would have helped me to tell you more—about everything."

"I tried once, and I said the wrong thing. I stuck my foot in my mouth. I hurt you. I didn't know how to talk about it."

I remembered that moment many years ago. I had dropped him off at his studio on my way to work.

"Have a good day at the office, baby," he said. "You gonna make 'em squirt?" My eyes had teared up. Is that all that he thought of my work? He had slandered my secret temple. A tear spilled down my face, and he realized the impact of his words. "Oh baby, I'm sorry. I'm so sorry," he said. He never discussed details after that.

Silence.

"Honestly, you are intimidating to me. You are a beautiful, powerful woman. I was jealous, too. I was acting out." Maybe he was trying to stroke my ego, but his words just made me even more sick. *It's bad to be too beautiful and powerful, apparently.*

"And...I had a hard time with how sensitive you are, sexually. But that's not an excuse."

"I need some air." I said. I abruptly stood up, went out onto the deck, and bathed my lungs in the sweet, clean night air.

I recalled, on the occasions when I was available to travel with him for a work trip, he'd emphasize how he'd need to focus on his work, as if to dissuade me. But all the while he was letting his inner monster out to play.

Of course he didn't want me there.

I was never very good at suppressing emotions. Never thought it did much good anyway. So I let that cold river of grief cut a path all the way through me. I took deep, panicked breaths that came out sounding like gasping. I gripped the railing of the deck with the same grip reserved for the raft in white water rapids. After a minute, Chor walked out on the deck and stood next to me for a cumbrous moment.

"You are my temple." I said softly, as I looked out into the night. *"My temple."* I felt my eyes spilling over. "It hurts me to think of you desecrating yourself with all that garbage sex."

"Those times...they didn't mean anything," he said.

"Maybe not to you!" I said. "It means something to me! If I told you that I'd fucked 50 men and masked it all for these years and 'by the way, it didn't mean anything,' would that make you feel any better?"

He looked down across the dark land. "You don't wanna get revenge?" he asked. Revenge hadn't even crossed my mind. Not for a split second.

"Revenge would be a waste of time," I said. "I have better things to do with my minutes here on planet Earth.

"Maybe I'm not enough for you," I added after some somber stargazing. "Or maybe I'm just too much for you." He enveloped me in his arms, defeating my halfhearted attempt to push him away.

"Do you really want to be with *only me?*" I asked. I couldn't comprehend how or why he would want to be with only me—with a virtual buffet of other women so readily available. "Why not just set yourself free and ravage the world? And set me free, too!"

"I only want to be with you! I do! I feel clean now. You are the one, baby," he exclaimed, earnestly.

How convenient that you wanna be with only me... now, after you've fucked the masses. My cynicism was having a field day.

"I don't know," I said, full of sorrow and shaking my head. "I don't know anything right now. I'm just glad you are still alive."

His secrets felt dirtier than the dirty acts themselves. I reminded myself: I had kept my own.

Throughout our relationship, I'd explicitly expressed to him, "Do whatever you want, love. Do whatever you *really* want. It's your life. And it's a precious life. You should seek your soul's true desires. If your desires lead you back to me over and over, that's wonderful. I love being with just you, but if you ever choose to be with other people, I just ask that you always be real with me." I didn't want to be the ball and chain. I wanted to be his queen and his hot haven and his best friend.

"This doesn't make sense," I reflected after his confession, carefully replaying all those conversations from the past in which I had invited openness and freedom. "We talked about all this!"

"I know, it doesn't make sense, but it happened. I understand how you are feelin.'" This was his classic line to calm me down, but it wasn't quelling the fire in me this time.

"Yeah, this is quite the cherry on top of everything."

What do I need now? That's the question of the hour.

I'd been revolving my life around his crisis for a while already, and his fake relationship status before that.

Do I even need a relationship at all?

I don't need anyone, said my ego.

I could be like a sovereign sexual nun—hunting as I pleased, a well-guarded mystery, owned by no one.

This had been a recurring fantasy whenever love had gotten messy and dangerous.

We stood on the deck for a while without speaking, digesting all the broken glass.

"It hurts my heart to hear you speak about other women like you did. All women are goddesses, even if they don't know it yet," I said.

"As a great man, you can help every woman to realize her goddess nature, with your noble actions. All those women, that you called bitches and whores, were somebody's daughter or sister or mother. Would you want someone treating your daughter or sister or mother like you treated those women? Would you want someone even talking about your sister or your daughter or mother like that?" Chor fell silent.

"I forgive you, love," I said, the words making their way past my inner security guard. The fresh work of the medicine and his freely offered confession helped me to be soft. Anger dissipated. Waves of tenderness washed over me. Sighs of surrender pierced my chest. I could almost feel the night air rushing into the gaping wound.

I understood what it was like to smother a secret, in shame and in pain. I felt for him. Still, touch was one thing. Sex was another. And he had gambled with my life.

"I just need time...to feel. I need to time to wait and watch and see how this healing unfolds for both of us."

I'd never felt more hurt by him. And yet I'd never felt closer to him. Talk about brutal honesty. At least he had confessed of his own free will, and I respected that.

We curled up in bed. I wept. I shed the tears of

10 winters. Ice melting. Armor breaking. Chor held me and absorbed my waves of sadness.

"I'm going to let the world know that I'm married," he said.

"Yeah, you *better* let the world know who your queen is," I said, "IF we make it through this." We locked eyes, acknowledging the uncertainty.

"You were hiding me," I continued. I was perpetually aware and even amused that he left me out of his endless stream of social media posts. He often highlighted other artists, friends, his immediate family, even fans. But I was the invisible other half. I did not expect to be put on a throne every day, but there was a natural dignity in me that longed to be acknowledged. We brought each other inspiration and support daily. We hashed out ideas for paintings and projects. We were shining lights in each other's lives.

"I *was* hiding you," he admitted. "No more. The world has to know."

"Just hold me. No plans now," I said.

I shivered in shock through the night, slipping in and out of dreams of him using other women—and other women using him. I saw a shadowy stream of drunken disposable bodies, rhythmic grunting, and empty expulsions of impulse. Secrecy and shame hung over the ambiguous forms like clouds of pollution. I died with grief that night, over and over again.

—

I woke in his arms. I lay for a moment with my eyes

closed, hesitant to greet reality. I released a breath, yielding to the stark, ugly truth of it all. I sensed that my torrid dreams were in part reflections of my own debased actions, when I'd been out of integrity with myself.

"I love you," he said, and showered me in kisses. I blinked. I lay there for a while, emotionally catatonic.

Finally, I rose and walked outside in a daze, looking into the morning sun. Cattle roaming. Creatures singing. Yes. The same paradise as yesterday.

My heart, shattered beyond recognition, was apparently still beating inside me.

I don't know what to do.

Is this the straw that's breaking my back?

What is love?

As I looked out over the land, a bigger picture came into view. In a relationship, every moment matters. Every thought matters. Small actions can have monumental ripple effects. True love demands vigilant full presence, every breath.

I had had so many negative thoughts over the past few years. A mountain of little resentments had accumulated. I kept a quiet tally of what was given and taken. Plenty of moments I had withheld my warmth when the scale was tipped. Devotion had lost out to simple accounting. Plenty of moments, I had fantasized about other people or about the perfect lover that didn't exist. Where had my own tainted thoughts planted weeds in our love?

I spent the day in quiet contemplation. I could barely eat. I wrote what I could bear. My stiff and guarded body threatened to break as I stretched in and out of gentle yoga poses, but it didn't.

I felt peaceful and horrified—all at once; the whole truth and nothing but the truth had been laid out on the table. I just knew. There were no more skeletons in the closet to jump out at me.

Chor and I sat together in the hammock, in silence. No expectations, no limitations, no hovering anger. I secluded myself from all the others that day. I wanted to be alone, aside from Chor's quiet, steady presence. I wanted to avoid their scanning, knowing eyes. A pleasant "how are you today?" would have sent me into tidal tears. I wasn't up for the public surgery just yet.

Midday, Chor went to visit with the men at the other house for a while. "I talked to Moughenda and Michael," Chor reported back. He shared with them that he had confessed to me. Though it was stated that no confessions were required here at Iboga House, they were still happy to listen and offer counsel.

"Moughenda said 'Wow, you are really ready, man.' They said I have to just let you be and let you feel," Chor said.

"Yeah," I concurred without any fanfare.

The sunset show came. Chor and I sat together in the bittersweetness of it all. The ultimate romantic retreat in the ultimate pain.

Nighttime descended. We lay in bed, resting, preparing, praying, opening. The suspense of our own personal cliffhanger was grueling. Where would this journey lead us?

CHAPTER 37

FIVE MINUTES TO LIVE

"Even though your innocence may have been stolen from you, you can always reclaim it."
— JENA LA FLAMME

MICHAEL FINALLY came to knock on our door. "OK, friends, you can meet us at the fire ceremony in a few minutes." We moved at a slow drip pace.

Another couple had joined us in the circle that night. We all introduced ourselves. There was a minimalist elegance about the woman, Dahlia. With her slender body, delicate cheekbones, pixie haircut, and dark, cautious eyes, she appeared to be a doe trapped in a human body. Dahlia greeted us with simple Spanish pleasantries. Greg, her husband, smiled warmly. His carefully spoken English was spiced with a friendly German accent. Both Dahlia and Greg exuded gentleness.

"Dahlia and Greg, I'm so happy to see you tonight," said Moughenda. "Welcome, everyone. Michael, would you like to begin?" Michael relayed all that Moughenda had shared during the first fire ceremony, about the Bwiti, the oral tradition, the ways of working with the medicine. Clearly he had paid close attention to

Moughenda many times. At a point, Michael derailed from his well-practiced oration and talked excitedly about all the synchronicity the medicine had brought to his life, until he realized how much time he'd taken. "Ah, sorry guys. I took a couple teaspoons of medicine earlier, and I'm feelin' it!" Michael and Moughenda chuckled. This was a deeply sacred affair and utterly playful all at the same time. Like life.

Moughenda turned to the group, "Dahlia and Greg live close by. Amazing people. They had me over for dinner, and wow, Dahlia is an amazing chef! Oh my God, incredible food," he smiled as Dahlia beamed. "Dahlia had been struggling with alcohol," Moughenda said plainly, without shame or reserve. "She had her first medicine journey a month ago. She has not had a drink since. So tonight she continues her healing. Greg is healing with her." The couple smiled and nodded.

"Ann-Marie is also here in ceremony with us tonight," he smiled kindly toward Ann-Marie. She would be taking the medicine, too. Michael and Moughenda had explained that the apprenticeship involved much personal healing, for being a great healer truly begins within. They'd walk in the shoes of the recipient as they became clear, strong, and healthy individuals.

Ann-Marie's petite body was wrapped up in a cartoon-print fleece blanket. She looked like an ancient child in deep concentration. "Ann-Marie struggles with negative thoughts," Moughenda shared with compassion in his voice. "What kind of negative thoughts do you have, Ann-Marie?"

Ann-Marie responded without hesitation. "Oh, like 'I'm stupid. I can't do anything right. I am weak.

I am a bad mother.' It just goes and goes, and gets me down. I'm a lot better than I was, but I still struggle," she spoke with a meek, lyrical voice.

After pausing to give her space to express, Moughenda said, "Now...do you *really* believe those things?"

Ann-Marie contemplated intently for a few moments, her brow wrinkling slightly, as though she had never looked closer to verify these statements. She lifted her face, eyes wide, and she shook her head no.

"Every human mind is an incredible gift! You can create!" Moughenda exclaimed. "You can make the most of your intelligence by being thankful for your intelligence," he offered with the tone of an invitation rather than an instruction.

"We have thoughts, but we are not our thoughts. They are only a part of us. It's the same thing with emotions. They come and go. You can hold on to them, or let them pass. You can ask the medicine for healing tonight," he said to Ann-Marie.

Moughenda paused in the dark. Michael had meticulously completed the evening's elaborate firewood masterpiece. "Chor is healing from heroin addiction. Elizabeth is his partner, here for her psycho-spiritual journey."

We looked around at our fellow inner travelers. Moughenda had introduced us all with both care and transparency. Here we are. As we are.

"People ask me about past lives sometimes," Moughenda chuckled. "There are all these different times: before this life, the past, the present, the future, and then after this life. Which of these really exists? Hmm? We really don't know for sure about our past lives. We never will! It's a heavy burden when people try to worry about resolving issues that they never even went through in this life. And then there's the past, in our current lifetime. Like all things in the past, we must let it go. Wild, huh? This is actually what the life review is all about. Not holding on, but letting go.

"Sure, we all get hurt. But you think that person who hurt you 10, 20, 30 years ago is thinking about you? Probably not. But you'll never know. Are you waiting for them to apologize before you let go? Are you waiting for them to fix it? Why? You don't even need to think about that person who hurt you anymore! Be free! Enjoy this gift of life!"

I felt like he was talking to me, but then again, this was a common human ailment. One of my unanswered questions had been, "How can I release the armor of post-traumatic stress disorder and be awake to the moment?" I had shared on my intake form that I had survived sexual abuse. Predators from my ancient past were long gone, yet they had taken up so much psychic space over the years. I had stoked my anger and stroked my fears. Sure, we all want to learn from our past wounds in order to protect ourselves, but with trauma, the self-protective instinct goes on hyper-drive. PTSD is a heavy muscle that can't stop flinching, even when it's exhausted. I prayed that the medicine would teach me the art of letting go.

"Life," Moughenda paused artfully, "waits for no one. You don't have to dwell on the past. This is YOUR LIFE. What do you want to create with it?

"You know, we all feel things. We all feel sadness. We all feel grief. But we don't have to let that go past

24 hours. *Life waits for no one,*" he repeated. His words resonated as a remembrance.

Michael lit the fire, and the collective past seemed to go up in its flames. The fire flashed upward and illuminated our timeless faces around this ancient communal fire of self-inquiry.

"So, does the past really exist? Think about it. *Can you visit it?* No!" We all laughed at the simple brilliance of Moughenda's analogy.

"Can't visit the past, ha!" Michael echoed, chuckling, as though this were his favorite joke that he couldn't get enough of.

"And the future, does it really exist? *Can we go to the future?*" We all shook our heads no. "The future is full of many possibilities. But the future is not here yet!" Michael nodded in agreement, amused. "Sure, sometimes we have glimpses of things to come, but they're not real—until they are.

"And what about the time after this life? Life after death? What's going to happen? We don't know! Have you been there?" Moughenda pointed at me. I shook my head no. "What about you? Have you been there?" he pointed around the room, questioning different people. We all shook our heads no. "So...which of these are really REAL?"

"The present," we said in chorus, catching Moughenda's contagious laugh.

"The past is history, the future is a mystery, and today is a gift; that's why they call it 'the present.' That's what my grandpa always said." Chor offered.

"Yes! Only the present is real," Moughenda affirmed. "Of course, we gotta make plans sometimes. I'm a hunter. Back home in the jungle, when we go to hunt, we make plans and strategize, but we don't *worry* about the past or the future. You can still be in the present, even when you are making plans."

Michael held up his five fingers. "See?! Here are all those times, right here on our fingers." He pointed at his pinky finger, then worked up to his thumb, one by one, "We have the past before this life, and here's the past of this lifetime, the present, the future of this lifetime, and the future after this life. So if we take away what's not real," he folded down all the other fingers besides the present, "we have...ta da!" He ended up flipping the bird. "Yeah! Fuck worrying about everything else! There's only now!" Michael laughed heartily, thoroughly delighted with his crass mystical show. We all laughed until our bellies ached.

Moughenda continued and the giggles simmered down. "You know in my family, there were 75 women! 75 women, can you imagine?! So I studied them, very carefully. I wanted to understand women. And you know, I saw...sometimes they hit a point when they are really done with a man. And that's it! They are just done! And there is nothing you can say or do to talk them out of it. And we don't even have divorce, but women can go if they want. A good woman, if you are lucky enough to have one, is like a diamond. A diamond! You gotta love her and cherish her," he said, not so subtly looking at Chor.

"Some men, they get a beautiful woman, and then just take her for granted! They take their diamond and just shove it under their chair and forget about their treasure! Then they spend their whole life complaining that they don't have enough; they want more; life sucks; life should be more amazing. They spend so much time complaining about their poverty, and then they get old. And then...with five minutes to live, the chair crumbles beneath their fat old ass and they find that diamond there." Moughenda pretended to search under his chair with flailing hands and then held up the invisible diamond. "'Oh,' they remember, 'I have this diamond!' But now I only have five minutes to live!" We all laughed at his show until we snorted and teared up.

Michael slapped his leg, "Five minutes to live!" He was the perfect sidekick.

Moughenda continued. "Now in the Bwiti, we can't tell you how to live, as you know. We do not command; we can only advise...." Moughenda turned to Chor. "You have this amazing good woman here, man! Don't lose your way! You know, my grandfather was the big shaman for many villages around. Many women wanted him, but he loved only my grandmother. She knew just as much as he did. She helped him with everything. She knew all the plants. He was the big shaman, but she...SHE held his power." Moughenda struck his pointer finger up in the air and paused in the firelight.

"And at the same time, women can be too much drama sometimes. I had to walk away from a woman before because it was so much drama. I loved her, but I couldn't live with her in a good way anymore. Sometimes people have to walk away if there is too much drama." We took a collective deep breath, each feeling the preciousness of our opportunity to love.

"From now on, you are 110% honest! Honest with

yourself and honest with each other."

Michael fetched the small wooden medicine box and brought it over to Moughenda. Moughenda took out several capsules and inspected each carefully. Then he held them in his hand and uttered beautiful, lyrical African incantations over them. Sweet chills came over me. Moughenda spoke the words with a voice that seemed to be thousands of years old. Then he looked up and kindly explained. "I was blessing the medicine to allow for Michael to carry it and give it to you." Michael brought us our medicine capsules. I took a moment to hold the medicine to my heart. Without words, I asked the medicine to offer its healing. I asked it to be merciful with me. We swallowed. We sat watching the fire devour the wood.

"What element is the king of all elements?" Moughenda asked.

"Air?" I offered. "This is the primary element in the yogic system, because all the other elements die without it."

"Yes!" exclaimed Moughenda. "Air! We are made up of all the elements, but air is the most important. Breath will carry you through this journey."

Michael went to get a glass jar with powder inside. He dipped his spoon and poured some into his mouth. His face pinched, as if he'd tasted the most sour substance on earth. He washed it down with a swig of water. Michael then distributed the powder to each of us.

"This is the ground bark of iboga," Moughenda explained. "It is very, very bitter. Just wash it down with water." When it came to me, I took it in my mouth. Ah yes, good medicine is always so bitter. I started to chew it a bit before drinking the water, as I had been taught in peyote ceremony. Michael and Moughenda glanced at each other, wide eyed.

"Wow, you're chewing it?" asked Michael, surprised. I nodded to confirm.

"Yeah, you can chew it. It's good. Most people can't stand it!" said Moughenda.

Even the taste itself felt cleansing. Pure. Astringent. I finally washed down the last bits with some water.

We let the fire burn as the medicine settled. "Does anyone have any questions before we go in tonight?" asked Moughenda.

I shouldn't say anything.

The words burst out before I could censor myself. "Yes," I said. "How much should I really take...before I break?" Moughenda had surely heard our whole story today. He knew what was up. I panted for a couple breaths, overwhelmed with emotion. "I love this man. I want to help him. And I don't know how much I should tolerate, how much I *can* tolerate, before I end up hurting myself."

Moughenda responded thoughtfully, "Ask the medicine tonight. This one is between you...and you."

Michael prepared the beds and lit the candles. We were each led to our individual space. The Bwiti music started, and the medicine began to stir within me.

CHAPTER 38
DOOR NUMBER TWO

"The bad news is you're falling through the air,
nothing to hang on to, no parachute.
The good news is, there's no ground."
— CHOGYAM TRUNGPA RINPOCHE

"Love is not just some chemical produced in the body.
It is the very matrix that births us."
— LAUREN HAHA

THE WARMTH RETURNED. The trembling was softer this time. A deep peace washed over me. My mind was a vast, tranquil ocean. I felt the sweet arms of Mother God and Father God wrapping gently around me, their adored child.

For quite a while, the medicine felt so subtle, and I felt a sense of relief. *Maybe it will be light tonight.*

Unbeknownst to me then, the medicine was slowly gearing up to gift me with a different kind of roller coaster.

It seemed intentional, even destined, that the Bwiti music was reaching me through space and time, on those particular nights, through that device, there in that little makeshift temple in Costa Rica. The benevolent sounds were healing many layers of my being. The elaborate patterns of percussion were continually disrupting the habitual downward spirals of my mind. I sent thanks to the musicians, wherever they were.

The exuberant music communicated:

Life! Life! Life! Keep dancing! Keep drumming! Keep singing! Keep on keeping on! Keep creating, exploring, hunting, feasting, giving, growing, birthing, being, loving, living! Yes! More life!

I could see Moughenda in my vision, watching over us like a good shepherd. There was a translucent collective of souls with him. I knew this was his tribe in Africa. They stood behind him, all energetically bonded and supporting him, forming a single being with many hearts. They had become intimate and synergistic in ways that felt alien to my individualistic American culture.

I remembered my questions. I wanted to dive deeper into them. I served as my own guide and inquired with the medicine directly.

How can I master my mind in order to release fear?

The medicine responded: *Imagine yourself to be a redwood tree.*

Hmm. Interesting answer.

I suddenly felt myself to be a redwood tree being: grounded, still, quiet, ancient, wise, strong yet gentle, immense yet inconspicuous. I perceived the timeless awareness of this noble tree: watching and waiting, protecting and whispering. My roots stretched deep into the fertile underground internet of Gaia. My branches and evergreen needles reached up and out toward the sun. Connected to all.

I was so interwoven with heaven and earth that my individual borders blurred into oblivion. I was but a thread in the infinite divine latticework.

I rooted around for that old familiar force of ego, but there was not a drop to be found. By nature, *a tree had no ego*. Any possibility of fear melted away along with my illusory armor of absolute individuality.

I had heard the teachings about ego death countless times in my yoga and sutra and psychology studies. I had glimpsed it, fleetingly, in deep meditation. No doubt these experiences had all seasoned me. Yet, never before had I experienced egolessness in such a fully embodied way. This method offered by the medicine sparked my imagination and gifted me with a potent direct experience.

Yes. That redwood tree thing really works. Brilliant.

I continued digging into my questions: *How can I be more patient?*

And the medicine responded in its silent, soulful language: *You can be a redwood tree for that, too.*

Well, that's handy.

Again, I dropped into my redwoodness and discovered that it was a remarkable practice for patience, as well! What a clever spirit!

I asked another question: *How can I experience acceptance—of the past?*

The medicine responded playfully, a sacred clown pointing out the obvious: *Redwood tree.*

I tested out the answer. I found myself resting gracefully in the present moment.

My mind wandered into different realms of my life. I looked at everything with a magnifying glass, and sometimes started down dark rabbit holes. Upon the first hint of fear or negativity, I responded with a resounding: *Stop!* Immediately following, I'd give myself a strong shot of the truth:

I AM love.

I AM strength.

I AM patience.

I AM acceptance.

Then I would return to being the redwood tree. Over and over.

I pondered the power of language and thought. Each thought, like each word, is an invocation. I felt it necessary not to just say "I *have* acceptance," for that implied a passing possession of something separate from myself. I felt the call to affirm the truth in a more intimate way: I *am* acceptance.

I saw the fire spirit in my vision. A collage of faces, belonging to abusive people from my past, dissolved into ash in the flames. It was my own attachment to heartbreak that was burning up in that fire. My pain was transforming before my very eyes, becoming the primordial substance that all things return to: ash.

Ash nourishes gardens for the growth of new life.

Dark thoughts about Chor's sexual exploits would occasionally erupt, manifesting as vivid visions. He slid in and out of foreign bodies like a hungry serpent as I watched, ostracized and mute, from behind a thick wall of mental bulletproof glass.

I observed my monkey mind, stroking its fear, righteous anger, and cynicism—with a death grip. Then the medicine interrupted my entropy.

You are the same.

You were both hiding.

You know how painful it is to hide.

I saw foreign fingers sliding into me and hungry mouths seeking my nipples. I felt that familiar filthy feeling of regret for a moment. The images were progressively magnified, until I had a close-up view, so close that I could not distinguish a finger from a penis or a mouth from a vagina. They were all just flesh puzzle parts, penetrating and being penetrated.

Same sins, just different body parts.

The medicine schooled me. I looked deeply at myself. I was flooded with compassion for both of us. Softness and surrender washed over me.

Forgive, whispered the medicine.

No holding on. No debts. No suspicion.

Just step into your bright present and don't look back.

I became aware that, in my primal efforts to stay safe and happy, I had harbored addictions to anger, isolation, and resentment. All utterly impotent strategies, it turns out. They were slowly incinerated in the light of the medicine. As these old, familiar patterns faded away, I felt a sensation of free falling. There was nothing to hold on to. As I discovered there was no ground to hit, the terror of rapid descent transformed into exhilarating liberation.

I waited for the storm of nausea and lucid nightmares, but they did not come.

From under my blindfold, I sensed footsteps shuffling over to Chor. "Hey man, take another capsule," said Moughenda. Good. Load him up. Clean him out. "OK, we are going to do your life review tonight," Moughenda said to Chor. His words permeated my field. I couldn't help but eavesdrop, and I enjoyed the intimacy of it all.

I could hear Chor trembling and shifting. "Now go to your house. Don't ask how. Just go," came Moughenda's familiar guidance.

"OK," Chor said.

"Go to your room."

"I can't. It's still black."

Then Moughenda said the magic words that seemed to set Chor free: "Just imagine."

"Oh, I can imagine!? Yeah! I can definitely imagine." As a visual artist, the realm of imagination was Chor's home turf. "OK. I just went through my front door. I guess that was 'the door' that I had to go through. I can see everything now. I am in my house." Yes. The medicine was rocket fuel for the imagination.

"Good. Now go to your room. Do you see yourself?" said Moughenda.

"I went up the stairs," reported Chor. "I'm in my

room. I found myself. It's misty. I can't really make out the face, but it's me. I can tell. It's my body structure. It's my voice. It's my spirit self. I am looking at my self and my self is looking at me. And...it's funny. In the background behind him—me—is a blown-up picture of myself...smiling! I can see that picture, but it's still foggy and dreamlike."

"Now ask your self these questions. Speak the questions, and your answers, out loud." Moughenda prompted Chor, just as he had done with my journey. This brought it all closer to home, I knew, to speak the questions and report each divine answer with our own voice.

"Ask, 'What is my purpose?'"

Chor repeated the question and reported the answer: "LOVE."

The interview went on in this call and response way.

"Will I be a part of art history?"

"Yes."

"How?"

"LOVE."

"Will I ever be free from my mind?"

"Yes."

"Why do I have negative feelings about people and what they do?"

"LOVE."

At first, it seemed like an odd answer. Then I instantly reflected on a gem of wisdom that Chor's grandfather often shared, "There's only one emotion: love." Love is at the root of every emotion, even so-called negative emotions. It's just love, be it clear or muddled, expressed or suppressed. All love.

"Do I really trust myself?"

"Yes."

"Can you guide me and give me answers and clarity on my artistic path?"

"Yes."

"Do I really love Elizabeth?" This was the moment of truth...with the greatest natural truth serum on the planet. Strangely, I was not offended by the question. I was happy that he felt he could explore anything here next to me.

"Yes," Chor answered, with a firm, warm tone. I could feel the hint of a smile on his lips, even though I could not see him with my physical eyes.

"What is the meaning of my life?"

"To create...to paint. Art."

"Who are my true friends?"

"You," Chor said, referring to himself.

"Who are my enemies?"

"You." The whole room chuckled, resonating.

We are our own worst enemy after all.

"Does Elizabeth love me?"

I answered him in my mind. *YES. I love you. You know I do.*

"Yes," Chor answered for me.

"Do I love me?"

"Yes."

"Will I achieve financial abundance in the art world?"

"Yes."

"Please show me how to achieve this."

"LOVE."

"Will Elizabeth and I have children?"

"Yes."

Wow. We are already to the topic of children, and we haven't even kissed and made up yet. The healing is happening at lightning speed, apparently. Hold on tight.

"Why did I disrespect my heart, mind, body, and soul?"

"Because you suck!" Chor reported, bluntly. His spirit self wasn't holding back any punches. "Yeah, that's me talking to me, all right," he added, snickering.

"Now apologize to yourself," Moughenda guided.

"I'm sorry, man. I'm so sorry."

"Now give yourself a hug." I could hear the fabric shift as his etheric arms wrapped around his spirit self. "Now ask yourself, 'Who am I?'" Moughenda continued.

Chor asked the question, but didn't respond. "He's...not answering," Chor said after a pause.

"OK, say goodbye to yourself for now. Now go to

the moon. Don't ask how. Just go."

A moment later, Chor responded. "I'm there, in a crater on the moon."

"Do you know any relatives who have died?"

"Yeah, my grandfather, John."

"Call to him," said Moughenda.

"John. John! OK, He's there," Chor confirmed. "John had one of those voice boxes, because he smoked for a long time and had throat cancer. He's there, but he doesn't have that voice box anymore. I see him, and there's a big picture of himself smiling right behind him."

"Ask him how he's doing," said Moughenda.

"He's doing fine! Good! He's chillin'."

"Ask him: Who AM I?"

"He's just saying, 'I don't know, I don't know.' And he's shaking his head."

"Oh, he's just joking with you!" Michael added, with certainty, as if he could see the scene. "He's a funny guy, isn't he?"

"Yeah!" Chor said, amazed. "He *is* a funny guy! He was always cracking jokes!" *Michael could see John's spirit.*

Moughenda continued, "Ask him again: Who AM I?" Then Moughenda addressed Grandpa John in the spirit world. "Come on now. Tell the troof!" His faint accent spilled over with the strong command.

Chor finally got a response from Grandpa John: "You...are...you!" The whole gang giggled at the simple brilliance of the answer.

"Now come back to Earth," said Moughenda. "Don't ask how. Just go. Go find the tallest tree in the forest."

"OK. I'm there. I see the mountain, the little mountain that's right next to the Iboga House here. I'm really far away...but I see a big redwood tree on top of the mountain. It's the tallest tree."

A redwood tree, what do ya know.

"Now, I'm there at the tree," said Chor. "It has a face on it, a wood face."

"OK, ask the tree these questions." Moughenda continued offering Chor's questions.

"Show me the root of my negativity," Chor said, repeating Moughenda.

"My brain."

"How can I overcome it?"

"LOVE."

"Reveal my life partner to me."

"Elizabeth." Palpable, rhythmic joy coursed through my whole being.

"Can I change?"

"Yes."

"How?"

"LOVE."

"Can I learn *how* to love? Show me how."

"Stay focused on your path of LOVE."

LOVE is the answer, to everything apparently. I guess that simple slogan is really true.

The medicine grew stronger in me. I traveled into myself: deep, deeper, deepest. The medicine took me down to the bottom of my inner ocean, yet it remained ever so gentle. I felt crystalline clean, light filled, and intrinsically beautiful.

Forgive, whispered the medicine again and again.

This is my love here next to me. My great love. My imperfect, brave, healing love.

I knew. The process of forgiveness would break my heart open. Wide open. Terrifyingly open. Big as the universe open.

"Now go back to your house," said Moughenda. "Find Elizabeth."

"OK, I'm there." Chor's responses became slower. "I opened the door. She's there."

I suddenly remembered Michael's story. People could traverse each other's visions with this medicine. *I'm going to play,* I thought to myself, lucid and brimming with benevolent mischief. I took an inspired detour. I felt myself leap over some kind of invisible fence into Chor's journey. *Tee hee. Here I am.*

I found myself in our house with Chor. I looked back at him and smiled wide. "She's smiling at me," Chor said.

Moughenda guided, "Apologize to her."

"I'm sorry, Elizabeth."

"Ask her to forgive you."

"Please forgive me," he paused.

I forgive you, I answered in my spirit voice.

"She forgives me," Chor reported.

"Tell her you love her." Moughenda offered. He knew the truth that Chor was longing to express.

"I love you," Chor said warmly.

"What does she say?" asked Moughenda.

Hmm. I could say ANYTHING right now. Chor didn't know that I jumped into his vision. And he didn't know I was ready to burn the past—and ready to sky-rocket into our new life. Up until that point, I'd been totally silent. No hints. No clues. No sounds.

For a split second, I pondered the virtual buffet of creative options for my response within his vision: *pink frogs, fuzzy dice, hang-gliding on Mars.* I finally decided on the pure, simple, sweet truth of the moment. *I love you,* I said in silence.

Then Chor immediately relayed my response. "She says, 'I love you.'" I let out a little audible squeal. It slipped out before I could censor myself. I couldn't contain my amazement and delight.

I could have said anything! Anything!

"Tell her you love her," said Moughenda.

"I love you," said Chor sweetly.

"Give her a hug." Apparently Moughenda saw Chor's lips purse under his blindfold. "Ah, is that a kiss?" Moughenda asked, with a sweet chuckle.

"Yes," Chor laughed, along with the whole room.

"OK. Good job! Good job," assured Michael, who was working in tandem with Moughenda. I understood. Though there are no "right" or "wrong" answers in the life review, but participation with full attention and an open heart were essential. "Now you need to launch," said Michael. "See the sky? You can take off. Fly into the sky."

"Ah, it faded. I can't see it," said Chor.

"Go back to the mountain where you were. See it?"

"Yes. OK, I'm there."

"Look up. *Now* do you see the sky?"

"Yes!"

"Now fly into the sky."

"Whoah," Chor said slowly, in awe. He fell silent, but I could feel him soaring and seeing.

Time to focus on my journey.

My inner landscape started to swirl. Images churned. *Oh, here we go,* I thought. But instead of the rapid conveyor belt of horror, my awareness was showered in countless images of beauty. Again, so many visions bloomed and morphed into one another that I couldn't linger over any one of them: warm pink hearts, flowers, trees, musical instruments, smiles, loving familial embraces, rays of sunlight, and countless other images that must have been the art of angels.

I flew over a scene on a beach. I looked down and saw myself in a long, white dress, smiling, peaceful, and abundant in the sense that all my human needs were met. Two small children and fuzzy figures of other family members played nearby.

The scene changed, and I flew over a colorful, cartoonish wedding. I became aware that the couple to be married was Chor and me. I was looking at bright, kitschy, Disney-esque reflections of our spirit selves.

How could this be? I am not ready. I need time.

But the wedding vision unfolded in spite of my fear and hesitation. All I could do was witness.

Life waits for no one.

I circled the ceremony from above in slow spirals, watching from this aerial view, as our spirits joined in holy matrimony. We kissed as cartoon hearts and confetti and streamers exploded all over us. Joy flooded my whole being.

The wedding scene faded into a vast night sky. Two vertical columns of brilliant cobalt blue light appeared before me. I understood that these two columns were our soul's hearts, the *sushumna nadis*, as they are called in yoga, the central axes of our beings. The columns slowly drew closer toward each other until they merged, producing a single circular flash of white light that then vanished into emptiness. This was the nature of sacred union, the highest yoga.

As I was a witness to this visual teaching, I was simultaneously a participant experiencing this process. I felt my ego dissolve yet again, in this cauldron of relationship. I felt my self-clinging and my self-protecting impulses melt away. Deep devotion swelled in me as I beheld this ancient process of two melding into one, and that one merging into the infinite. The terrifying and beautiful truth: the sacred garden of two can lead to supreme oneness.

SHARE, said the medicine, as clear and kind and simple as a kindergarten teacher. I understood: Share with Chor. Share everything, without reservation or accounting. Share without looking back. The grip in my heart softened. My palms opened.

The world of nature began to burst out of a visionary night sky. Then the sun began to rise, within me. Plants and creatures unfolded from splitting cells. The earth sprouted and grew in fast motion, green and lush. I saw every blade of grass up close, stretching toward the sunlight. I observed: Each blade of grass, and every living thing, was wildly in love with light—and light was in love with every living thing.

The mysterious source of all the burgeoning life was revealing itself right before my inner eyes:

All life is the love child of matter and spirit.

All things are made of love and live on love.

All is love.

The universe was one big, beautiful, messy love affair. All living beings were in love with all other living beings, in some way, within a great dance of mingling, mating, sharing, hungering, hunting. The lion is in love with the gazelle even as it devours it, in perfect balance with creation.

I beheld the nature of Nature: infinitely fertile, opulent, playful, generous, and even humorous as it created every possible type of being. An endless stream of various life forms were being born and then morphing and evolving into other beautiful and funny creatures.

Nature was also fierce, for life was made precious

by its temporality. The full glory of a form could only be known by its eventual absence. Every moment was made golden by its impermanence.

Enjoy the gift of life, Nature whispered.

My spirit was bathed in grace. I felt a smile spread across my face. I flew, content and effortless, through this flowing multidimensional visual ocean of fecund beauty.

At a point just before dawn, the earthly creatures started their opening musical selection, heralding the wondrous gift of the day to come.

Thank you for this day.

I peeked out from under my blindfold at the pre-dawn sky. I caught a glimpse of Chor in my peripheral vision. *Stay focused,* I reminded myself. I felt him stirring, and then I sensed he was brimming with a message. I let go of my disciplined focus and turned to glance at him. His blindfold was lifted and he was looking at me and into me. He took a long, deep sigh, ever so lightly shaking his head in wonder. He whispered the words: "I...LOVE...YOU."

I was so overcome with emotion that I couldn't speak. I could only bring myself to communicate with a gesture; I placed my hand over my heart. I closed my eyes for a moment and breathed deeply, receiving his expression as if it were carried on the wind. *He will know that I feel him. He will know what I am saying.* His hand escaped his sheet and he tenderly reached toward me, like a newborn learning to use his limb for the first time. It seemed to take all the strength he had. He touched my pinky finger with his. We looked at each other and smiled knowingly.

He is sincere, the medicine expressed. *His healing is complete.*

Now the real adventure begins. Will you accept?

He is your blue moon, honey.

The moment ripened, and we both returned to our blindfold and our personal journey. Chor swooned and sighed next to me. I wondered where the medicine was guiding him, yet I relaxed in trust. Then I felt Chor, feeling for me—from inside my vision. His spirit tapped on my inner door. I knew that he wanted to enter my being.

Sure, love, come inside me. Come all the way in. Enjoy. What a wonderful world, eh?

I sensed this gateway to my inner garden, and it was beautiful to open it consciously. Chor flew through me, like a streaming hummingbird zipping around in all directions inside me. He was inquiring again, testing his transmission....

Yes, Chor. I LOVE YOU.

The swirls of beauty slowly came to a peaceful, shimmering stillness. The first rays of dawn kissed my face, and I cracked open my blindfold a sliver. I admired the illuminated landscape with my vivid perception. All was sparkling and polished.

Michael pranced over, all smiles. He topped off my water and encouraged me to take a sip. Moughenda had gone into the guesthouse earlier for a brief rest, but he came out just in time to see Chor stir and look out at the world with yet another layer scrubbed off his inner vision.

I was bubbling over with excitement to reunite with the revived Chor. We'd just traversed the whole universe and shed our old skin. We were meeting yet again for the first time. A deep knowing vibrated within me. Our hearts would surge back together and fructify into some brilliant new life, but we hadn't yet said the words. I looked over at Chor.

What did you discover, love?

He looked at me and his smile spread like the vast rays of sunlight across the land.

CHAPTER 39

REWIRED

"Sacred Marriage is a double-headed Eagle. We don't oppose, contend or compete with one another because we only have the one pair of wings."
— GEORGE BERTELSTEIN

MICHAEL HELPED ME up, and I tested out my trembling legs. Chor rose, his legs steadier than mine. Again, we greeted our pilots with zeal and gratitude. "Thank you, Moughenda! I feel amazing!" proclaimed Chor.

"Thank you!" I exclaimed. Hugs were freely shared; this was a family reunion after multidimensional travels. Smiles and laughter popped off like fireworks.

Then Chor looked at me with astonished eyes, and his jaw dropped. He gasped the longest gasp I'd ever heard. The corner of his mouth curled and I knew this was a happy gasp. "Celestiaaaaal!" He said. "You...are... CELESTIAL! You are a GODDESS!"

I giggled. "Ah, well thanks for noticing!"

"I was kissing your feet! I saw you—in my vision! *I really saw...your soul!*" I laughed, grateful and gracious.

Our love nest in the main house beckoned. Chor

and I glanced at each other, both in telepathic agreement to migrate as swiftly as our freshly reborn bodies
would allow. I held onto Chor's elbow with one hand
and Michael's with the other. We made our precarious
journey back to the main house. We were drunk on the
fruit of knowledge, stumbling across our earth boat in a
sea storm of bliss.

Back in our room, Michael checked that the bottles of water were next to our bed, cracked the curtain,
and made his polite departure. We knew the drill. We
settled into our haven and melted on the bed.

My vision still fluttered with glittering tracers. The
medicine was still strong. I was molten love. I nestled
into Chor's mountainous frame.

We had not said a word about our future. We
connected first with a silent full-body knowing. Chor
showered me in delicious kisses again. How they
flowed—seeking, sticky, fresh, virginal. His lips were
warm, sweet, moist butterfly wings. They danced over
mine, melding, mingling. Seamless togetherness.

Again, I relished the adoring, authentic affection.
My heart gushed warm honey. We explored each other
with purified hearts and awakened hands.

*There is nothing more between us. We are naked
together again.*

"I'm exquisitely exhausted," I said. I longed to drift
into rest with my lover, but Chor was too excited for
quiet time.

"It was like a real-life cartoon comic-book movie!
Some of the answers I shot out there were a little funny.
I kinda had everybody laughing at some points." We

chuckled together, appreciating the brilliant simplicity and humor of the medicine.

"When Moughenda told me to go and find you at the house, I did, like *sszzhh*," he made sound effects for his flying. "As soon as I opened the door, you were there, in the living room. Maybe you were *really there* in my vision!" he pondered with a smile as he held me closer. "You had a smile on your face. I knew it was you." I smirked.

"Moughenda's having me ask myself all my questions and he's telling me basically, I had to ask you for your forgiveness. And you really forgave me. I felt it. And then I told you 'I love you!'"

"I was really there, in your vision! I jumped in!" I told Chor, quick and excited. "I said 'I love you!' right before you did!"

"Whoah! When you squeaked I thought, 'Huh? Why'd she squeak?' And then...it happens to be that you had really said 'I love you' in my vision, right before I said that you did! What!?" he said, amazed and delighted.

"Yeah, I sure did!" I concurred.

"When you are in vision, you are fully aware—and aware of your surroundings. It's incredible. After I gave you the hug and the kiss goodbye.... Michael helped to launch me off. He said I did a good job." He smiled proudly.

I jumped into the replay. "It was amazing when they told you to find the biggest tree, and you saw a redwood tree. Well, I was the redwood tree. I know it. The medicine taught me to become a redwood tree, on the inside, for strength, patience, and acceptance. I really felt what it was like to embody that redwood tree. Our visions were definitely woven."

"Yes, love, yes. You are the tree I've been looking for my whole life," he said. We laughed at the strangely romantic statement.

"And so," he continued, "Michael told me, 'You see the sky? Go up into the sky and take off.' At first it was there, and then it went away. I told him that I couldn't see the sky. Then he said to envision the mountain and go there. It was kinda like my landmark. From there, I was able to look up and see the sky and take off flying like *yeeaahh*! I finally launched—into the sky!

"I launched into my imagination, my thoughts... my heart, mind, body, and soul...into my Self. I was flying through my own brain! It was like a big smorgasbord cyborg map. I actually gave my brain a hug! Whoah!" Chor amazement poured through his clear, sparkling eyes.

"I remembered: 'Yo! I need to focus on myself! Yeah! All right! All right! I need to clear my mind. I need to clean this junk out. Because there was still dark stuff everywhere. It was murky. It looked like there was monsters or dark smoke. It was the negativity: pride, ego, greed, lust, pain, dishonesty, drugs, all the negative aspects of life.

"Then...that's when I turned into 'LOVE MAN!' I literally turned into a love superhero. I had a suit and cape and everything! And a backpack full of hearts filled with love potion number 9." We laughed. His vision was deep and hilarious, all at once. Classic Chor. He had loved comic books growing up.

"Do you remember what colors you wore?" I asked.

"I was all in reds and oranges, all bright! Everything was! I was grabbing colors and throwing 'love bombs' everywhere all in my head, and in my body. I said to myself, 'Yeah! I gotta fix my mind!'

"So then, I saw this little sign that said 'NEGATIVITY.' So I said 'OK. There's negativity! Grab that! I gotta get rid of this.' A trash can suddenly appeared right there, like one you see at a park or something."

"Like a classic old garbage can," I said for him.

"Yeah, exactly! So I threw the negativity in that trash can. Then I thought, 'Man, that's not good enough. So I poured some gasoline on top of it and lit it up with a match, and all that negativity burst into flames. But no, that still wasn't good enough. So then I threw a grenade in there and POOF! It blew up. Then I thought 'Yeah! That works! All right!'

"There was so much negativity. I kept throwing all that dark stuff in the trash can, lighting it on fire, and blowing it up! It was like a little video game: *Ba-ding ba-ding! POOF! POOF! POOF!*"

"When you were throwing the negativity in the trash can, did they appear as forms or as words?" I asked.

"Words!" he said excitedly, and I could envision his cleanup scene, like some kind of Sesame Street inspired action movie. "The negativity came out as black signs, dark signs, with dark smoke. This was the medicine healing my body. It was slowly turning everything from dark to light.

"It was crazy because I could look at myself from this other perspective, as a microscopic little guy. I watched myself grab all the stuff from inside my body and put it in the trash can. It was like a movie that I was both watching and starring in. Then, finally...there was a final, big atomic bomb explosion like *ppff*."

"Because you packed a whole bunch in there?" I asked.

"Because I packed a whole brain load! A whole brain load of negativity," he reenacted the explosion, flinging his arms out, encouraged by my giggles.

"And then everything started flipping and tossing and turning. It was like the big bang theory. Everything transformed into bright colors and light. I went into this whole new love world!" He paused, eyes glancing around, as if to discover that this new love world also happened to be our very own room.

"You know, the negativity is always gonna be there," Chor reflected. "It's gonna creep back in, but the iboga gives you tools to fight it off and to hold it back and not let it take over.

"There were points when I started thinking about my family. The first person that popped up was my dad. I couldn't really make out his face, but I *know* it was my dad. I could hear him. He said, 'What are you doin' here?' And I told him, 'I love you man! I love you!' And it was like I was in *his* dream."

"Well it probably would have been about that time of the night. Dream time. Maybe you really *were* in his dream." I said.

"Yeah. Maybe. The next person I saw was my mom. Right when I saw my mom, it started off happy but then I started feeling all cold again because I thought about my mom's diabetes. She's sick and everything. She started deteriorating before my eyes. She was in a hospital bed. It was just sad. I said to myself, 'You gotta take care of your mom. She'd not doing good. She needs you.'

"When my heart was getting cold again, I remembered, 'Think happy thoughts! Think happy thoughts!' You can be in control the whole time, really. I said, 'No! My mom's gonna LIVE!' Then my heart started warming back up. And then everything lightened up. I thought, 'I wanna see my mom when she was doing good, when she was healthy.' And she came back when she was younger like in her late 20s. She gave me a hug. Ah, I love her so much. I said, 'I love you, Mom!'

"Then I asked the medicine, 'What's up with my sister?' So BriAnn came in the vision. I was in this color world, and she was coming out of all the colors. I said, 'What's up, Bree!' I went over and gave her a hug. It looked like she was around 15 years old or so. She was making these funny little faces that she did when we were younger. She still makes those faces a little, when she's joking around. Then I thought, 'I need to see my sister as she is now.' And so there she was, older.

"I wanted to see my niece and nephew, Caylah and Zion. They came out and everybody was happy. I picked 'em both up and gave 'em hugs. Yeah!" He petted my head as he chattered on. I was in heaven, lapping up all the closeness.

I bubbled with gratitude for the visionary gifts he had received, chief among them was this vivid affirmation of the preciousness of family, a common theme with all the sacred medicines. The plant teachers, though growing on different continents, are, no doubt, all in cahoots to keep the humans heart-centered.

"After that, there were some points where I felt like I was going crazy. I started thinking about our relationship. My heart would start getting cold, when I was saying to myself, 'Oh no....'" His last words came out in slow motion.

"What were you thinking? Were you worried or sad—or guilty?" I asked.

"Yeah all that. And I was thinking, 'Does she love me? Does she love me?' Then I could literally feel you in my head saying, '*Yes, Chor.* I love you! You know I do!'

"I had to tell myself, 'Just relax! Relax!' Then, I knew: I had to not *worry* about you."

"I had to not worry about you, too," I said.

"And then," he continued dramatically, "I was tempted to ask, 'Let me go inside your head.' But na, I thought, 'I can't worry about that right now, I have to go back into myself. I have more work to do!' So I go back into Love Man mode, grabbing more negativity, throwing it away and blowing it up and blowing it up. Everything kept getting brighter and brighter.

"Later, after more clean up, I came back to you. I was outside your head at first, in front of your brain, like a spirit. And there were all these other spirits floating around there. You were in your vision. Then I went into...your...head! I could see the iboga working in your head. I thought, 'Yeah! It's beautiful in here!'"

"You were inside my mind?" I asked.

"I wasn't just in your thoughts, I was inside your *skull!*" he responded, astonished. "I said to you, 'I'm sorry, baby. I'm so sorry. I love you.' Then you said, 'I know! I love you, too!'"

Chor continued. "I asked you, 'Can I go all around inside your brain?' And you said yes! So I did! *Sszzhh*." He reenacted flying through my head with his Hollywood-caliber sound effects.

"I heard you, in my vision! And I really did say yes!" I added.

"Whoah."

"Yeah," I said, "I felt you knocking on my door, so to speak, and I invited you in. I was communicating my love to you." Our foreheads drew together and our third eyes kissed for a moment, the cherry on top of our shared story.

"So I went all through your brain, in quick flashes. There were so many colors!" he said, like a kid raving about the biggest ride in the amusement park. "Then I thought, 'I gotta go back and focus on myself again. Yes!' So I said, 'Bye! I'm outta here! I love you!'

"I went back into my own body. 'Yeah! Love Man! I gotta get you, negativity!'" He spoke with the resounding resolve of a Marvel comic book hero.

"So I was doing more cleanup work, and then...all of a sudden, you crack through the bottom of my head!"

"Me?" I asked, innocently.

"Yeah! Right through the bottom of my head, through the darkness, through all my negativity. You had golden skin. You were rising up and up, getting taller and taller...like a goddess, a gold queen. And there were all these fairies floating around you. I gasped, 'wooowww!' It was the longest gasp of air I've ever taken. I said to myself, 'Oh my God! Celestial! She is so *celestial!*'" He acted out his epic gasp several times, drawing more giggles out of me every time.

"As you were breaking up through my negativity, it was all just going away, and everything was turning to light. The sun was shining brighter and brighter.

"I was looking up at you, and then I stepped out of my body and looked at myself—from outside myself. I saw my eyes and mouth start turning into hearts. My jaw just dropped. My big mouth was cartoonish, but everything else looked real." He replayed his silly expression, eyes wide like they were about to engulf me and jaw dropping to the floor. "I was just looking up at you, hearing my spirit self saying, 'Celestial!' over and over. I looked back down at my spirit self, and he's looking back at me saying, 'Yeah! Yo. She is *celestial.* You need to listen to her. You need to learn from her, she knows the way.'

"The medicine also said, 'You guys need to understand each other. She loves you. You love her. And you gotta treat her good.' I thought, 'I'll never disrespect a woman, especially my queen, ever again in my life. I'll never disrespect *myself* ever again in my life.'" We both drank in a grateful breath, letting his powerful words sink in deep.

Chor shared more fresh scripture, straight from the earth's heart. "LOVE was the answer to LIFE, and to everything. The medicine also said, 'Don't let your mind control you. You control your mind.' Then all these messages were coming through in big flashing words: SHARE! SHARE! SHARE! 'Oh right,' I thought, 'I'm gonna share everything with Elizabeth. *Everything.*'"

"I had the exact same message!" I said, amazed. "SHARE. Share everything with you—without hesitation or reservation. But I also knew that the medicine was communicating all this—because you were sincere and so willing to do this work with me. The medicine told me: your healing is thorough.

"The medicine expressed that I should really treat you like my king, because you have risen to take your crown. I need to prioritize our relationship above all others. That's what it is to be married, for real. Before, it felt like it was me out for myself and you out for yourself. Everything was separate."

"It was like that," concurred Chor. "But it's not like that anymore. It's a team effort. It's a love effort."

"Yesss," we said together, culminating in a kiss.

"And I saw Moughenda," Chor continued. "He came into my vision wearing his African shaman gear, with his hands on his waist and a big smile on his face. He came closer and closer, in slow motion. The ceremonial body paint was all runny, like he was sweating from working so hard. He's gotta help to get all this darkness out of there.

"Then I saw two traditional Western-style wedding scenes going on at the same time. *Both were our wedding.* It was crazy. Moughenda came over and said, 'No no no no no no no no. Don't do it like that. That's not the way.' He knocked it all over like everything was all a bunch of Monopoly pieces. 'Do it like this.'

"Moughenda grabbed us, and we were like two little African dolls. He set us up on this African altar. Everything was African. And boom, he put us in this hut, on this little stage. 'Here you go. Now face each other,' he said. 'Put your hands up like this and hold each other's hands.'" Chor took my hands to demonstrate, weaving our fingers together, bringing the visionary ritual to life.

"Then Moughenda said, 'Now look into each other's eyes. Now kiss.' And we kissed. And it was like 'aaahhh!'" sang Chor, belting out his impression of an angelic choir. "'Now you are married,'" he said with Moughenda's voice.

"I flew out and had this view from the back, my spirit's view," said Chor. "Our heads came together. There was a third eye surrounding our heads, and together they formed a single pupil. It looked like the Egyptian eye of Chorus—or the eye of Horus, I mean." We laughed. Eye of Chorus.

"Two becoming one," I said, amazed. "Ah, love, I had the same visions. Different images, but the same messages!" I exclaimed. I relayed my visions of our colorful wedding scene and sacred union. Clearly, the medicine had us on the same page.

"There were so many beautiful moments..." Chor tapered off, in awe.

"Well I guess we are having a wedding, then!" We said at the same time. The medicine had guided both of us home to this primordial human ritual. It was extravagant—and absolutely necessary. No time to waste.

Life waits for no one.

"We are going to Africa," said Chor, "for full initiation."

"Yes. I feel it. I know it." I concurred.

"I wonder if Moughenda can marry us in Africa!?" he pondered aloud, excitedly.

"Let's ask!" I chirped.

"Chor," I looked into him, "I'm feeling the call to apprentice. After I've seen what it's done for you, I know I need to be of service. I'm a healer. I have that in me. There must be so much to learn, but I feel like I should ask Moughenda about it."

"Yeah...me, too," he said thoughtfully.

"Really?" I asked.

"Yes, I need to study this medicine. Let's do this together." We vibrated, united.

Chor continued recounting his epic inner adventure. "And so, the wedding happened toward the end of my vision, as things were starting to wind down. The medicine was starting to wear off. And the medicine told me, 'Before I leave you...this is the last time you are gonna do it for now. You are going to come back within a year and take it again.'

"The medicine told me again that it was already in my DNA. It was like déjà vu for my spirit."

"Maybe this was the medicine of your ancestors," I said.

"Yeah. I feel that. I just knew, I'm already entitled to learning this medicine and being with this medicine. This is the medicine for me."

I imagined his ancestors, watching Chor and cheering him on as he played the game of life in this great arena of embodiment. He'd come home to his roots, and the ancestors had surely left a trail of mystical breadcrumbs for him to follow. He found the magic elixir. He got the girl. Most importantly, he fell in love with his life. He won—this season. With their help, he'd win many more.

"At that point," Chor continued, "it's after 8 to 10 hours in vision, at about 6:30 in the morning. I didn't throw up at all. I just dry heaved a little bit. That medicine wanted to stay in me. But it was definitely cleaning stuff out of me. The whole time, I'm just pissing.

"One of the apprentices said it's in your system for up to six months. Moughenda said it can be in your system for up to two years depending on how good you treat yourself. So I'm gonna treat myself good and keep it in my body for life."

Chor paused for a moment and closed his eyes. "Whoah. I'm still in vision." He opened his eyes back up, just a sliver. "It's *really real,* like I'm in this other world. It's like my visions are are getting more clear, because my body is more clean and pure. I can see Moughenda, in my vision." He closed his eyes again, looking inwardly.

"No more porno," Chor said staunchly.

"What?" I asked.

"Yeah. Moughenda just told me in my vision, 'No more porno.' It was his voice. That shit is like junk food. It drains so much of my energy and attention."

"It's a shame," I said. "Erotica can be high art. Porn has the potential to be so creative, sensually authentic, intellectually stimulating, heart-quenching.…Porn could transmit teachings of sexual yoga—or just good sexual skills in general. But in most porn, the women are just getting slammed and faking orgasms. It's so empty and mechanical; it's like watching puppet sex. Great porn is all too rare."

"I know," Chor concurred. "The trashy stuff is so addictive.... 'Just love your woman and whatever she asks.' That's what the medicine is saying now," he smiled. "I'm getting all these teachings!" He said. "No more horror movies."

"Ah, thank God," I said with gusto, through giggles.

His eyes closed again, reconnecting with the channel. "Now I'm checking in about what kind of music I should listen to. Hip-hop is OK, good hip-hop, but not that kind of heavy, dark, ego-tripping, woman-dissing rap music. I'm definitely changing my life."

He paused as more teachings streamed. "I don't want to eat meat anymore."

"Really?!" I was shocked. This man had always relished his fried chicken and pepperoni, and he'd always hated my hatred of fleshy food.

"Yes. I am a vegetarian now. I am not going to eat meat—unless I hunt it wild in the bush in Africa with Moughenda." I was in awe, privy to the live-streaming transmission.

"I have no desire to use drugs or drink alcohol or smoke cigarettes or disrespect my body. I know who I am, and I love myself." *Music to my ears.*

"Because you are amazing," I said, dreamy eyed.

"Because I am amazing. And we are all amazing."

"Yes," I added, "We are all miraculous masterpieces of creation."

Kisses. More kisses. So many kisses. Waterfalls and avalanches of kisses. Kisses arising from our perfect commingling. Equal partners in lip tango.

I remembered chasing him down, for little shreds of affection. I needed his lips and his touch like I needed air. I would trap him on his pillow before bed for a goodnight kiss. He would peck me a few times, as if just to get it over with. I was grateful for tongue when I could get it. "OK. Go to bed," he would grumble sweetly as he grabbed me with his herculean arms. Yes, he always wanted me close, but not too close. I realized that it wasn't that he didn't love kissing me, for clearly he did. It was the sick secrets that kept a layer of psychic saran wrap between us.

We seemed to be making up for the past few years. Our purified body temples coalesced. Our limbs were slowly winding serpents in love. Our hearts formed a subtle tapestry of interdependence.

This is the way it's meant to be.

My treasure map of inner knowing had always been leading me here, to this sacred union, though I had started to doubt it in recent times. Bitter words had echoed in my mind: *Maybe love is just a fairy tale.*

Love is a fairy tale, I realized, and it's better than I ever dreamed. It just requires some heavy-duty elbow grease and big medicine.

"SLOW DOWN." Chor said profoundly.

"Hm?" I said, slowly emerging from the watery

world of our kisses.

"Yeah, I need to slow...down...way down. I was going too fast. Too much, too fast."

"Yeah, baby. I have been feeling that you need to slow down. I know that you will be even more successful and potent in your art when you live a more balanced life. Spiritual practice, family, good food, and love makes the fertile ground from which to grow."

He nodded thoughtfully. "True true. I'm so lucky I have you in my life, baby, my loveness queen."

"You know it."

"The medicine showed me," he went on, "we are made of the five elements. Everything is made of the five elements. I saw it."

"That's what the ancient Vedic texts say!" I added. "All that info is really free for download, but it's still fun to read books and relate with other humans."

"Yeah! Free for download! I downloaded all that!" He pressed me sweetly into his warm, iron body. "This medicine is teaching me the laws of life," said Chor.

We slowly closed our eyes again. Just as I drifted off, Chor piped up again. "I also saw my aunt Phyllis last night, who just passed away. She was smiling. Didn't really say anything, but she was happy. I saw my aunt Harriet. I saw other members of my extended family. Their souls are all happy. I was actually giving them telepathic hugs.

"And then..." he said with dramatic flair, "I saw a future vision of me and you with kids. I saw you from a bird's-eye view, on some sand like at a beach home. I saw you playing with a little boy. And there was a little girl laying there—and another lady with a kid, but I couldn't quite make it out because it was a little dark in that area. Might have been a nanny."

"Oh, a nanny would be nice," I gushed, in the misty liminal place between waking and sleeping.

"And there were visions of Moughenda coming in, like an old family friend. He had some grey hair. I said to him, 'what's up!' and I gave him a hug." Chor's voice shimmered through my whole body as he spoke and seemed to ripple out into the fabric of all existence.

"Whoah," he said with closed eyes, reporting live from his vision. "I'm on top of a mountain now, near our home. I'm diving off the mountain, landing in water. It's like a beautiful jungle island bliss land! This is heaven! Yeah...the medicine is about to leave the building...I can just tell." We took a long pause, savoring the medicine as it faded, and dripped into the edge of sleep.

"Aliens!"

"What?" I asked.

"Aliens—on spaceships!" he said exuberantly, as if it were some kind of vital cosmic clue.

Oh, here's an interesting detour.

"Darling, this might just be the churning of your mind. Or it might be symbolic. Don't take everything literally. Let's ask Moughenda about this."

"Yeah, what a show," we chuckled as he contemplated.

CHAPTER 40
THE LAWS OF LIFE

"And while I stood there I saw more than I can tell and I understood more than I saw; for I was seeing in a sacred manner the shapes of all things in the spirit, and the shape of all shapes as they must live together like one being."
— JOHN G. NEIHARDT,
BLACK ELK SPEAKS: THE COMPLETE EDITION

AFTER WHAT SEEMED like an eternity in each other's arms, we stretched like lazy kitties and stood up. "Oh, my back feels tight," said Chor.

"I could guide you through a few yoga poses that might help," I offered, expecting his familiar, blunt "no." I couldn't help but to try and help, even if it was rarely received.

"Yeah, please. I should listen to you more," Chor said as he jumped onto my yoga mat. My eyes widened, and my lips curled into a silly smile.

"What's so funny?" he said.

"Wow," I said. "It's a miracle." We laughed as he stretched and twisted. His simple act of receiving was revolutionary.

I went to the bathroom and discovered crimson. I had been a couple days late for my menstrual cycle, and

I knew, my body had waited for the medicine.

Moughenda had mentioned that a woman should not take medicine on the first few days of her moon time, because her moon time was medicine enough. This made sense and reflected the customs of so many other nature-based cultures. I thanked my body for its patience.

"Oh, baby," I said on my way out. "I just started my moon." We shared a sigh and silent gratitude for our shared flights.

We teetered downstairs for brunch. It must have been early afternoon already. I fetched a plate of fruit and followed Chor into the dining room. As I entered, I beheld an astonishing sight: Chor sat with this head bowed over his plate and his palms together at his heart.

"Wow, love. You are *praying* over your food!" He looked up, surprised. The act had been so natural that he hadn't even thought about it.

"Yeah. I *am* praying over my food!" We both laughed, for he never prayed over his food. He had always wolfed down his grub like a starving wild animal, usually while standing in the kitchen, hunched over a takeout box, or in front of the TV. I'd always prayed over my food, but he had never showed much interest in joining me. I loved taking that moment to savor the gratitude and transform the molecules of the food into magic. Plus, pausing to pray made everything taste even more delicious.

"Yeah, the laws of life!" Chor affirmed.

Michael joined us at the table, curious and vivacious as usual. "So, how are you guys doin'? You went through that door, didn't ya?" Wink wink.

"Oh yeah, we went way in." I answered, returning the smile.

—

We spent the day in each other's arms again, talking, laughing, kissing, strolling, stroking, laying in the sun. Another day with no to-do lists. We relished each moment of luscious peace.

We meandered between the hammock, the outdoor sofa, and the bed. I filled my journal with fresh pages, turning every moment of our experience into a diamond in my mind. Chor looked at trees again for long, lackadaisical epochs, studying them with the same attention that he once reserved only for his smartphone. Between my chapters, I studied this new Chor.

I felt so clean, even cleaner than the day I was born. Clean body. Clean mind. Clean soul. Content. Blissful. Beautiful. No poisonous intoxicant with its fleeting buzz could ever compare to this supremely intelligent medicine. And I was so grateful that Chor had been able to get a taste of it.

I sensed that this superlative state was just the beginning. The medicine had planted seeds of change within us that whispered of many more miracles and blooms of beauty to come.

A couple times, fearful thoughts flickered by at the speed of light. *How long will this last? It's so good. Too good.* These thoughts would almost instantly fade. I saw them for what they were: mental mosquitos, just staying busy.

There's not a moment to waste on such banter, I

reminded myself. I needed every drop of my attention to behold beauty and nurture love.

Dinnertime came, and I remembered Chor's last odd vision, the straggler. "Hey, Moughenda, Chor had a vision of aliens in spaceships. I was saying that sometimes the vision is just a vision."

Moughenda chucked. "Yeah, lots of colorful stuff will come through. You gotta watch your mind," he pointed to his head. "An African will never have aliens in their visions, because they have never seen one anywhere. Aliens are in American movies, so Americans see aliens sometimes!" Moughenda's laugh spread like wildfire. I understood: the medicine speaks through familiar images.

"Frankly," said Moughenda, "I don't think that aliens exist. There might be secret government stuff, but aliens are a human invention." He tapped the table with both his palms as if to close a case. "Humans can create anything."

Nighttime returned with its mysterious show of charming creatures. We slipped into our box seats on the deck. "Oh my, we have fireworks tonight," I said. A jungle forest fire raged in the distance, too close for comfort. The fire devoured a generous bite of our little mountain next door. At least half of a square mile lit up the deep indigo sky with glittering smoke signals.

My vision still shimmered a little. I felt a wave of fear wash over me. Then my panic subsided as swift and smooth as an ocean wave returns to the mother. I remembered the fire spirit in my vision, eating my fears until only embers remained.

Chor came over to the railing to get a better view. "Whoah. That's crazy," he said.

"Can you go let Michael know?" I asked. Chor went to check in with Michael. I faced the fire alone for a time. There was no frequency of fear left in my body, yet discernment remained. Redwood steady.

I kept my eye on the fire. My cautious gaze morphed into fascination. The sparkling flames seduced me into the present moment.

"Yeah, it's fine," Chor said, walking up behind me. "Michael said it happens all the time here. Sometimes lightning strikes, and sometimes they do a controlled burn. It never spreads too much because it's too moist."

"Good to know." Nature had provided an initiation of her own, an opportunity to transmute fear and practice what iboga preached. Medicine ceremonies simply created a boot camp for the grander journey of life itself.

We curled up to watch the ballet of fireflies and diving bats, accompanied by the concert of nocturnal tropical life. After a timeless time, we nestled in bed. My body still didn't seem to need much sleep, yet I was replenished by the stillness. Chor purred lightly next to me, and I savored the wondrous, simple gift of his presence.

CHAPTER 41
ANIMAL MEDICINE

"I realized that most thoughts are impersonal happenings, like self-assembling machines. Unless we train ourselves, the thoughts passing through our mind have little involvement with our will. It is strange to realize that even our own thoughts pass by like scenery out the window of a bus, a bus we took by accident while trying to get somewhere else."
— DANIEL PINCHBECK, *BREAKING OPEN THE HEAD: A PSYCHEDELIC JOURNEY INTO THE HEART OF CONTEMPORARY SHAMANISM*

"Think your own thoughts."
— LYDIA LUNCH

WE BEGAN the next day interlaced in the light of the nascent sun. Nature was threading us tighter together. Hot unity. Abundant laughter. Fresh fruit and inner light. Yes, please. More, please.

We strolled over to the guesthouse where Moughenda was enjoying morning coffee and a hand-rolled cigarette with Ann-Marie and Michael. We rapped about the art of life.

"So, Moughenda, did you learn all these teachings from your grandfather?" I asked, curious about the roots of his aphorisms and instructions.

"The medicine is the real teacher," he answered. "The teachings come straight from the medicine. The Bwiti is just the study of life.

"Let me tell you about the Bwiti.... We don't have one single person who is dictating things. That's the way of the tribe. If you have a question, you need at least three different people to verify something. You ask three different people in different places to go into ceremony and ask. If you get different answers, then you keep looking for the answer." Truth could only be found firsthand, and yet with the aid of the collective. This way was both empowering and humbling.

"And when we make decisions...we use at least three senses to make decisions. Most people go on their mind alone these days, or their emotions, or just one of their senses."

Chor listened intently as Moughenda spoke. Yes, Moughenda was the perfect guide for my outspoken giant. "Yeah, that makes sense!" Chor concurred.

"We practice the art of thinking," Moughenda continued. "People don't realize...depression really starts from negative thoughts. You know...there is NO depression in Gabon?!"

I gasped. "No?" Depression was considered such a normal ailment in the Western world. Signs on public buses drew awareness to this serious epidemic. Hotlines and healers beckoned to those in need. Doctors and drug companies made a fortune selling meds to the afflicted. My own mother had been a psychotherapist, and I remember her coming home with anonymous tales of this travesty. All the signs in my society said *depression happens*. I didn't doubt that depression is very real for some people, yet I wondered: perhaps there are things to learn from a culture in which it did not exist.

Moughenda continued, "I first heard about depression when I moved to New York City a few years back. I thought, 'What is this thing, depression?! This is crazy. Life is a GIFT!'" His hearty laugh was ever contagious.

"Yeah! Life IS a gift!" we said, laughing. Depression, viewed through our polished lenses, in that moment, was absurd. The medicine had a sense of humor, and it played through us.

Exhausted with laughter, I sighed, offering a moment of silence for those who suffered, and I prayed that they would find the medicine they needed to enjoy their lives.

I pondered the absence of depression in Gabon. The regular presence of the medicine must be a factor in this phenomenon, along with the integration of its teachings. Surely the ceremonies also figured into the recipe, with their all-night drumming, dancing, and singing. And all the togetherness, the daily intimacy of tribal life. And plenty of nature.

"Yeah, depression starts with thoughts," Moughenda affirmed, "so we practice the art of thinking. Every thought matters. Every thought is magnetic. Every thought can manifest in the world. We are very powerful creators! I practice the 10-second rule. I play with my thoughts! I move my thoughts around like those 3D computer screens. I fill my mind with happy thoughts!" He laughed, delighted with his mental sport.

"Wow," I said. "As a society, we generally assume that

thoughts are just automatic. It makes sense. We can be artists of thought, but I know it must take some practice."

"Yeah, it can take some practice," said Moughenda.

"Hmm. Depression is often called a chemical imbalance, and perhaps it is, but I see how it can all start with thoughts," I mused. "Every thought creates either biochemical medicine OR biochemical poison in the body."

"Yes!" affirmed Moughenda. "Of course we all feel things. We all hurt at times. In one year, four of my family members died. Four. My grandfather, my brother... but 24 hours is the time I give myself to grieve. And I grieve fully. But then that's it. I move on. Because life waits for no one," Moughenda affirmed. "Attachment is slavery, and people can even be attached to sadness. People can really hold onto their sadness for a long time, and they make themselves sick with depression."

I imagined that depressed people wouldn't last too long in the African jungle. Trekking through the bush to get your food has got to keep you on your toes and tough as nails. Move it or lose it, for real. They had lions to deal with. Indulging the force of inertia likely came with life-or-death consequences.

"We are strong people! If someone hurts themselves, we laugh at that person! We don't coddle that person like, 'Oh you poor thing.' No! We say, 'Hey man! Why are you so stupid?' But we make it funny. Even that person who hurt themselves laughs. That's just our way.

"Once, an American man came for initiation. He was helping us build a structure. He cut himself pretty bad with a tool, and he was so surprised when everyone started laughing at him!" Moughenda laughed, gripping his knees as if to avoid falling over. "Yeah, he was so confused. Everybody kept laughing and laughing, until he finally laughed too. When kids hurt themselves, then they get a little spank. They get hurt worse. They learn quick to be strong and look out for themselves."

Moughenda relished another puff of his tobacco. I asked, "I've noticed that you and Michael smoke these hand-rolled cigarettes. Doesn't the medicine remove your desire to smoke? I know that some people take iboga specifically to quit smoking."

Moughenda chuckled. "Yeah, I enjoy my tobacco. And the spirits love it," he said with reverence. I noticed that he did not handle his cigarettes in the same desperate way as most smokers. He rolled them ritualistically, and he took a long time between puffs. The smoke itself seemed to be an offering as it slowly poured out. "The thing is, iboga can help people to quit smoking, or anything else, *if* that is their true desire and *if* they set that intention." Moughenda said with satisfaction. Michael concurred as he rolled one for himself.

I sensed that Moughenda was loaded with stories and wisdom treasures. I wanted to lap up as many chapters as I could with the time we had. "I bet you hear some wild things, working here," I coaxed.

Moughenda went on, happy to share, "Oh, yeah. One time there was this crazy woman who came here. She was very sad about her dead dog. She came all the way here, and she actually asked me to conjure up her dead dog's spirit, and I said, 'No. Sorry lady. That's not what I do.' And I gave her her money back! And you know what? That dog had died nine years earlier! *Nine years!*" We all cracked up together, amused and astonished. "How long do people have to hang on? That's the pain of attachments!"

"How did you wind up in New York City?" I asked.

"Well, the medicine guided me there," said Moughenda, matter-of-fact. *Of course.* "The medicine taught me how to work with addicts. I was leading a lot of underground healing ceremonies, but then I saw that there would be trouble coming for me soon if I didn't move on. That's when I looked into Costa Rica, and this place and the money and this land all came together like magic! I knew as soon as I walked onto the property, this was the place. I had seen it in my vision. I wanted it to be legit. I had to get permission from the government."

I admired Moughenda's seemingly endless reserve of enthusiasm and stamina. "Sheesh, Moughenda. How do you have so much energy?" I inquired.

"Think about it," he answered mysteriously, smiling.

"Let me guess. Happy thoughts?" I answered the pop quiz.

"You guessed it! Is it possible to have low energy if you are really happy? And is it possible to be happy when you have really low energy?"

"Nope," I said after a pause. "They just don't go together. Happy thoughts are apparently going to put energy drinks out of business."

Our circle migrated to the main house for lunch. I walked out onto the back deck. The world sparkled. It wasn't enhanced. It was just revealed.

The ladies in the kitchen double-checked Chor's new dietary preference. "¿No carne para su esposa?"

"No carne para Jwakeeeeeen!" Chor said jubilantly, answering for himself. We sat down.

"No meat for you?" Moughenda asked Chor curiously.

"No. I don't want any meat. I have no desire. That factory meat is not calling to me anymore. Like I said, I might eat meat—if we hunted it in the bush in Africa," he laughed. "I'm sure that wild meat is totally different!"

"Oh yeah! That bush meat is so good! I love me some bush meat! We'll go hunting. You gotta camp out there and be still for three days straight." Moughenda tested Chor for his reaction.

"Sounds good! Let's do it. What's your favorite kind of meat?"

"Porcupine meat!"

"Wow, porcupine." Chor said with great curiosity, pondering the possibility of consuming the spiky little creature.

We stopped to silently pray over our food. Chor utilized his new signature mudra: a gentle bow, drawing his hands together at his heart, then opening his arms wide to shine his love back out into the world.

"Thank you for this day!" I said. The crew concurred.

"Give thanks to the earth. I love this beautiful earth!" Chor said. He was a new man, indeed. This experience brought a whole new meaning to the catchy phrase. With every illuminated word out of his mouth, my heart shimmered with gratitude for his new life, for this new day.

"The earth IS amazing," Moughenda concurred. "You know, there's all this concern over saving the earth these days, and so much external action to accomplish that." Michael giggled with recognition. He obviously knew Moughenda's lyrics well enough to know what was coming. "Saving the earth begins within. With... happy thoughts! And in the long run, this earth will outlive us. This earth is powerful. This earth can cleanse and balance herself in ways we don't even understand."

It clicked for me, though it was counterintuitive at first. "When people find inner peace, they stop harming the earth. Naturally," I said.

"Exactly," said Moughenda.

"So, do couples always find harmony like we did?" I asked the team.

"Yes, often, but not always," Michael said. "We worked with this couple that had come for their OxyContin addiction. They had both been hooked, for years. Once they broke their addiction, they broke up. They realized that the shared addiction had been the only thing keeping them together. They parted ways on very good terms. But you could say that they did find harmony, because they both went on to explore their lives and find personal fulfillment. The medicine offers the truth."

"Wow. There you go," I said. Chor and I let that soak in.

"All right, guys, we are going to the beach today!

We'll leave around 10:30."

"Yay!" I said, feeling my inner kid. Ah, mama ocean. My favorite earth temple. We gathered up our things at a leisurely pace. Time did not seem to behave in the same way here, likely because there were no clocks anywhere in the house and I wasn't constantly checking one. Time wise, I was off leash.

We lounged on the deck for a while and snuggled in the sun. Hours seemed to pass. Surely this was after 10:30, but it didn't matter. "We need a retreat like this every year!" Chor said.

"Yeah! That's what I've been sayin'!" I teased again. Yet another point that seemed to be a brand-new idea to him. "We need to step out of time once in a while."

"Well, it's a new me, loveness. This is so good."

We wandered over to the guesthouse and took a moment to reconnect with our families via the internet connection. I sent out good news via text: Chor is a new man! The medicine worked!

It was impossible to express the totality of the miracle I'd seen in a text message, but I at least had to get them an update. Chor reached out personally to his family as well, sharing pieces of his vision. "Hey, my dad dreamed about me that night! When we were in vision!"

"Yeah, that makes sense. Perfect timing!" Chor really had been flying around as Love Man, visiting people. The medicine seemed to open inner gates and dissolve the ordinary restrictions of the flesh to an extant.

"OK, let's go!" Michael had finished packing up the car. Moughenda drove. Michael joined us. We drank in the lush jungle scenery as we drove to the beach.

I thought about the strength of Moughenda's people. "Hey Moughenda, I've heard of these languages in the world where there is no word for try. There is only *do* or *not do*. Is your language like that?"

"Oh yeah! There is no word for *try* in my native language! Ha!"

"There is no word for it when the concept does not exist," I said.

"That's right!" Moughenda said. "I'm going to leave you two at the beach with Michael for a few hours. I'm going to look at another property. If we can get the right place with more rooms, then we can lower the price a lot. I want to have a separate luxury treatment center that is more expensive so that I can support the affordable medicine for the people. I want to make it more accessible."

"That would be amazing. So many people need this!" I said.

"Yeah, I have friends who really need this," said Chor. "Addicts. The people I used to party with. When I told them I was going to do this, they were happy for me. They would love to try it, but they can't afford it."

I thought of his friends, his toxic crew. Some of them were fathers. Suddenly, I felt all the hungry addicts in the world. I felt all the suffering family members of the afflicted. I felt all the lovers whose relationships had been ravaged by addiction. People were watching their loved ones die, without any knowledge of this medicine. I felt a surge of desire to assist them. Iboga called to them through me. The gift of life was waiting to be enjoyed.

We filed out of the car and admired the quaint beach village and the serene, sparsely populated beach. We vetted a cozy spot and spread our blanket over the sand. "OK, guys," said Michael, "I'm just gonna run over there to get some water from the store—and a little gift for my son. I'll be right back!"

Chor ventured into the ocean. He baptized himself. He smiled back at me and raised his arms up to the sky. My heart sang to see my love enjoying such simple pleasures.

About five minutes into his ocean dip, Chor grimaced and crumpled over. He hobbled out of the water. My heart skipped a beat. "Something stung me!" He panted and pouted as he made his way over to the blanket. He clutched his foot and took a good look. I could see a plethora of fine black needles embedded in the ball of his foot.

"Oh, baby, those are needles from a sea urchin," I said.

"Pull them out!"

"I don't think I should. Those snap super-easily and can end up stuck in your skin. The deep puncture wounds can easily become infected. There's a whole bunch there—and they're deep. We need to get you to a doctor." Michael lingered on his errand. Fifteen or so minutes passed. Chor writhed in pain and squirmed with concern. His sensations and emotions passed through my body. Ah, the blessing and the curse of deep love.

Chor sighed. "That's why I don't go into the ocean!" He laughed. "You know, before I would have been fuming. It hurts, but I'm still happy." We rested on the blanket, surrendering to the situation.

Michael finally emerged from the street and tore over to us, realizing that something was terribly awry. "Oh God! I'm so sorry! I shouldn't have left for so long!" He panted, and suddenly his frantic concern seemed more tragic than Chor's sea urchin spikes.

"No worries. We're just glad you are here now," Chor said.

Moughenda arrived soon after Michael. "Let's go to my doctors, guys. They are not too far away." We held Chor up as he limped to the SUV. We sped on our way.

Moughenda left a couple messages for his local doctors. "Hey, man, don't worry. If my doctor is not available, I can just cut out those things myself with my knife!" He joked, Bwiti style.

"Hm. Something tells me he won't be gentle!" I said. We all laughed. "Hopefully your doctor is available."

"So these are the doctors that help you with heavy detoxes?" I asked.

"Yeah. They are present for heavy detoxes. And they run EKGs and physicals for some people when they can't get them done before coming. It's funny because when they 'help with detoxes,' I basically just pay them to come and sleep on site. I never need their assistance. The medicine tells me everything I need to know to heal someone. But those doctors sure help some people to relax. It's a private joke now. I call them up and say, 'Hey, man, you wanna get paid to sleep at the center tonight?' And they say, 'Sure!'" The whole car cracked up. "But they are also available for any kind of medical issue, like now. So that's good."

Moughenda's doctor finally responded, and we

drove to their office. Chor lay back on the table and let the doctor have a look. Moughenda rapped with the doc in Spanish. The doctor knew his way around sea urchin spikes, apparently. "Yeah, he can help. But it's gonna take some time," Moughenda reported. We all settled into the doctor's examination room.

"OK. Let's do this," said Chor, cheerfully. The doctor pulled out as many spikes as he could with tweezers. He took his time, employing a delicate and meticulous approach. Then he whipped out a formidable syringe. He spoke in Spanish to Moughenda, who translated. In order to reach the last shards, he'd have to shoot Chor up with some local anesthesia and make some incisions. As the long needle penetrated, Chor threw his head back, clenched his teeth, and screamed in silence. His whole face contorted. I'd never seen my tough guy in so much pain.

The doctor had to dig deep into the wound to finish the job. One by one, the recovered spikes clinked into a dish. It was tedious. Even with the anesthesia, Chor winced and growled.

Moughenda kept us cracking up as we endured the predicament. The office took on the atmosphere of an impromptu fiesta. Smiles even broke through the thick wall of pain on Chor's face. "Moughenda, how did you get that scar on your cheek?" I asked. His laughter immediately poured out. There must be good story behind that question.

"In the West, people have a certain idea of what a 'power animal' is. They think it's an animal that you 'like' or that you feel some connection with." He chuckled as he shook his head side to side. "In Africa, we have a very different understanding of a power animal.

"Finding a power animal is one kind of initiation. We go into the jungle, all alone, on some medicine. We are looking for our power animal, and our power animal is also looking for us. So I found mine, a tiger. This is a different kind of tiger than the ones from India. They are not 500 pounds, but they are still big, wild cats. Maybe five feet long." Moughenda outlined the height and width of the size in the air with his hands.

"And so?" I asked, wide eyed.

"And so...we come face to face with our animal. We test each other's strength. There is a battle. *If you survive*, you absorb the power of that animal's soul into your own. That tiger lives on through me and helps me do all my work. That's why sometimes people see a tiger in my face in ceremony." Even as Moughenda told his fantastic tale, there was no tone of vanity in his voice. Between the bursts of laughter, he was just a man answering the question asked of him.

"I had only a knife, so we got close. He got me good here," he pointed to the scar.

"Sheesh. Tough people," I said. As a devout vegetarian, I loathed the idea of harming an animal. I also realized that Moughenda came from a whole different world where interfacing with the forces of nature was an essential part of life, and it was vital to test one's strength and skill. I understood a different perspective through his eyes.

When Chor was good and patched up, we helped him to hobble out. The knife fight with a tiger had put things into perspective, and suddenly Chor's sea urchin spines didn't seem all that bad.

CHAPTER 42
TALKING TREES

"In this union—the union of masculine and feminine, spiritual and physical—the personal was transcended and the divine entered in."
— Nancy Qualls-Corbett, *The Sacred Prostitute: Eternal Aspect of the Feminine*

"The JOYourney is the BLESStination."
— Michaelah "Miraculah"

AFTER A LATE LUNCH, we all lounged on the porch of the guesthouse. Chor took the opportunity to jump on the wi-fi and sift through his smartphone. With my polished energetic vision, I could almost see Chor's mental energy being sucked into the device.

"Hey, Moughenda," I asked. "What do you think about smartphones, the internet, Facebook, all that?" I knew he'd have something to transmit, and Chor would listen.

"Ah, the matrix! These are valuable tools, of course. The internet is how you found me, right?" he said smiling. "They should be tools...tools to connect with the right people and tools to do your work. But these devices can become another addiction. It's a lot of fantasy. They can suck people in for hours and hours: liking this and liking that and looking at all the 'likes.' It can be a constant distraction from the present moment. It can be food for the ego, too. It's just good to keep it all in balance."

Chor looked up from his device. "Think about it," Moughenda continued, nodding at the smartphone. "All these people, the thousands and thousands of people that you are connected with on Facebook or Instagram or any of those things. Do you really hang out with most of them? No!" He chuckled. "I know you are not hanging out with all these people. Your family and your work need more of your attention. Use those things wisely, and use them in balance, man. You gotta unplug from the matrix sometimes and let your mind breathe." Chor smiled sheepishly, like a kid caught with his hand in the cookie jar. He had come to treat his smartphone like a lifeline, checking it countless times each day.

Moughenda's words resonated. From my own experience, I found that too much time on the devices pulled me off balance. I regularly carved out periods of time to detach from the matrix and reconnect with my human animal nature.

"I know you must need a lot of time to create," Moughenda said to Chor.

"Yeah," he agreed.

"To be a great creator, you really gotta go beyond your own imagination, man." Moughenda advised.

"What do you mean, *beyond* my own imagination?" Chor asked.

"Great creators and geniuses go beyond their own

personal imagination."

"So where do they get their ideas from?" I asked.

"From the universe!" Moughenda exclaimed. "And no one says no to the universe!" His laughter lit up the lazy afternoon.

"I've heard this; I've felt this," I said. "Truly genius ideas don't come from our own little mind. They come from some greater intelligence. I like calling it the universe, too."

"Yeah, I like to talk a lot," Moughenda laughed at himself. "But I'm not better than anyone else because I'm a shaman. That's gotta be known. Just like Chor is not better than Michael because he's an artist, or Elizabeth is not better than Chor because she's a dancer, or Michael is not better than anyone because...he's Michael!" We all laughed at ourselves. "We all just have different skills to share. That's all. That's what it is to live in a tribe, a real community, where we are all helping each other all the time, through thick and thin. Nobody is the boss. Nobody is the king.

"Granted, sometimes I help people work out issues, but I am just a counselor. This is my skill that I share." I imagined it could be seductive for someone to get carried away with the power of such a vital role. I appreciated his humility and humor and tribal sensibilities.

"Moughenda, do you have any suggestions for integrating this experience and staying on our path when we get home?"

"It's good to let things go, to let go of all attachments. Don't hang on to things. I have this practice: Every night before bed, I mentally review my day. Then

I let go of everything," offered Moughenda. "It's really simple, but it's powerful, too."

"I see, it's your way of digesting your day," I said.

"Yeah. And stay clean!" Moughenda peered at Chor, both stern and loving.

Moughenda shared his ideas for educating the mainstream through a documentary. "The Bwiti are so elusive when it comes to outsiders. They don't want foreign interpretations. It's funny, whenever anthropologists or filmmakers try to penetrate the Bwiti communities, nobody will admit to knowing anything. They won't share anything. If they do get footage, then it will end up coming through all messed up, indecipherable! Ha!" He laughed. "I can do a documentary right, because I am coming from inside the tradition. I can communicate from the right perspective.

"The world needs to know about this medicine, and these ways need to be understood. I am almost done with this documentary...it's 80% done." Moughenda was bridging worlds. He was willing to share his magic and his precious medicine, on his terms. The world was waiting.

"I have this idea for a reality show," he went on, his eyes impassioned. "And it will be a good one! There are so many shitty reality shows out there these days!"

"Oh yeah," I agreed. "There's so much trashy, trivial fluff! I would love to see a reality show with substance. What's your idea?" I asked.

"It would be the *real Extreme Makeover!*" he laughed. "I could take any junkie from off the streets, like people on the verge of death, and detox them. I would give them a new life—and then return them to their families. Maybe their families had lost hope or lost touch. Their families might have even disowned them. Those moments when the transformed people are returned to their families would be priceless. I want to help facilitate that. People would see the miracle of this healing and transformation. It's all for love, really. Love for the people and love for the medicine.

"People also need to know how to respect this great medicine. The medicine needs to be grown properly and taken properly. It starts with a prayer to the earth; we ask to grow the medicine in that particular place and make offerings. There is ceremony as we grow the medicine. There is ceremony as we prepare the medicine. Then there is ceremony when the medicine is sent away. A lot of ceremony! This is the way."

The words came bubbling up before I could edit anything. "Moughenda, can we apprentice with you?"

"Yes. We are both feeling this," said Chor, purposefully.

"Good! The world will need more good providers who are working with good medicine!" He laughed, welcoming us home. "You can work with the medicine that my tribe makes in Africa."

Michael smiled knowingly, sprawled out on the hammock next to us.

I pondered people's patterns in the quest for healing. "I'm just curious, do people ever make reservations here and then cancel?"

"Oh yeah," said Moughenda. "People can be pretty shifty. They get scared. Some will put it off, over and over. Addicts might even cancel a few times."

Michael added, "People often go for their 'last hurrah' and then it leads to seven more 'last hurrahs.'"

"Yeah," Chor laughed. "That's what I did. I definitely had my last hoo-rah, but I'm so grateful that I made it here."

Then Michael said something so chilling that it will be etched in my mind forever. "Sometimes, people make a deposit and then go on their last hurrah, but they never make it. They OD and die. We send their money back to their families. That's really sad when that happens, when freedom was just waiting for them." We all lowered our eyes in reverence for a moment.

The hard-core addicts are so enslaved, I imagined, that they probably cannot even imagine a decent life without their fix, much less an extraordinary existence. And to think, this earth magic is just waiting to love them up.

"So, the tree in your vision...did it have a face?" Michael asked Chor, lifting the somber cloud over the conversation.

"Yeah! It was talking to me and everything!" said Chor.

"Trees *do* have faces!" Michael smiled. "I have a talking tree story!" Story time. Michael's face brightened. During a ceremony one evening, he shared, he'd made friends with a particular tree. About an hour after a second teaspoon of medicine, Michael began feeling dizzy and slightly nauseous. After staggering to the washroom, he purged for what felt like hours, though it was probably only a few minutes on the clock. Michael stumbled outside and found himself with his head in his palms. After a few deep breaths, he looked up toward a massive almond tree. He began to focus, and a gnarled face formed on the trunk of the tree. He smiled and the tree smiled back: a big, warm smile.

The tree spoke to Michael and said, "You have a nice smile there."

Not even slightly shocked that a tree was talking to him, Michael replied matter-of-fact, "Yeah, you too."

The tree squinted up toward the right side of its head—or trunk—and asked him, "Hey, would you be so kind as to remove this nail that's been jammed into me?"

Michael, ever happy to help, approached the tree as he responded emphatically, "Yeah, for sure. Where?" It was quite dark, and he could hardly balance himself, let alone search for a nail in a talking tree or wrestle it out. "Ah, I'll come find it later for ya, buddy," Michael promised. The face slowly disappeared, and Michael laughed, enchanted and amused, as he made his way back to the fire.

Later the next day, while lounging under that same tree with another apprentice, Michael shared his interesting conversation with the tree from the previous night. His fellow apprentice laughed and shared that there was in fact a nail in that tree. One had been pounded deeply into the trunk a while back when they were putting up a hammock, and the tree bark had grown over the nail. They went back to that talking tree, and after just a short search they were able to find the nail and remove it.

"To this day it's still one of my favorite places on

the property to nap." Michael said, beaming and basking in our sighs of awe. Michael's tale was so fantastical that it could have been a scene from a Jim Henson movie, and yet it seemed completely plausible at that point. The medicine clearly had the power to reveal an omniscient intelligence through multiple beings and various life forms. Earth magic, indeed.

—

We all headed to dinner, trailing Michael on the dirt path to main house. "Michael," I asked, "you know that there are these stories on the internet of people with heart conditions dying sometimes while taking iboga? Do people ever die with iboga in Africa?"

"No." Michael said, firmly, as he stopped in his tracks and turned to look me in the eyes. "People are not known to die on the medicine in Africa, at least not where Moughenda is from. Growing up in Africa, people have a deep connection with their tribal healers. The shamans come to understand people. They can use the medicine like an x-ray and discover whether there are any conflicting health issues. Then they can often treat problematic conditions with the right plants. They have a whole apothecary in that deep jungle that we don't even know about. And they have ways to sense the right dose of iboga to give. But learning these healing arts and developing such deep relationships takes a lot of time. Nobody needs to die on the medicine."

I nodded, receiving the transmission. I contemplated the good use of EKGs and medical screening for modern shamans treating tricky addictions and afflictions—with only eight days to work with.

Before I could make a clever comment about "x-ray vision," Michael went on to the next important topic.

"You guys hungry?"

—

After dinner, we retreated to our bed, which had become our holy altar of hot love. Chor enfolded me with caresses. His fingers danced over my high-voltage body; my skin threw invisible, palpable sparks upon contact. I climbed all over his formidable, fragrant frame and bathed him with my tongue. He was super charged, crystal clear, and finely tuned. My purring mouth coaxed a climax out of him. His clean-heart nectar dripped down my throat. Naked church.

No more secrets.

Pure truth, the ultimate striptease.

I offered quiet gratitude for the medicine, and for the great creator who dreamed it into existence. We had been given a rare second chance. We would not have made it to this heaven on earth without this wildcrafted grace. Our lives would have grown ever deadlier and our hearts, ever colder. This rare gem of true love would have been buried or broken.

I looked up. Chor's eyes were intoxicated with bliss, and his skin glowed with pleasure. Yes, love, drink it in.

I felt so proud of him. And proud of us. The medicine was indeed a miracle, but we had both jumped into the deep end, together.

The stark truth, born of our woven rebirth, was being carved out of the moment. Chor was the only naked man I wanted to touch, and I sensed the intelligence of my desire. Spirit was demanding a tighter alchemical container for our passion. I didn't know exactly how it would work, but I knew that I would have to abandon my temple work in order to experience the wedding whispered by my visions and the depths of sacred union with Chor that my soul longed for. This was what was right *for us,* as unique beings in a new era together. It was also high time for me to evolve professionally. I was ready to express my talents in different ways. I would let all the logistical possibilities percolate in my dreams. And I would keep dancing—and making chocolate.

We surrendered to sleep. Sated and free.

CHAPTER 43
BAPTISMAL WATERS

"Have we forgotten the true source of our yearning? Take note of who birthed you and reclaim your source."
— MIRIAM ELYSE

"Dare to declare who you are. It is not far from the shores of silence to the boundaries of speech. The path is not long, but the way is deep. You must not only walk there, you must be prepared to leap."
— HILDEGARD VON BINGEN

IT WAS OUR last day there—and the first day of our limitless forever. We were each to have a spiritual shower, a traditional Bwiti cleansing and blessing ritual. What would it be like to be bathed of the past? Our curiosity was piqued.

The ancient protocol, Moughenda explained, called for a nearby river. We'd enter the water with one set of clothing; then after being bathed, we'd change into a new set. We'd leave the old clothing behind, along with the past. When we walked away from the river, Moughenda emphasized, we could not look back. The spiritual shower would mark the completion of our work there and the segue back into the world.

After breakfast we joined our crew at the guest-house for the daily jokes and deep wisdom. "What happens in the Bwiti rite of passage?" I asked Moughenda.

"Oh, they break you down. They break you good!" He spoke with zeal, like this was a joyous thing. "They scare you! They make you think you're gonna die! But you don't die," continued Moughenda, chuckling. "After they break you down, they build you back up again."

"Yeah!" said Chor, smiling. "I wanna do it! Let's go!" Ever the adventurer. Somehow I sensed that the rite of passage would be more intense than an upside down zip line ride for tourists in Costa Rica.

I imagined this would be a test of strength, a ritual ego death, and an initiation into adult tribal life. My mind reeled with possibilities.

Michael pulled out a laptop to show videos of their trips to Africa. Bwiti women taught their earthy dance to awkward initiates, barefoot on the dirt, their hips shaking in complex rhythms. Children played against the backdrop of lush jungle. At night, the tribe drummed and danced by firelight, covered in leaves, grasses, brilliant colors. Vivifying music and broad smiles abounded. *Yes, we are going there.*

"In my vision, you married us," Chor said. "Moughenda, can you marry us—in Africa?" Chor and I looked at each other. Yes, I told Chor with my eyes.

"Yeah!" said Moughenda, enthusiastically. "We can do that! We can get shamans from all the nearby tribes to come and participate. It's a big deal. It's like three days long!" he smiled.

"Wow, that's a party!" I said.

"Yeah. And..." Moughenda paused, "in this ceremony, there is no divorce!"

"Yeah, no divorce!" Chor said with force, joy, and clarity in his voice. "You ready for that, loveness? No divorce?"

"Yes." I said firmly, looking back into his soul.

Then unexpected guests arrived. Seemingly out of nowhere, a young couple with two small children wandered up to the guesthouse on foot. "Is this...Iboga House?" asked the man with a raspy, wavering American accent. Despite being fairly clean cut, he looked weak and weathered. His red, hungry eyes leaked pain. I could see the heroin all over him with my clean eyes.

"Yes! Yes it is!" said Michael and Moughenda, almost in unison.

"Thank God. Thank God. Bless you. We made it!" said the man, hanging onto life by a thread. "I'm Joseph. This is my wife, Katherine, and our children, Naomi and Sammy." Katherine looked exhausted, but she was clearly sober. They held the hands of their beautiful, cherubic-looking children.

"Please come in!" said Michael. "How did you get here?"

"We took a bus from San José. I'm begging. I need help," said Joseph. "I don't have much money."

"You don't need to beg," chuckled Moughenda. "I'm going to help you. We'll work things out later. Can we film you for an initial interview? This will help other people."

"Yes, anything you need," said Joseph.

"Chor, can you help film?" asked Moughenda, as he handed him an iPad.

"Yeah, sure," Chor said, standing ready and alert.

"Tell us a little about yourself and what's bringing you here," said Moughenda. Joseph shared openly, as if relieved to spill all that he'd been holding in. The children played on the floor with a few toys that Michael had procured. They seemed utterly oblivious to the tragic details of the adult conversation.

"I'm addicted to heroin. I'm using at least a gram a day. I know I am gonna die if I go on like this. Soon. I have these two beautiful children. I wanna see them grow up. I can't take this bondage anymore. I don't know where else to go. My wife found this place."

"We didn't even know if you'd be here," said his Katherine, "but the situation just got to be so urgent. I feel so terrible...I encouraged him to wait to get off the junk, because it was bad timing. We couldn't afford the time off work, but then he just couldn't go on any longer."

"OK," said Moughenda. "You came to the right place," he assured them warmly. He motioned for Chor to hand over the iPad so he could check the footage.

Chor took the opportunity to speak up. "I was in your place a few days ago, man. I was headed toward destruction."

"What?" said Joseph, wide eyed and befuddled. "But you look...so...good!" And Chor did look good. He beamed—happy, healthy, and squeaky clean. He actually looked like he'd just rolled out of a triathlon— and a great facial.

"Believe me," continued Chor, "in a couple days, you are going to feel better than you ever have in your whole life."

"Really?" said the astonished mystery man, lighting up with a spark of hope as he stood at the gates of hell. "What about withdrawals?" he implored.

"There are no opiate withdrawals with iboga," I assured him. "There's a detox, for sure, but no withdrawal symptoms."

"What?" his jaw dropped. "No withdrawals?"

"Yep."

"Oh my God. Thank you, thank you, thank you," he whimpered.

"You just gotta be 110% honest with yourself," advised Chor. "Give up all the ego and pride. Just open your heart and open your mind." I looked at Chor with awe. He was already stepping into service. I saw the budding healer in him, the holy man, the guide.

I recognized that it's never enough just to heal ourselves. Complete healing happens when we share our particular medicine with others. Service is the final and everlasting phase of healing.

"You ready to take your medicine tonight?" Moughenda asked the man with a big smile.

"Yes!" said the man, enthusiastic and depleted all at once.

"Good. Good. You're gonna be OK, man," assured Moughenda, smiling.

"Am I going to trip out?" Joseph asked, with just

the hint of a grin. "Is this *psychedelic?*"

"It's visionary," responded Chor, "but it's not for kicks. This is not like acid or some kind of casual trip. This is deep, man. You are gonna get schooled."

"Wow," pondered Joseph.

"You two can go relax and get ready for your spiritual shower," Michael told Chor and I. "Be sure to wear something you can leave behind," Michael reminded us. "We'll be back soon. We are gonna take our guest to our doctors to get his EKG and full physical," he said cheerfully, with a wink. "His first ceremony will be tonight!"

We had a leisurely lunch as the kitchen staff whipped up extra meals for our guests. Soon enough our stewards returned. Joseph had the green light for his treatment, and we were all excited for his imminent transformation.

Michael stayed with Joseph while Moughenda and Ann-Marie drove us to our spiritual shower. Moughenda pulled over and parked on the side of a remote jungle road. As we walked along, Moughenda picked many kinds of wild plants, inhaled their natural perfume, and pressed them into his hands. He started handing them off to Ann-Marie to carry. "There's good fresh herbs here! Beautiful herbs!" he said.

Moughenda plucked one delicate, young branch of tiny leaves and suddenly slapped it up against Chor's shoulder. It left an exquisite pattern of white dust imprinted on his arm. "Oh, that would make a nice tattoo," I said.

"Yeah, it would," he said. "We should both get one." Our eyes locked. Committed, clean, surrendered to love. Riding impermanence, in holy union. Here we go.

The sound of rushing water welcomed us. Moughenda went ahead of us, disappearing down a stone path leading to the river below. We followed and found him wading into a shallow part of the river. He artfully arranged the fresh plants he'd gathered into two separate mounds on a large, flat boulder. He lit a white candle nearby.

"Come down into the river and face me," Moughenda said to us. We walked in ankle deep; Chor and I stood side by side. I wore a long, thin dress adorned with exotic prints. Chor wore black boxers. Ann-Marie waited nearby, ready to assist as she studied the ritual. Moughenda began to sing a soft, enchanting song in his African language. He took one mound of the prepared plants and plunged it into the river in front of Chor. He shredded and softened the greenery with his hands. Moughenda was absorbed in his task as he sang.

Moughenda took the dripping mass of plants and held it over Chor's head. Chor eyes widened as the cool, aromatic water awakened his senses. Moughenda sang as he doused and scrubbed Chor's face, arms, legs, belly, back, and chest with the plants. He dipped the plants into the river again and then firmly drummed Chor's heart several times with his plant-filled palm, just as the goddess had done to me in my vision. Moughenda flung the excess water forcefully behind Chor into the river, as if to discard any last drops of darkness downstream. Chor took deep, intentional breaths.

Then Moughenda took Chor's hand and filled it with the cleansing plants and instructed, "Now clean yourself." I looked steadily forward into the oncoming river, into the future, into the destiny that awaited us if we walked the path that the medicine had offered to us. I could see Chor out of the corner of my eye, attending to his baptism with care. He packed the plants into his shorts and thoroughly washed his penis, pelvis, and buttocks.

Yeah, baby, get all those ghosts off you.

He washed his head, neck, and hands, finally sitting down in the river to wash his feet, thoroughly absolving every inch of his precious body.

Moughenda came over in front of me and looked me in the eyes. His magical song activated the moment; the water felt more refreshing, the air sweeter. He began to cleanse me in the same way. The pristine water poured over my crown, washing away my limited thinking. He scrubbed the burdens from my shoulders and the cynicism from my forehead and the stagnant habits from my hands.

The fragrance of the moist, crushed greenery was intoxicating, pure, fresh. These plants in the river water felt cleaner than soap.

Moughenda dipped the plants again and tapped my heart open, cleansing the fresh wound inflicted by Chor's transgressions. Our past was carried downriver, to be composted and purified in the belly of the earth.

Moughenda then handed me my earthen washcloth to complete my bath. I kneeled into the baptismal river. I washed away the residue of shame from my holy yoni lips and inner thighs. I washed my feet along with the passages of yesteryear. I plunged the plants under my neckline and sanctified my breasts.

As Chor and I washed ourselves, Moughenda gathered fresh river water into his cupped palms and

drenched us over and over. We gasped for air in between
the cool splashes. I held the crushed plants in front of
my face and breathed them in to bathe my lungs.

"Now stand back up," Moughenda guided. "Let
your plants go into the river behind you, through your
legs. Remember, *don't look back!* Not even a glance!" Our
plants floated behind us, into the stream of eternity. "Now
pour the fresh water onto yourself as I did." We gathered
the wet life force in our bowled hands and showered ourselves again. Clean bodies. Clean minds. Virgin hearts.

Moughenda ascended the stone stairs back to the
road. Ann-Marie respectfully turned her back to give
us privacy as we changed into our new clothes. We
left our old clothes on a tree branch. I imagined some
fairy would make good use of the abandoned threads.
We made our way back up to the road. "Let's go!" said
Moughenda, smiling, delighted with a job well done.

I clutched my king's arm, and we marched in sync
back to our chariot.

—

Back in our room, Chor and I dressed for dinner. "I
have to talk to Moughenda," I said. "I have to tell him...
about my dakini work." I was feeling that inner green
light to share the sensitive information. I knew I had
great changes to make, and I wanted Moughenda's perspective. I also needed to know that he'd take me on as
an apprentice, colorful past and all.

"I still don't understand why you kept this so secret,
if it's so sacred and good," Chor said. It was a point he
couldn't seem to grasp, and every time he mentioned it I

felt a little thorn in my heart. He wasn't understanding me.

"I kept it secret for the same reason why Moughenda kept his treatments in New York City a secret. He had to, in order to protect it. These forms of healing work are still controversial." Maybe he would finally understand, I thought, with that comparison.

"This country has yet to decriminalize desire," I elaborated. "People are still legally persecuted for giving or receiving professional sensual care. This should be a basic adult freedom. I've known gifted and sincere dakinis who've been raided and arrested for offering their beautiful work. Others have been discriminated against; they've been barred from other academic or professional pursuits. Others have been judged and branded socially. Many people need us, and yet the mainstream persecutes us. I always kept it a secret not because I'm ashamed, but because it's precious and vulnerable. I needed to protect this work, and I needed to protect myself."

Chor shook his head. He still didn't get it. He repeated his simple philosophy.

"Yeah, you're right," I said, "I shouldn't have to keep it a secret—in a perfect world. I know that one day we will evolve, I saw it in my vision. We're just not quite there yet."

I let it go for the moment. He let it go for the moment. We sighed and wove our hands together.

❧

Chor and I walked over to the guesthouse at sunset to see Moughenda. We had agreed to share our testimonial on film. We wanted to give something back to others. We sat down in front of the camera. Light was fading fast. We looked at each other for a flash; then...action! Our testimonial came out concise and potent.

I started speaking, without hesitation. "My husband relapsed on heroin after many years of being clean. When he first told me, I was saddened to learn that heroin addicts have a 90% chance of relapse in the first year, even in the best rehabs...." I continued with my tale.

Chor sat next to me and spoke in turn, baring his truth for all the world to see. "I went back into lesson. I disrespected myself. I disrespected my wife. I disrespected women...." We told our whole story in a nine-minute nutshell.

"Good job, guys! Thanks!" said Moughenda. "Check it out." We peeked at a few seconds of the footage. Yes, it would speak to the people that were ready to hear it.

"Moughenda," it was time for me to reveal. "I need to tell you about a private part of my life. I don't generally share it until I really trust people...."

"Oh, yes?" he said, curious and attentive.

"There is one more kind of work that I've had, in addition to my work with yoga, dance, and holistic health coaching. It's very...unusual...and very beautiful, to me.

"A long time ago, I apprenticed with a tantric priestess. She was a shaman, of sensuality. She taught me the practices that can transform sexual energy into spiritual energy. And she taught me the art of sensual healing touch. It's a very taboo idea for some people." Moughenda took in my wild tale. His face remained calm, open, and kind. I continued.

"That work has been so good, but now it's time to let it go, for my own evolution—and for the evolution of my relationship. The medicine guided me. And I need to know if you would still accept me as an apprentice."

"Well, this is good." he said, "I hate surprises! I am glad you are telling me now."

I knew that Moughenda must have heard a lot of things, but probably not anything like this. "In Bwiti, we don't tell people what to do," he emphasized again. "I can only offer advice, then you go see for yourself. Find your own truth!"

His advice started with a question, perhaps the best form advice can take. "When you are really and truly in love with someone, and your love is mutual and strong, don't you naturally want to share all your love with that person?" I looked at Chor with my purified eyes. His face was so ancient. So familiar. This was no ordinary lover. This was my twin flame, my mate, my ultimate consort. My heart melted. Yes, this was true, for us at least, and Moughenda knew it. I wanted to give Chor all of me. I wanted to share every hot moment with him. I wanted to need only him. He looked into me. Ditto, he said with his eyes.

"Yes," I answered Moughenda.

I continued, "It's also how I've made my living, and I don't know exactly what's next. I feel like I'm jumping off a cliff into the unknown." I looked at Chor. "I'm going to need more support from you, baby. I've been carrying the brunt of the bills for so long, and frankly it's taken a toll on me. It's not good for team spirit.

"And there's more. There is a priestess in me that was born to share these intimate arts, like there is a painter in you. All my treasures are for you now." Chor nodded, receiving my expression.

"Ah, money. Don't worry about money," advised Moughenda. "Every day, follow the medicine. And you make a plan. Me, I'm a hunter. I make a plan and keep my eye on the target. You can do that. Make a plan and keep your eye on the target.

"And...you gotta love money. I mean really *love* money, but without being *attached* to money. You gotta know your higher purposes for money, but don't have fear around money. You receive it and let it go and enjoy it."

"OK," I said reluctantly. I was still stuck in some limited thinking, but I was willing to crack my mind open enough to entertain some fresh possibilities.

"Love," said Chor, looking into me, "Love is the answer...to everything." I grasped his panther paw and took a deep breath. He spoke the simple truth. Maybe the road wouldn't be that simple. Then again, maybe it would be.

Chapter 44

Healing The Future

"If we doctors threw all our medicines into the sea, it would be that much better for our patients and that much worse for the fishes."
— Supreme Court Justice Oliver Wendell Holmes, MD

Our last fire ceremony had arrived. Ann-Marie and Michael were both present. One of the medical doctors that Moughenda regularly worked with had decided to join us.

Joseph was already laid out in the open temple behind us, his candle placed behind him. He churned and cooed and sighed. "Whoah," he would occasionally utter. He actually sounded like he was experiencing some bliss. Good for him.

"Joseph's wife is putting their kids to bed in the guesthouse," shared Moughenda. "How are you two doing?" Moughenda asked us.

"Good!" we said, as one. "I feel clean and new and ready," I said, "ready for our new life."

"Yeah!" Chor concurred. "I'm a new man. I'm so grateful."

"OK, you two," Moughenda addressed us. "You take this experience and these teachings back home—and back into the matrix. Support each other. Remember, happy thoughts are the best medicine for the mind," he emphasized. "You are artists of your thoughts!"

Moughenda leaned forward, as if to share a secret. The flames grew in the fire pit, licking up toward the sky. "The medicine will keep teaching you. You have to listen closely."

Moughenda straightened up and looked around the circle. "Everyone, we have a guest here tonight, Dr. Rodriguez."

"Hello," said the doctor as he nodded kindly in our direction.

"Dr. Rodriguez, how are you? What brings you here tonight?" asked Moughenda.

"Thank you, Moughenda. I'm here to sit and talk and be with all of you. I have felt the call to experience this medicine. I've seen so many healing miracles here, things I couldn't have imagined were possible." He paused and looked down, pensive.

"I feel hindered sometimes, as a doctor," he said, lingering on an edge within himself. "There are so many ailments that I cannot heal. We, the doctors, cannot truly heal people, in a lot of cases, except for the broken bones and stitches and a few emergency procedures. I went to medical school because I wanted to heal people, and we are so limited by the confines our institutional education and the powers of the pharmaceutical companies. We just end up with this palette of pills to give people, and they all have terrible side effects that create a chain reaction of other ailments.

"I want to *really heal* people. I want to understand the healing arts that you hold, Moughenda. And I am looking forward to experiencing this medicine soon."

Moughenda sat thoughtfully and responded, "There is a new time coming. More and more people will learn about this medicine. More and more people will want true healing. We will need many good doctors on our side. The earth gives us everything we need for healing. And Western medicine has certain gifts, of course. We can work together. And we will need some good apprentices!" said Moughenda, as he smiled at us.

"You two get a little booster, a homeopathic dose," Moughenda smiled at Chor and me, as he rifled through his little wooden box of capsules. He carefully chose one for each of us and handed them to Michael to deliver to us. "Chor, this will help to heal your wound from the sea urchin. Elizabeth...this will just help!"

Joseph purred softly in the background, as he shifted endlessly in his bed. "Ah...this is...amazing," he crooned. We all smiled, sharing the cosmic inside joke, the ineffable joy, the inner miracle.

—

We nestled in and savored our last night out of the rat race. I wondered, how would Chor be, back in his flow of things? How solid was this healing? How would our lives change?

Only one way to find out.

I felt our homeopathic dose of medicine. It was

barely perceptible, but it would be just enough to bring the spirit of the medicine into our journey home.

CHAPTER 45

RETURN TO
SO-CALLED REALITY

*"We live in a culture where everything tastes good
but nothing satisfies."*
— DANIEL PINCHBECK

*"All desires are the inappropriate substitute for the desire
to be at one with God."*
— RUSSELL BRAND, REVOLUTION

EARLY MORNING. Clocks and phones existed again. Time to reenter the matrix.

We packed up and drank in another view from our deck, doing our best to memorize the scene and take it with us. I stretched in and out of a few yoga poses as I basked in the morning light. I'd made it eight days without caffeine and chocolate, the longest run I'd had in years. Stripped of my trivial yet constant crutch, I felt delicious in my body, attuned to natural rhythms, energized yet calm.

Moughenda gave us a ride back into the metropolis. We walked into the human swarm. I could see people in a new way with my new eyes. I could see each person's flavor of sadness or joy. I could see their

particular poison and the well-worn stories spinning in
their heads. Ruddy, swollen skin on some faces begged
for alcohol. The grey hue of others revealed the perpet-
ual longing for the next cigarette. The weathered, gaunt,
scabby skin of one arguing couple whispered of meth-
amphetamines. Almost everyone had a monkey on their
back, laughing from the other side of an unseen veil:
Cheetos, chocolate, porn, money, fancy purses, or the
illusion of control. For a few, their pleasure was prayer.

The truth became clear to my inner eye; addiction
begins with the seed of desire—for satiation, peace,
pleasure, transcendence, union, and ultimately, love.

Desire is the very essence of embodiment. All
things are born of desire, and all things are sustained
by desire. There is no crushing desire. And there is no
transcending desire, except for temporary exalted stints.
We can only honor it and guide it and love it.

Yes. Love...is the answer.

To walk the path of celebrating life, we must meditate upon our desires, our heart's true and essential
desires, every day. We must ask ourselves: *Why* do I
desire that particular thing or person or experience? We
must keep asking, until we reach the root of all desires,
until we are left looking into the face of love itself.

Through practice and purification, returning to love
again and again, we can transform desire itself into an
offering, and addiction into devotion.

—

We settled in for the plane ride home. This time, I nestled

onto my love's shoulders to find his warm, welcoming fingers stroking me. "I'm excited to go home...to our new life," I said. I thought of our bed, are critters, our little kitchen, our rhythm—all seen with our fresh view.

"Yes, loveness, me too," he said.

"Are you gonna tell the world about what you went through?" I asked.

"I have to," said Chor.

CHAPTER 46
SEEDS OF
SYNTHESIS

"The evaluation of entheogens needs to be in terms of how productive these experiences are for healthier approaches to the issues of living in these times, in this world."
— RALPH METZNER

WE MELTED into our bed after a long day of travels. That first morning back home, Chor showered me with sweet, warm, soul-quenching kisses. He leapt out of bed, buoyant and joyous. He went straight out to the backyard and took a deep breath. He gazed at the trees with awe.

I joined him outside. He saluted the morning as he had done in Costa Rica, bringing his palms to his heart in prayer, then throwing his arms wide open. "I love my life!" he exclaimed. My love had new wings.

"Share. Listen to her. Honesty. Tell the truth...." He softly uttered the messages that the medicine had given him, taking deep breaths between each one.

He turned to me. "Let's meditate—every day," he suggested, "together." We sat before my altar, which had previously been my solo zone. This sacred art installation was an organic expression of all the traditions that mingled in me. Tibetan and Hindu deities, Native American sweetgrass braids, palo santo wood, an Egyptian statue of Bast, a vial of water from the Ganges River, small works of art, and other sacred objects sat together peacefully in this universal shrine.

"I need to be in there, too," said Chor, looking at my altar. "I know just the thing." He traipsed upstairs and returned with his signature collectible can of Spanish Montana spray paint. It had been smeared with red paint during a racy art video we'd made together for its promotion, blessed traces of our colorful co-creation. "Here's me." And he placed the can next to the Bast statue on the altar.

We sat for meditation, watching the brilliant and endless spinning of our own minds. I felt his breath. He felt mine. We savored a sweet, silent awareness of each other. Occasionally, one of us would take a deeper breath to return to mindfulness, and it was a two-for-one deal. A radiant sphere pulsated between us. I felt a new force in meditation that I hadn't ever felt in quite the same way before: synergy.

Kyle returned to our home later that day. He had been able to stay with his dad for our healing retreat. My heart melted into rosewater as I watched Chor welcome him with open arms. "Hey, man. Good to see you," Chor said. Kyle stepped back and looked at him with one raised eyebrow. The Chor he knew didn't offer warm hugs. Chor just enfolded him in his state of shock and shook him up with some manly pats. "Hey, I want you to know. I'm your dad, too. I'm not just your stepdad. I'm your other dad. I'm sorry for the way I've been. We're gonna change the vibe in this house."

"Okaayyy," said Kyle, stunned. "What happened to you?" he asked with some cooler-than-thou teen attitude, before scampering up to his room.

We made dinner together that night. This ordinary act was a miracle for us. We both chopped and stirred and experimented. Chor proved to possess the same creative genius in the kitchen with veggies and tempeh as he did with spray paint. We sat down at the table and lit a candle and prayed. We looked at each other and talked about our day.

⌒

The days rolled on. The beauty only magnified. We moved through our days in sync, sharing that certain kind of silent communication that only mated beings can have. New rituals formed fluidly. Each day, Chor would wake me with a shower of kisses. We'd migrate outside to our backyard to gawk at the miraculous trees that he'd been overlooking for so long. We'd utter prayers and cleanse our lungs with breath work and drink down a big glass of warm water. Then we'd sit for meditation. Some people might call all of this discipline, but it was simply superlative pleasure.

"I love taking good care of myself!" he'd say with delicious enthusiasm.

"Meditation before the matrix!" became our household slogan. The devices and the rat race would have to wait until after our morning practices, when we were well rooted in our hearts and attuned to the universe.

Nature called. We'd take a walk after meditation on most days. Chor continued to look at mama nature with a green reverence. Chor started photographing flowers. We couldn't walk or even drive by any great flowers without him saying, "Ooo, ooo! Stop! Let me get a shot of those."

His tastes had indeed evolved. Chor played the Bwiti music daily. He grew a new appreciation African Pygmy music, African jazz, and many forms of traditional world music. His favorite flavors of hop-hip were conscious rhyme and lyrical activism. The horror movies died along with the drug addiction. The house would no longer be filled with shrieks of pain.

After six years of unaccepted invitations, Chor finally fell madly in love with yoga. This physical and spiritual discipline helped to further integrate the gifts of the medicine into his daily life. I loved feeling him practice next to me. I loved hearing his artful breath and glimpsing his glittering strength out of the corner of my eye. I loved sensing his inner journey, so close to mine. He inspired me. He charged me up. And I had a feeling it was mutual. More synergy.

My own yoga practice became ever more luscious. Limbs and joints and breath were liberated and celebrated beyond previous milestones. My mantra practice deepened; the medicine had unlocked greater mental freedom and focus. The different paths were mingling happily within me.

—

"Let's create canvases with the messages from our journey and place them all over our house!" Chor suggested. He spray-painted bright backgrounds on a bunch of tiny canvasses. We both painted them with festive lettering:

Celestial

Listen to Her

Learn from Her

SHARE

You are You

Slow Down

Honesty

I know myself

Life is a gift

Let it go

Tell the Troof!

LOVE is the Answer

We framed a picture of Moughenda as a daily reminder to appreciate our miracle and live in a sacred way. Chor wanted even more souvenirs, so he promptly tattooed "IBOGA" and "LOVE" onto his neck in thick, dark script. Nothing like a neck tattoo as a note to self. They were a blessing for me as well, for they graced my gaze every time I looked at his radiant face.

⟂

Chor immediately translated his iboga blessings into a series of paintings, *Love Visions,* all masterpieces of visual medicine. Spirited, benevolent African faces donning ceremonial adornments looked straight into the viewer: challenging, inviting, and celebrating life. Rays of shimmering light emanated from their third eyes and flowed across multidimensional landscapes. White hearts bounded across the canvases, shamelessly joyful. Gazing at them, I experienced the same dynamic combination of unbounded flight and deep stillness that I had in our ceremonies.

Next, expanding on the series, Chor painted portraits of mystical mortal goddesses, expressing his baptized perception of women and his deepened respect for their inherent earthly divinity. Love lasers burst from their chakras, and they seemed to levitate amidst a backdrop of stars and Chor's signature Boogie Birds. The women were everyday saints of every color and shape, simultaneously regal, sensual, and sacrosanct.

This book poured out of me, and it flowed so fast that I felt like I wasn't writing it. I was tapping into some universal source, beyond my personal imagination. I felt like a divine writing utensil. This story wanted to tell itself.

Our artistic mediums helped us to turn our raw experience into tangible treasures that would reflect back the light of our visions for years to come.

—

Love Man was busy. He preached nondenominational and unconditional love in his casual conversations and public postings. He began filling his social media feeds with messages of inspiration and gratitude along with his fresh iboga-inspired art—and photos of all the flowers he'd fallen in love with.

GIVE THANKS.

Love.

Practice daily.

What are you manifesting?

Chor utilized his public voice to share openly about his relapse and the miraculous medicine. We both did. We aired all our dirty laundry in order to hopefully save some lives and contribute our two cents to the collective awakening.

Chor birthed the public campaign of love that he had dreamed up in Costa Rica. From the rooftops of the public internet, he sang the praises of our relationship and shared sweet photos of us. "We gotta get a picture with our wedding rings together!" Chor said excitedly. He shared: "MARRIED WITH LOVE...I am announcing to the world I am HAPPILY married to my goddess Queen @enectarbast. Been together for 7 years 'til infinity.... Our official ceremony will be in GABON AFRICA. ONE LOVE. I love her because I love myself."

"Show 'em how it's done, baby," I said, touched. "On behalf of lovers everywhere, thank you for honoring your queen." His public professions made the world a sweeter and more noble place, and they helped to nurse my healing heart back to robust health. I was no longer the invisible heartbeat of his life. Queens like to be crowned, of course.

The past, smothered in love, fades into oblivion.

Chor sat at his freshly organized desk, very busy spreading all the love, when I glanced into his closet. After returning from Costa Rica, he had purged a lot of old clothes. What remained sat in neatly folded stacks. "Ha!" I started laughing.

"What?" he asked.

"*That's* what the medicine did to your head!" I said, pointing to his clean closet. He chuckled. It was true. As above, so below. The state of the closet is the same as the brain.

"We should have a date day every week!" Chor suggested.

"Yes, pleeez!" I shivered with delight. So we found a new religion, our date day. Sometimes a hike, restaurant, movie, yummy mutual massage, or all of the above. This was romantic indulgence and so much more, for I knew that we were cultivating gold together. Our delight and devotion would eventually magnetize us for greater and greater abundance.

Chor became more and more artistic with his touch, and I marveled at his virtuoso in this medium. He received my guidance in the inner yogas of tantra, and the priestess in me purred. It felt right as rain to shower my lover with all of these intimate gifts, as he had become so willing to receive them.

"Wow, baby," he said after making some luscious love. "You're different now." We quickly discovered that my body had changed. It was as if some internal scar tissue had melted away. When we made love, I could take him deeper, wilder. I still enjoyed my refined sensitivity, but I could more easily receive his raw, primal power. My body felt ripe, luxurious, juicy.

I felt spirit drawing our beings together, ever closer, to create new life, be it in the form of human babies or creative offspring. *Soon.* Spirit wanted to crack me all the way open. The way had been cleared, and we were finally ready to merge completely.

The medicine had sensitized me, as well as Chor. Simple pleasures held my attention, even more than before. A sweet breeze or the sight of a tree or a kiss would overwhelm me with beauty. I could feel my dopamine flowing abundantly. My adrenal glands felt replenished. My natural energy had returned.

I felt the redwood tree presence living within me. I summoned it to center stage when I needed strength, patience, or acceptance.

Each night before sleep, we sat side by side in our bed and prayed in silence. I practiced the daily review that Moughenda had taught us—with a twist of gratitude. I'd add a "thank you" for every event that happened that day, then I'd let it all go. Feelings of warmth would flood my being. I felt the healing power of this practice in my body as my breath deepened, oxytocin gushed, and heartbeat relaxed.

"You've been touching me more," I told Chor one day. "You've been kissing me and hugging me. You've been speaking to me with such kindness. You are here, now, and you are being real with me. These little things are better than diamonds. I don't feel lonesome for you anymore." I realized, for the first time ever, I felt truly unified. "I'm all yours now, love."

More and more I started to overhear, "Let me talk to my wife about this, and I'll get back to you." When opportunities for travel came up for Chor, he started consulting with me about them instead of just telling me. And he would find a way to include me. If he did travel on his own, he'd keep it short and sweet. We didn't want to go more than a week or two apart. We wanted to nourish strong roots.

This new depth of intimacy was simultaneously comfortable and uncomfortable, but it was a good uncomfortable, the kind we all experience when building new muscles. We were two tigers in a tight room: no escape, no distractions, no leaks. No groupies and no acolytes. Every human poison was brought to the surface to be viewed and purified. We had become infinitely more intertwined in every aspect of human life. My heart seemed to expand beyond my little body. My ego's armor was fading away.

Two lights became one and entered the infinite.

—

"You know, I spent a lot of money partying," Chor confessed to me one afternoon, as we were discussing our upcoming Iboga training. "It was ridiculous. I could have paid for my whole training that we are going to do, and then some. But I was learning lessons."

I was amazed to hear about these secret splurges, as he'd always been so religiously frugal, but not entirely surprised, considering how sick he was. "Wow," I said, feeling all the extra hours of labor on my shoulders with which I carried the household. A spark of resentment flashed and then immediately burned up in my deep breaths.

He's being honest with me, I reminded myself. *He's a new man.*

Money. The topic had been building pressure for a long time. I had to talk about it. Could I say it without exploding?

"Love, we need a revision of our household finances," I said, with neither fire nor ice in my voice. "I've been feeling it for a while. We need to be in this together."

Before I could say anything more, he calmly said, "I know. I feel it. I'm going to give more." I sighed, feeling the burden already falling away. He was stepping up as a husband and a king. We would soon share everything, taking the medicine's invitation to heart.

⸺

I had to swiftly transition out of my dakini work, though I was still a devotee of the dakinis. I was called to deepen my service as a facilitator and an activist. A natural new sense of openness manifested in regards to sharing about these chapters of my life. Free and clear of it, I could speak out—without fear of the pleasure police breaking down my door. More importantly, the quiet voice of the medicine prompted me: It's time to be loud about this.

I wasn't quite sure what was coming next, professionally. There would be fleeting worries about finances; then I would engage my new inner dialogue:

STOP!

And say the truth:

I am open to miracles.

I am open to all my needs being met in a good way.

I am open to the wisdom of the medicine.

Other realms of work blossomed for me. New

opportunities appeared as if out of a mist. Magic was afoot. New yoga students manifested. I scheduled more teachings, and they tended to fill to the brim. I made mounds of my artisanal organic chocolates, and gave them away at every opportunity. They were always a magical cherry on top of all my other creations. I sensed that they pollinated the prosperity of every project, like all sweet and sincere gifts.

Chor and I dreamed up new art collaborations. "She's so...BEAUTIFUL," I gasped as Chor painted on a life-size photograph I had taken, depicting a graceful naked Madonna. Chor gave her the visible halos and rays and lush mystical embellishments that I could only imagine. We unveiled her at the BALANCE show at 111 Minna Gallery in San Francisco. The exhibit also featured Chor's fresh visionary paintings of women from the *Love Visions* series, along with the sleek floral works of Jet Martinez.

For the opening reception, Chor painted me and my esteemed fellow performer, Lady Eternal Love, for an avant-garde burlesque piece. We transformed from veiled to unveiled, dark to light, whore to sacred mother—and everything in between, before dousing the audience in sweet feminine blessings: rose petals, feathers, oils, and fresh fruit sacrament.

The mutual idea erupted for me to serve as his executive assistant. I found that my passionate energy was just as activated in this new arena of business. My high-end client relations skills came in very handy; the dakini in me loved serving in an authentic way. Naturally, I could serve as my love's greatest advocate. I believed in him and protected him like no other. An inner spiritual compass led me to high frequency professional associates and fertile opportunities that were in alignment with the Beauty Way. This new path was illuminated by synergy and synchronicity, and, of course, love. I was shocked to discover that I actually enjoyed studying legal contracts and the esoteric inner workings of the fine art world.

Go figure. Mermaids can walk on land.

My presence magnetized substantial fresh abundance straight away. Apparently I was the professional genie that he'd been waiting for, and he was the benevolent king that I had needed all along. We'd been hiding, right next to each other, for years.

Sometimes, I learned, the answer to all your prayers is already there, perhaps even in your own bedroom, waiting for the right medicine and the willingness to take it.

The more we offered, the more was offered to us. The universe seemed to be conspiring to carry us, perhaps because we had so fully surrendered to it's auspicious current.

—

One day, while visiting a friend's housewarming party, I shared about iboga. I met a woman there who had been sober for three years after her iboga ceremony with another Bwiti provider.

"Everything changed for me at that point," she told me. "I no longer wanted to dishonor myself. The cravings left my body, though I had to make a lot of positive changes in order to stabilize my new life. I couldn't hang out with my drinking buddies anymore. I focused on my new business, which I loved. There was no more space in my life for destruction." This was familiar music to my heart. This was why I felt drawn to serve. I wanted to hear more stories like this. Yes, the medicine goes the distance.

The medicine was whispering, and I was listening closely:

Keep on keeping on this path of love.

CHAPTER 47

TEMPLE DANCE

"You must dance until everyone is completely intoxicated with LOVE."
— SHOSHANNA ROSE

"Today, I would describe a priestess as a woman who lives in two worlds at once, who perceives life on earth against a backdrop of a vast, timeless, reality."
— JALAJA BONHEIM, *APHRODITE'S DAUGHTERS : WOMEN'S SEXUAL STORIES AND THE JOURNEY OF THE SOUL*

W HERE ARE YOU, love?

From the balcony, I scanned the audience for my lover's face, the face I've been looking for since the beginning of time.

The stage lights cast a soft glow and heavy shadows onto the people. The room was slowly filling with the human hive. I watched the chaos transform into order as people filed to their places and took their seats. It was just minutes until show time. I called to Chor through the ethers.

Please, love, I need my king here by my side.

This night, one year ago, had been devastating. Never again, I thought.

This was a landmark. Our journey had come full circle. *May tonight be a crowning jewel for us,* I prayed.

This event was my gift to the community: the Nouveau Devadasi Fusion Temple Dance Festival. For three consecutive years, I had produced this series of workshops and performances celebrating traditional and fusion forms of temple dance. It was a labor of love, inspired by my first sacred dance teacher and my fellow modern temple dancers.

Master teachers of different sacred dance lineages would impart not only their choreography, but also the history, sacred myths, and esoteric teachings embedded in their mysterious movements.

I would witness the all-female student body tap into their authentic, volcanic, awakened femininity. They would take flight within their own skin and transform into unique goddesses before my very eyes.

We'd sit in circle and speak our truth, finding strength in solidarity. We'd make moving magic together and bear witness to each other's deeper beauty. Peace was cultivated within our own bodies as multiple traditions mingled.

That evening was the teachers' performance. I'd been carefully crafting my dance for weeks. It was my full-body prayer and ritual of transformation—inspired by my love for Chor. I would speak to my king with movement, let the world watch, and let the unseen heart nectar trickle out into all that is.

The previous year, the teachers' performance started much the same. I searched the darkened faces of the audience for Chor right before my dance, the last on the program, but I couldn't see him anywhere.

I finally saw him after my performance, wavering in the crowd as everyone was beginning to file out. He was drunk. "You were amazzzing. Yeah baby. Woo!" He was with an artist buddy of his who was equally tipsy. He'd arrived so late that he wasn't able to meet any of my revered allies, but when I saw him, I was glad that he hadn't.

After the performance that evening, I asked him to hang out and help me load up.

"Ah, love," he said, "there's this art opening tonight in the Mission. I really should stop by, just real quick. You are gonna be all right. I'll meet you at home, loveness."

"Love," I pleaded. "Please at least stay with me—and come home with me." I longed for his strength by my side at the end of that long day, even in his inebriated state. And I knew that if he ran off in that state, he'd likely launch into a terrible drinking binge. He wouldn't make it home until late, and when he did, he'd be a stinking handful.

"Na, loveness. Gotta do this. Don't worry. I'll be home soon." He pecked me on the cheek and bolted.

I made it home on my own. 2 a.m., I texted and called Chor a couple times. No answer. 3 a.m., still no Chor. I was exhausted, yet strung out on worry.

Where are you, love?

At 5 a.m., I worried for his life. He'd never stayed out so late. He'd never not responded to me. My panicked heart pounded in my chest along with every tick of the clock.

I called him again at 7 a.m. At last, he answered. "Oh...love!" he said, groggy. "Oh shit. What time is it?"

"It's 7 a.m. Where *are* you?"

"Oh, I passed out at Billy's house. I drank too much I guess."

"Jesus, Chor. I was worried sick! I couldn't sleep a wink. Now I have a full day of teaching ahead of me. How could you do this to me? And last night, of all nights?"

"Oh, baby. I'm sorry," he said.

"I'm just glad you are safe," I said with rough love. "When are you coming home? I need you to take care of the dog today, remember?"

"I'll be home soon, yeah. I got it." After my long day of teaching, I returned home at 9 p.m. to find that Chor had arrived just moments before me. Our dog had been stuck inside our house and hungry all day.

I found him in the bathroom, swaying as he pissed. He reeked of liquor. He was not only hung over; he was still drunk.

"What are you doing? I was counting on you! You left our poor dog inside all day."

"Ah. Relax. She's all right."

"What?" I asked, shocked at his blasé attitude. "I need to be able to count on you. I need you to take good care of our animals when you say you will."

After some confrontation, I drew an apology and a vow from him. Never again.

My king had lost his crown during my most important creation of the year.

—

It was a new night and a new year. "Chor is here!" said my fellow performer and dear friend, Aradia, as she peeked her head through the balcony door. "He's there, standing in the middle, against the wall." She pointed toward him with a little hop, excited for my excitement. She knew how much it meant to me that he was there, and strong.

My eyes followed her words and sure enough, there was my king. His eyes were scanning the room. He was searching for me, too.

I'm here, I said silently. His gaze finally found me on the balcony. I smiled.

I hurried down to greet Chor along with his uncle Douglas and aunt Esther. Chor's eyes sparkled as he poured adoring compliments on me. I blushed and beamed under his gaze like a flower under the sun. I threw my arms around him and tickled his cheek with my lashes. "I'm so glad you are here, love." *And radiant, regal, clean.*

I made my way to center stage. "Welcome, everyone. Thank you so much for coming to receive our offering. This is no ordinary dance performance....

"It is said of the devadasis of old India: just the dust from their feet was more precious than gold. Here is why. Each dancer has cultivated a unique shakti, or creative power. Everything around her becomes infused with it.

"Drink this shakti in with your breath. It is a blessing. Let the energy awaken your whole body and spark your heart and pollinate your life with beauty. This is how you receive a temple dancer."

An array of sacred dance forms lit up the night: classical Indian Odissi, Nepalese, Balinese, African fusion, Sufi spinning, Persian, Gypsy fusion, Buddhist Tara Mandala, temple bellydance fusion, and modern shamanic fusion.

When it came time for my turn, I stood behind the stage entrance, deepening my breath and slowing my heart rate and invoking divine energies into my body like a lightning rod. The words of my first dance teacher, ShoShanna Rose, echoed through my mind, "Intoxicate everyone with love."

The traditional Bwiti music began with the strumming of simple string instruments, rapid drumming, and wood-on-wood percussion. I walked in slow motion onto the stage with ceremonial Odissi steps. Following my own rhythm, time decelerated to a near standstill.

My fingertips cast invisible rose petals around the room through honoring mudras. My limbs and eyes and breath silently asked: *My love, Where are you in this forest of people?* My fingertips reached through the dark, honing in on Chor like a compass needle landing on North.

My palms turned up, questioning and challenging.

Are you ready to marry me in Africa?

My hips struck an invisible drum, awakening the earth. Slowly turning, my body began to spin, casting sparks around the room. I worshipped the audience with my eyes, yet returned my focus to Chor again and again, my king, my pillar, my redwood tree.

Look at me. I am celestial—and embodied.

My shoulders shook off the past like an old coat. My shimmies started a sacred fire.

Chor's eyes widened. His lips curled into a smile.

I slowly walked toward the back of the stage, reaching toward some unseen future. Then I looked back toward the audience, inviting.

Will you join me for the journey to this next horizon?

On the last beats, I tested my new visionary wings in the wind of my mind.

Let's fly.

CHAPTER 48

FAIRY TALE ENDING

"We are multidimensional beings living in a cyclical world. When we reject or ignore any part of ourselves or our experience, then dis-ease ensues. Embrace the dark and light equally, with breath, with 'yes,' with love."
— LUCID DAWN

"Love breaks my bones, and I laugh."
— CHARLES BUKOWSKI

DID WE LIVE "happily ever after?"

To tell the truth, it was no fairy tale, but true love is far more interesting than a Disney recipe.

We were still very human. We would still snicker about minor things (I want those lavender flower dryer packs for the laundry; he doesn't). We still had family squabbles and moments of duress. Kyle was keen to test the limits of Love Man. He pushed any button he could sniff out.

Those pesky negative thoughts would occasionally sneak in through some unattended back door in the brain, but we had become far more aware of their tricks. The medicine, the Bwiti teachings, and all the sweet spirits called into our ceremonies had blessed us with fresh strength, dexterity, and ingenuity. Our new tools were hardwired into us, present wherever and whenever we needed them. We were more aware of the menu for our inner state. Lots to choose from: 10,000 flavors of happiness—or misery.

We battled our demons daily, as a team. "Demons are really just angels in drag," I mused one day, from our new vantage point. "Those demons keep you on your toes. They test you. They make you build spiritual and mental and physical muscles. They complete the contrast in the great drama of life that seasons our soul."

"Eh. Demons are just demons," Chor growled. Yes, we balanced each other.

As we learned, iboga was no magic bullet, nor was it a cure-all, but it would be no fun if it were. The maturation of consciousness seemed to be the name of the game here on Earth, and that would not happen if an all-powerful pill could turn everyone into healthy robots. Iboga was indeed a miracle, and yet fully and forever participatory.

"FEAR, negative thoughts, I throw 'em in the trash can bomb! Psh!" Chor said one night as we lay in bed, throwing some imaginary mental refuse with his hand. "Then I just say the word 'LOVE' and they go away!" It was such a simple practice, yet I knew, the medicine helped to cleanse and rewire him enough to utilize it.

"I'm still a non-perfect human being," Chor admitted. "And at the same time, we are gods and goddesses. We need to respect that and know that and use that divine percentage of our brains.

"I am awake. And awakening. This medicine woke me up. After the fact, I'm still feeling good. The negative thoughts still come, but like Moughenda said to me, 'You already know what to do. You know the answers.'

"There's no more 'I hope' or 'I try.' There is only 'I know' and 'I do.' I make it happen. Now I practice the art of thinking. I don't let my mind control me. I control my mind. I love my life! I know who I am. I still go through things, but the desire to destroy myself is not there anymore.

"It not only detoxified my life; it detoxified our relationship." He held me tight and rocked me sweetly.

"I struggle with my mind sometimes, too," I shared. "I have smooth days and rough days. Ultimately, there are no 'good' days or 'bad' days—because I'm grateful for every single day!

"On smooth days, it's all inner sunshine. On rough days, our whole story hits me hard. This mischievous voice started up in my mind, saying, *You've missed out, hon. You have some catching up to do.'* It was so fleeting. I caught it. I know, chasing after empty adventures wouldn't help anything. Nothing would ever satiate or fulfill me like this pure love does."

Chor's eyes widened, perhaps surprised that I wasn't as strong as steel. "Demons," Chor said.

"I wouldn't really be catching 'up' with you anyway. I'd only be catching 'down' with you," I said, making light of my dark side. "Yeah, I catch those thoughts redhanded; then I return to my heart at lightning speed. My truth is here, now, with you, my reborn king."

We found that regular confession shined the light on any nonsense. "I looked at a little porn today," Chor would occasionally reveal.

"Oh?" I'd ask curiously. *Yeah, baby, I'm your best friend.* "Tell me more."

"It's so much less than before," he explained one day. "It's not fulfilling anymore. It's just a tired, old fix. There's still stuff to work on, and choices that we must make every day. I'm just glad that we are talking about everything now." I appreciated his openness. Porn was not deadly, at least. We could navigate that one together.

"What's the positive addiction that needs to be there?" I asked. "There's clearly a need revealing itself to you. I feel that humans actually need erotic stimulation, just as we are coded to need intellectual stimulation. We are driven to explore, in all realms. And more, we require regular relief from the tyranny of logic. Porn can definitely do all that, though most of it really is like junk food for the soul." I paused, contemplating. "Maybe there's some artistic or high-vibe porn out there somewhere?"

"Na. There's no 'good porn' out there," he said, but I wondered if perhaps he didn't know where to look. We scoured the internet together. It was true: finding amazing art porn was like searching for a needle in a haystack. We found a few crumbs, but not much more. So we created our own unfilmed porn in our bedroom. We attended to each other's needs and fantasies as erotic devotees. "Healthy, vegan, organic true-love porn just for you, baby," I joked via text when occasionally sending him homespun sexy pics.

Still, it was difficult to avoid factory-made porn entirely, as it infested nearly every click on the internet. Chor took it one day at a time, and I encouraged him to be compassionate with himself. "Focus on filling your time with fulfilling things," I offered. "And if you feel that sexual energy arising, don't suppress it. *Direct it.* Let it be jet fuel for your tantric practices."

⁓

As the weeks and routines rolled on, I would experience some aftershocks about Chor's cheating. I had forgiven him completely, but it wasn't an instant recovery for me. There was some primal reverb, for Chor had risked my life with his risky choices, as well as his own, and our triumph was still green.

There was no anger. No nasty comments. No withholding. Ultimately, I trusted the direction that spirit was guiding me. Yet, there was still a vigilant little bird in me that kept a lookout.

I didn't want to milk any sad stories. I wanted to get on with our sweet, carefree love, but it would simply take some time for me to get acquainted with the reborn Chor—and to feel his new strength in a wide variety of different terrains.

⁓

After our first few short trips apart, Chor asked repeatedly: "So...do you have anything to tell me?"

Am I missing something? I thought at first. "Let's see...I love you!" I'd answer.

Finally, he shared, "I figured you'd probably go and...do something. You sure you don't want...revenge?"

"No, love," I affirmed, emphatically. "I meant what I said. Revenge is a waste of my time. Don't you know that yet? And our clean slate is such a treasure."

Even with our profound healing experience, I learned that rebuilding trust, once punctured, is as delicate and organic of a process as reseeding a garden. Naturally.

—

"So...do you think he will cheat on you again?" asked a girlfriend one night, as we sat chatting over an intimate dinner.

The words flew out of my mouth, swift and straight from my heart. "It's not my job to worry about that," I said firmly. "It's my job to listen to spirit—every day."

CHAPTER 49
RUBBER MEETS THE ROAD

"I have figured out after all of these years of recovery that addiction is really a wild lust for life acting out, a seeking of the feeling of being fully alive gone awry. It went awry because of the fear and pain beneath it. Clear that old shaiza out and, YES! Lust for life!! So good...."
— NONA FENDER

"Live your YES."
— SOFIAH THOM

AFTER A FEW MONTHS, we could feel the strength of the medicine leaving our bodies. As I sat out in the backyard one day, watching the trees, I felt the last silent whispers of the plant teacher within me.

This is where the rubber meets the road.

This is when you feel the strength of your own legs as you walk the path.

Don't be attached, even to the medicine.

"You feel this, babe?" I asked Chor that night in bed. "The medicine is fading, but this is the time for us to walk on our own."

"Yeah," he said. "I feel that...and I feel steady on my path. *I am doing this, Elizabeth.*"

"A true medicine will lead you to the medicine within," I reflected.

We would stay connected to our inner medicine through meditation, yoga, prayer, love, clean living, good company, and the art of thinking.

Serving people was another mainline to the inner medicine. We spilled our story about iboga to anyone who would listen. The miracle wanted to be shared. Most people had never even heard of iboga. The few who had were generally misinformed. We offered information and resources to anyone who asked.

Chor and I made preparations to journey to Africa for our wedding and full initiation into the Bwiti tradition. "I can't wait to marry you in Africa," he said often, with zeal. We loved having this destination on our horizon.

CHAPTER 50
MESSENGER FROM BEYOND

"It's important that we share our experiences with other people. Your story will heal you and your story will heal somebody else. When you tell your story, you free yourself and give other people permission to acknowledge their own story."
— IYANLA VANZANT

M Y BIRTHDAY rolled around three months after we met iboga. Chor took me to my favorite hot springs resort, a quaint idyllic paradise.

Clusters of carefree beloveds sprawled on the lawn for picnics and soft chatter. Others lounged languidly in the mineral pools in various states of undress. A quiet reverence pervaded the otherwise Bacchanalian scene. No clocks. No wi-fi. No cell reception. No matrix. No electronic distractions of any kind. Only nature, healing waters, and naked love.

In the nourishing water, we became mermaid and merman, sliding over each other like sinuous strands of seaweed. I memorized every inch of his skin with my fingertips as we floated weightless. The heat melted our feisty minds. Our bodies soaked up sunshine. Time slowed down to the pace of pouring honey.

We re-attuned ourselves to nature. Our schedule for the day was determined solely by the natural intelligence of our bodily desires.

"Let's eat outside," Chor insisted when we made lunch. I smirked, as this had always been my line. Everything tasted better in the fresh air, serenaded by birds and kissed by breezes.

We explored the surrounding trails, all guarded by ancient redwoods. I snapped a photo of Chor in front of one old grandfather tree with a proud trunk as wide as a road. He leaned into its quiet strength as he posed for me, glowing and happy and peaceful.

Thank you, redwood medicine, for whispering to me from the very beginning.

We made love in the afternoon and napped in each other's arms. Our eyes opened to the sight of a mama dear and her three babies nibbling outside our cabin window. "Aaahh," said Chor. "I gotta get my camera!" Love Man loves nature.

Warm, clean, and calm, we were seduced into a deep and luxurious sleep that night.

Yes. This is what it's all about. The extraordinary beauty of the ordinary.

We savored our second day of soaking. As I left to head to the sauna for a while, I noticed Chor chatting to a lady in the outdoor tub next to his.

"That was crazy," Chor said, joining me in the sauna a few minutes later.

"What?" I asked.

"That lady I was talking to, she was apologizing. She said to me, 'Sorry for staring. Don't mind us, you just look so much like our brother. And he just passed away three weeks ago.' So I offered my condolences and asked them how he passed away. They told me, he died—of a heroin overdose." Chor and I took a reverent moment in silence for the fallen.

"Oh, love, that is humbling," I said.

"They are all here grieving together," Chor explained. "The mother and his two sisters. So I told them, I used to be addicted to heroin, too. It just felt right to share. Then I told them about iboga. I want to tell everyone. I explained that it's not only for addiction, but also for emotional and spiritual healing."

"So how did they take that?" I asked. I imagined that would have been quite a blow. They just lose their brother, and then their brother's doppelganger tells them about the antidote that might have saved his life.

"They were really grateful to know about iboga, and grateful for the connection. Then I told them, with a lot of love, 'He transcended to a better place.'"

Chor and I moved outside, into one of the pools. I fell quiet. My heart felt for the mother especially. That must be like having your beating heart ripped right out of your chest, to lose a child. Just as I was saying a quiet prayer for the unknown woman, she walked over to us. Chor introduced us. "Lina, this is my wife, Elizabeth."

Lina smiled warmly. She stood natural and naked, a voluptuous Venus of Willendorf crone. "It's so very nice to meet you, Elizabeth. Oh, aren't you just lovely."

Her voice was filled with tenderness.

"I was telling her a little about what you are going through," said Chor.

"It's been a hard time," said Lina. "I've had my heart broken, but it's been broken wide open. I feel my son, everywhere. I know he's talking to us, through this web of life. He's talking through this nice man, right here." She nodded affectionately at Chor.

"It's no accident that we are all here together," said Chor.

"Yes, I feel that," said Lina. "I'm so grateful that we could spend three full days with Tyler's body in intensive care before he died. He wasn't conscious, but his spirit was still close by. We took our time saying goodbye, before it was finally time to take him off life support.

"The hardest part was having to tell my grandson that his father had died. His lovely wife was there, stroking his closed eyes, over and over.

"The strangest thing...I received this text after he passed away. It didn't show the number that it came from, like it normally would. A lot of it was gobble-dygook, but a few phrases stood out. 'She's strok-ing my eyes,' and 'I love you all. You are all here.' It was crazy. Then I learned about all these cases where people received bizarre phone calls and messages that were clearly from a loved one who had recently died. Apparently it's a phenomenon."

"Yes, I have heard of this." I said. "The departed souls are still in the electromagnetic field. Something like that. Maybe he was communicating through a channel that he could utilize." I had come to learn so intimately that stranger things were possible.

"Yes. Could be," said Lina. "We talked to him a lot when he was dying. We told him that we love him so much—and it's OK for him to let go and be free."

Chor and I listened to this beautiful mother, our eyes soft and open wide. We both knew, Chor had come so close. That could have been him. That could have been the words—and the pain—of his own mother.

Later that afternoon, we said farewell to our new friends on our way out of the front gate. "Thanks for letting us borrow this guy," one of the sisters said to me with a kind smile.

Chor hugged the grieving sister. "Goodbye, sister," he said. She melted and sighed in his arms. Her eyes welled up and spilled over. She took a moment to look into Chor's eyes. "Goodbye," she said, purposefully. "Thank you so much. This is such a gift. I was able to say goodbye to my brother, through you."

We were messengers for each other.

The universe was speaking intimately through us, echoing the tender truth:

Human life is indeed a precious, and very fragile, gift.

CHAPTER 51

THE MARRIAGE OF
MATTER & SPIRIT

"The mystics and the churchmen talk about throwing off his body and its desires, being no longer a slave to the flesh. They don't say that through the flesh we are set free. That our desire for another will lift us out of ourselves more cleanly than anything divine."
— JEANETTE WINTERSON, *THE PASSION*

"The Goddess is not a mental concept or a figure from an ancient past. She is alive in you."
—JENA LA FLAMME

IT WAS a sweet summer eve. The full moon beamed upon us, and the trees watched as Chor and I strolled around our neighborhood. "Do I *have* to get naked?" he asked.

"Only if you want to," I said, smiling, brimming with possibility and mischief.

I had orchestrated a very special date for us that night. Neither of us would have been truly ready for it before that very moment. All was perfectly timed. Life had ripened and refined us, side by side. Spirit had served as our steady, quiet guide; it had always been leading us to this place. Two very different traditions were weaving a beautiful tapestry, through the loom our lives. I offered quiet thanks to the medicine, as this had become my regular practice.

We would visit one of my teachers, Janice Craig, a tantric yogini and priestess hailing from a rare stream of the Sri Vidya tradition. "What *exactly* are we going to do there?" Chor asked, seeking to extract a concrete answer out of the ineffable. I did my best to respond with plain language.

"It's a ritual. It's full-body prayer. And it's worship. Naked worship." I said.

"Hm," he said, keeping an even stride.

We ventured to our unlikely temple, a charming, unassuming apartment in Sausalito. Janice greeted us at the door. Dressed in her brilliant red sari and adorned with Indian gold jewelry, she appeared to be Kamakhya herself, the goddess of *generous desire.* We entered the candlelit interior. The floor was strewn with rose petals. An elaborate altar, glowing with ghee lamps and decorated with fruit, flowers, incense, and deities, filled the room with a palpable loving energy. The humble space had become opulent and sanctified, transporting us to Andre Pradesh in India, where Janice had practiced passionately for many moons.

I made offerings to our priestess: a fresh mango, sandalwood oil, sacred herbs, and my homemade aphrodisiac cacao elixir.

Janice would be guiding us through a kalavahana, a traditional tantric devotional rite of the varma-marga, also known as the left hand path, the forbidden path, the hero's path. Instead of worshipping the Divine as represented by a statue, we would worship the Divine as represented by a far more provocative icon, our living lover.

Chor and I sat, face-to-face and facet to facet. "Tonight, I will offer many Sanskrit mantras as I touch many places on your bodies," Janice explained. "These sacred words are meant to awaken divine energies within you. I will translate them into English, so you have a taste of the meaning. It is called *twilight language*, which is cryptic and embedded with multiple layers of meaning. It is mysterious, but your heart will understand. Tonight, you worship each other as Shiva and Shakti, God and Goddess."

We left our limited minds behind and offered ourselves as pure vessels for the primordial polarities of feminine and masculine, matter and spirit, individual and universal. Polarities, forever in love.

"Now, we create our intention, our *sankalpa*," said Janice. She demonstrated the mudra, or ritual gesture, for sealing our sankalpa. "State your intentions."

I jumped right in. "My intention is to worship the Great Mystery, *through* my lover. I offer myself to love."

Chor spoke, clear and resonant. "My intention is to channel my sexual energy for spiritual awakening—for the Most High."

Our triad vibrated with synergy. It was a powerful dynamic to have another priestess present with us. We transcended our ordinary drama and unconscious habits under her penetrating gaze. The precious and measured time with her made for a potent container, inducing intense awareness. Her graceful formality made sharp students out both of us.

"You may disrobe, if you would like to." I rose to undress with the enthusiasm of a tiger escaping a cage. Chor stripped without hesitation. *What a good sport.* Janice removed her clothing along with us, infusing each movement with sensual mindfulness. All revealed, we created a perfect balance of vulnerability and power. Our bare skin felt holier than any holy cloth.

Even in this garden of nakedness, Janice was regal and poised. As a true priestess, she was in service as our guardian and guide.

Janice explained a familiar principle, "Being naked simply sparks more energy for the ritual." As soon as our clothes dropped, it was evident. Our bare bodies threw off heat waves of excitement.

"There is no goal, other than to be present. There is no pressure to perform in any particular way. There are no mistakes, when all is offered with sincere devotion," Janice said. She guided us through mudras that activated our entire brains and our many human superpowers. She encircled us with her velvet voice and hypnotic mantras. The tips of her fingers seemed to conduct a cosmic orchestra as she gently touched a myriad of points on our bodies.

The ancient poetic prayers poured through her touch and sprang to life within us: "Imagine an unending flow from God and Goddess into you. May this fill you with nectar, giving you the ability to create like Him and Her. Awareness manifesting as wetness, waters of life. Imagine awareness that unites you with all that you see. May your intelligence go beyond your personal limits."

Chor and I locked eyes. Looking into my exquisite naked lover ignited a sweet fire within me that fueled our ritual. His soft, loving gaze seemed to envelope me in a deep current within him. We swam in each other's souls. Our breath began to dance in sync.

Janice anointed and activated our chakras, the power centers of the body. At the throat, the center of conscious expression, she offered this prayer: "At vishuddhi chakra, imagine sky, the womb in which time moves, creating matter. May Brahma with his knowledge create new forms of life. May the year seed the plentiful creation. May the coitus of space and time never end." Janice then guided us to anoint a multitude of precise points on each other's bodies.

When we were both covered in blessings and fully charged, Janice then invited me to lie back in her arms and expose my breasts. "Yes, please." *When in Rome.* Her mantras serenaded me as she massaged my breasts in a way that only a woman can, teasing my nipples into fertile antennae and cultivating life-giving biochemical potions within me. My generous chest glimmered with the sheen of ghee in the amber light.

Chor sat before me as Janice worshipped my breasts. He was invited to offer yoni puja, in other words, to worship the Divine in the form of my pussy. That night, the queen in me shined and I wore an invisible crown of pleasure. I felt my desire as one with the original erotic force of creation. The goddess dressed up as me that night, and she was dreaming the evolving universe through my mortal womb.

Janice sweetly instructed Chor in the art of touch, in the same sweet rhythm as her prayers: "Dear one, touch your beloved as if for the first time." His hands were articulate, artistic, knowing, as never before. I looked at my love as he coaxed fountain after fountain of bliss out of me. In that moment, I received a vision of him catching our newborn children one day.

Just as I was about to dissolve entirely into an ocean of ecstasy, we were invited to exchange thrones. We paused, breathing heavy and slow. My body swayed, liquid, as I moved into the place where Chor had been sitting. I was drunk with pleasure, yet pristinely alert.

God is so generous to create such masterpieces, I reflected about our human forms. I imagined that God would be very offended if we did not fully, and respectfully, enjoy the gift of sensuality.

Chor leaned back into Janice's arms. I worshipped him as a naked God: stroking, teasing, adoring his powerful pillar with my hands. I offered the pleasure to Shiva through my lover's form. Janice stroked his chest, ears, face, and head as she showered him in the stream of mantras. I relished seeing another priestess blessing him with bliss, and I loved playing an intimate part in it all. This scene expressed the light that lived on the other side of our shadows, fantasies, and indomitable longings.

I enveloped his thunderbolt of awakening with my lips. The fire of his pleasure intensified; he drew closer to his boiling point. He struck spontaneous mudras with perfect concentration, intuiting this advanced yogic sexual practice all on his own. He lingered on the precipice of volcanic ecstasy for a time.

Finally, I drew an explosion out of Chor and drank

his nectar into me. He surrendered with a monumental howl, swiftly followed by shivers and a joyous laugh. "Oh, save the seed!" said Janice excitedly. "It is offered to the deity." She swiftly fetched an ornate little golden plate just for this purpose. I poured the liquid gnosis from my mouth onto the plate, and Janet placed it on the altar.

Yes, our pleasure itself can be an offering to the Divine.

Chor sat up and we converged in yab yum, a yogic meditation position just for two, with our hearts connected and legs wrapped around each other. We balanced passion and peace—within our own bodies. We traced each other's spines with our fingertips and looked into each other's eyes until we could see only one eye. We tasted indivisible Unity Consciousness, through the portal of the "other." Two became one.

As we rested in the resonance of our bliss, covered in a perfume of sweet sweat, ghee, and layers of incense, Janice offered us puja. She lit the arati, the sacred flame, and wafted it around, adorning us with light. She handed the arati to me, and nodded for me to do the same for Chor. Slowly, ceremoniously, I circled Chor's face with the arati. I relished just looking at him without rush or distraction. His face, illuminated against the darkness, was, again and again, an ancient memory. The most beautiful face in the world to me, my lover-king. I passed the flame to Chor, and he worshipped me in kind.

Janice then set the camphor aflame. After circling our faces with the bright and fragrant heat, she handed the camphor to us to gift each other with this offering. The sweet sandalwood incense followed, settling over our heads like halos.

Our priestess gave us rose petals with which to shower each other. I realized, I was always showering Chor with rose petals in my mind. It was such a treat to shower him with real rose petals in this tangible dimension.

Next came the jasmine oil. I dipped my fingertips and gently traced the golden skin of his miraculous brow, temples, neck, collarbones. The aphrodisiac aroma left me naturally intoxicated. Chor returned the favor.

Janice invited us to turn toward her. She painted our feet with turmeric, rendering them a vibrant yellow. Our path together was blessed. She offered us kumkum to anoint our third eyes. As we pressed the rich red powder into each other's forehead, I felt us both awakening through our senses.

We were on the human-world clock only for a few hours, but time had stopped. My heart was quenched, to truly see Chor, and to truly be seen, in this timeless space of noble presence. We had both fully arrived into the moment. Laughter. Joy. Surrender. Kisses.

Chor, once addicted to heroin and hungry women, became addicted to inspiring love in the hearts of all beings.

CHAPTER 52

SHINE ON

"All is Sacred. We can never honor All enough. It is that
effort that will create more love in all our lives.
Let us continue."
— GEORGE BERTELSTEIN

WHAT EVER shall we do, without the tyranny of darkness to distract us?

Forward, into the miraculous we go.

Forward, into the fire of love where ego dissolves into a thousand butterflies.

There is the endless play of beauty to create—as paintings or poems or rituals or ordinary moments. There is gratitude to express—as kisses, homemade chocolates, handwritten love notes, or honey-filled words. There is bliss-ipline* to attend to. Let's get our luscious on. There is our unique flavor of magic to cultivate. There is meditation to indulge in and the nectar of stillness to drink. There is sunshine to bask in and sweet breezes to savor. There are babies to make. There is training to do and people to serve. There is the art

bliss-ipline is the literary love child of bliss and discipline, a new word birthed by the poetess and oracle Michaelah "Miraculah" Ivie.

of thinking to practice and the limitless adventure of awakening to enjoy. And there is a wedding in Africa to plan.

EPILOGUE

THE END of the ceremony is just the beginning.

The visionary gifts given by sacred medicine are a new starting point for more adventures, great life changes, fresh challenges, and many long, ordinary days of extraordinary practice. The physical, mental, and spiritual healing prepares us for new tasks. The revelations of love must be carefully tended as sacred flames. From here, in the afterglow of ceremony, we honor the teachings and blessings of the medicine through our daily choices. We take the divine map and walk the journey, one step at a time.

The end of this book is just the beginning.

From here, we spark conversations about related issues: holistic addiction treatment, harm reduction practices, drug policy reform, enthnocentric and religiocentric politics, indigenous peoples' rights, respect for sacred medicine traditions, plant medicine sustainability, our over medicated society, the skyrocketing rates of abuse and overdose with pharmaceutical drugs, corruption within the Western Medical system, and sex workers' rights.

We expand our collective understanding of addiction itself, and we revolutionize the way addicts are treated. There is a common blasé judgment:

"They did it to themselves." This stems from ignorance of the conditions that create, sustain, and heal addiction. Addiction is mistakenly regarded solely as a life-style choice, rather than a complex psychobiosocial health issue. It is time to evolve and elevate through compassion and skill.

We stop sending addicts and drug users to jail, and we begin to address addiction and drug use as the health care matters that they are. We face the fact that the United States imprisons more of it's citizens than any other country, by leaps and bounds, with the majority of those individuals being people of color convicted of nonviolent drug offenses. We face the fact that this abundance of nonviolent prisoners conveniently provides cheap prison labor for private corporations. We end the racist and classist "drug war" along the lust for profit and political control that fuels it.

We stop sending medicine people to jail. We examine how we can safely integrate traditional uses of sacred medicine in our society and truly honor the religious freedom that this country is supposedly committed to. We burn our puritanical prejudices and examine the overwhelming clinical evidence that asserts the benefits of psychedelic medicine. We lift the iron wall of prohibition, thus eradicating the darkness that festers in the black market and the obstacles to further medical psychedelic research, and we open our minds.

From here, we practice the art of being human. I invite you. Walk forward with us.

THANK YOU

Thank you for being a part of our love story. If you have found this book to be beneficial in any way, please share about it via social media, email, phone, word of mouth, or message in a bottle. Post a review where it is sold online. Read bits of it at your local open mic. Leave copies of it in unlikely crevices of your town, with dried flowers and found feathers and original drawings tucked into the pages. More, reach out to host a talk and art event for your community. You will help this book to thrive—and help people learn how to approach sacred medicines with care and respect.

In Service,
E. Bast & Chor Boogie

ABOUT THE AUTHOR

E. Bast serves as a writer, poet, yoga teacher, visual & performance artist, fusion temple dancer, and musician. She studied at New College of San Francisco with an emphasis on Art and Social Change. She's led a colorful life, to say the least, and she's grateful for every bizarre and miraculous moment of it.

WWW.EBAST.NET

CPSIA information can be obtained
at www.ICGtesting.com
Printed in the USA
FSOW01n1252040417
32684FS